THE GIRLS WHO WALKED AWAY

THE GIRLS WHO WALKED AWAY

Fairfield Girls:
Their lives and times and the female struggle for equality
1796-2013

ANNE MCGARRY

Matador
9 Priory Business Park
Kibworth Beauchamp
Leicestershire LE8 0RX, UK
Tel: (+44) 116 279 2299
Fax: (+44) 116 279 2277
Email: books@troubador.co.uk
Web: www.troubador.co.uk/matador

ISBN 978-1783062-546

British Library Cataloguing in Publication Data.
A catalogue record for this book is available from the British Library.

Typeset in Aldine by Troubador Publishing Ltd
Printed and bound in the UK by TJ Books Limited, Padstow, Cornwall

Matador is an imprint of Troubador Publishing Ltd

For all Fairfield Girls – past, present and future

THE GIRLS WHO WALKED AWAY

(With apologies to Thomas Hardy)★

What of the faith and fire within them,
Girls who walk away.
When the learned say,
Tried and proved are they,
Gaining all that school could win them,
What of the faith and fire within them,
Girls who walk away?

In their heart of hearts believing,
Victory crowns the just,
And that idlers must
Surely find the dust,
Press they into the world ungrieving,
In their heart of hearts believing
Victory crowns the just.

Hence the faith and fire within them,
Girls who walk away,
Ere their juniors say
They have had their day,
Taking all that work could win them,
Hence the faith and fire within them,
Girls who walk away.

Form Lower V. Alpha (Year 10)
School Magazine
Fairfield, 1930

★Thomas Hardy's poem *The Men Who March Away – Song of the Soldiers'*
was written in 1914, a few weeks after the start of the First World War.

CONTENTS

INTRODUCTION

Women have come a long way since the Moravian Girls' Boarding School welcomed its first pupils in 1796. This is the story of that journey – a journey which includes the demographic, political and social changes of the period as well as an examination of the lives and times of the girls who attended the school over a period spanning four centuries.

The school which is now Fairfield High School for Girls (a state comprehensive school) was established by the Moravian Church in its Settlement at Fairfield, Droylsden near Manchester. It is one of the oldest girls' schools in England and over many years the lives of its pupils have mirrored those of numerous other women living in this country.

Five years ago, as a former pupil, I decided to write a history of the school. I had read a number of books devoted to the history of various schools and had found them dull and impersonal and I knew that what I wanted to concentrate on were the pupils themselves. Only by learning about their personal lives - their hopes and fears, their ambitions and their experiences - would I be able to understand, in some small way, what it was like to be a young girl or woman during this period.

It was relatively easy to research the social history of the time and the place but to uncover the lives of girls who had studied at the school over such a long period was a different matter. It was to become a combination of detective work and the completion of a jigsaw puzzle - albeit a jigsaw puzzle without the usual indication of the end result.

That day in 2008 I only knew about one girl. She was Mary Moffat née Smith who was Fairfield's 'favourite daughter'. In 1819 she married Robert Moffat who became a famous pioneering missionary during fifty years in South Africa. Mary actively assisted him in his work during all this time and their eldest daughter married David Livingstone. She even has a blue plaque in her honour on the school building, so that was easy. One down, but how many more to go? The school only had a very small archive and the papers were mainly concerned with the school after it had been taken over by the Lancashire Education Committee in 1919. I spent many hours sifting through Headmistresses' Reports and Speech Day programmes. It was like panning for gold but once in a while just a single sentence would leap out at me and this would then lead me on to investigate further .

Fortunately, in 1919 the school set up its Old Girls' Association and until the mid-fifties it had its own news section in the School Magazine and after that it started its own yearly magazine, featuring letters from Old Girls. These letters, which over more than ninety years have numbered many thousands, provided a rich source of information and I am greatly indebted to those Old Girls who supported the Association over many years and kept and protected this material. Here again, just a brief sentence would be the starting point of an investigation which would lead on to an enthralling story. For example, in the 1960s one Fairfield girl mentioned that she had gone on a world cruise, stopping at Perth, Australia where she had met up with an old school friend, Christobel Taylor née Hall, who was still practising medicine at the age of 65. I desperately wanted to find out more about Christobel. I knew from information in the school magazine that she had married a Dr. Benjamin Taylor of the Malay Medical Service in 1930. Apart from that, I had nothing more to go on other than she lived in Perth and I decided, with the aid of the internet, to contact the main paper serving that area, the "West Australian". They printed my letter in their "Wanting to Find" section and the day it was published I had an email from a lady who had known Christobel for over sixty years. Ann Fisher went on to tell me that Christobel had escaped from Singapore when it had been invaded by the Japanese in World War II and arrived in Perth at the beginning of 1942 with her husband and three children. They had nowhere to stay. Ann's grandmother took them in and provided a temporary home for them. Over the next few months Ann was able to give me much needed information about Christobel's life in Australia.

These post 1919 sources were no help, of course, in tracing girls who were at the school during the nineteenth century or in describing the lives they may have led. For this I was able to carry out research in the archives of the Moravian Church in Fairfield and also in the Church's main archive in London. Fortunately, copies of the Moravian monthly magazine "The Messenger" covering the second half of the nineteenth century are held at the John Rylands Library here in Manchester and they also provided an insight into the life and beliefs of the Moravian community. A former Minister of the Fairfield Church, the Rev. F. H. Mellowes, published a Short History of Fairfield Moravian Church in 1977 in which the Boarding School is mentioned and life in the Moravian Settlement is described in full, and this too has been extremely valuable. The use of the internet for viewing census returns and genealogy web sites and contacting former pupils in many parts of the world, has also been a great help; likewise the information in the National Archives at Kew.

All these Fairfield girls, like most other girls in the country, were influenced by the social conditions of the time and the inequalities suffered by the majority of women. I found many astounding examples of the abuse and derision that women were subjected to, as well as the more subtle ways in which their confidence was undermined. I have examined the contemporary literature of the various periods including the works of Mary Wollstonecraft, Charlotte Brontë, Elizabeth Gaskell, Vera Brittain, Betty Friedan and the women journalists of today who are deeply concerned about a woman's place in society. I have also explored the lives of a number of influential women who encouraged and inspired others in the struggle for equality as well as examining the gradual progress made in women's education.

So at the end of five years, how did the jigsaw turn out? By the time many of the pieces were in place it became obvious that the main theme of the book was the tremendous struggle for female equality that had been taking place. The school started at a time when the education of girls was seen to be unnecessary and work outside the home was unheard of for a middle class woman. The book ends in 2013 when one girl, who spent four months in 2009 deployed in Afghanistan, has just been promoted to Squadron Leader, and another girl, who was the first female oil trader for the UK branch of an international energy company, is now their Director of Commercial Development in the European section of the company. Both women are married and have children.

For more than a hundred years the school was a private fee-paying school available only to the relatively wealthy. Then in 1919, when it was taken over by the Lancashire Education Committee, it had to provide free schooling for 25 per cent of its pupils. This meant that a number of ordinary working class girls, for the very first time, had the opportunity to fulfil their potential. Further Acts of Parliament, over the years, have increased that 25 per cent to 100 per cent.

Great strides have been made during the life of the school – the original seven boarders would be completely amazed to see the progress that has been made both socially and technically. Each generation has played its part over the last two hundred years – two hundred years which have taken the girls through the Georgian and Regency period, the Victorian concept of the 'angel in the house', the male opposition to university education for women, the poverty of the thirties, two World Wars, right up to the modern independent girl of today.

I should like to think that this book will go some way towards providing a sensitive view of the past and an empathy that statistics alone cannot give and that it will show what it was really like to be female during the last two hundred years. It is also my hope that learning about the lives and aims of Fairfield girls over the last two hundred years will encourage the girls of today and help them to realise what can be possible.

I hope you will enjoy this journey into the past as much as I have enjoyed writing about it.

August 2013.

CHAPTER ONE

THE EARLY YEARS
1796-1825

"If you happen to have any learning, keep it a profound secret,
especially from the men"

Dr J. Gregory

It was on a warm summer's day, during the last week of June 1796, that the first seven pupils entered the Moravian Girls' Boarding School at Fairfield, Droylsden, near Manchester. They were a fortunate group of girls. Considering the time and the place, it was quite remarkable that such a school had been established in the first place.

The year 1796 was one of fear and instability, brought about by the French Revolution and the fact that Britain was now at war with France. Except for Austria and Britain, France held all Europe from Holland to Rome. As well as the fear of invasion the harvest the previous year had been bad and the cost of wheat had risen by nearly 100 per cent. Not only did most people think that it was an unsuitable time to be planning the opening of a girls' school, they also considered that the education of girls was unnecessary as well. In 1796 within about a twenty five mile radius of Manchester there is no evidence in available records that any similar school existed.[1]

Most girls were frequently made aware that they were not equal to their brothers. During the eighteenth and nineteenth centuries there was much argument about the status and education of women and many writers contributed to the debate. Daniel Defoe wrote in his essay '*The Education of Women*' that he thought it was barbarous that women should be denied the advantages of learning and that their education consisted of learning to read and write their names and being taught to stitch and sew and make baubles. He went on to criticise man's attitude to women in that they were considered only fit to be men's housekeepers, cooks and slaves.

Mary Wollstonecraft was the first major feminist and her book "*A Vindication of the Rights of Woman*" published in 1792 called for an equal education for boys and girls. She attacked the view that women were purely decorative and docile and pleaded that they should be respected for their own work and not thought to be inferior to men.

On the other hand, the French philosopher Jean Jacques Rousseau in the 18th century thought that a woman took second place to that of her husband. In his work '*Emile*' he wrote that women were expressly formed to please the man and that education of women should therefore always be relative to man. Their purpose was to please, to be useful to men, to make men love and esteem them and to make men's lives easy and agreeable.

Dr J. Gregory in his book '*A Father's Legacy to his Daughters*' published in 1774 advised his readers that they should be cautious in displaying good sense as it would be thought that they were assuming superiority . He went on to say '*If you happen to have any learning, keep it a profound secret, especially from the men, who generally look with a jealous and malignant eye on a woman of great parts and cultivated understanding*'.

The low esteem in which women were held can be judged by the notes published in a book on electoral law written in 1790. It stated that '*women, infants, idiots and lunatics lie under natural incapacities and therefore cannot exercise a sound discretion, or are so much under the influence of others that they cannot have a will of their own.*'[2]

The opinion that women were physically and mentally inferior to men would last to the end of the 19th century and even into the 20th century. Male writers maintained, without supplying any proof, that there were biological differences between the sexes which made women inferior. The physiologist Alexander Walker wrote in 1840: '*It is evident that the man, possessing reasoning faculties, muscular power, and courage to employ it, is qualified for being a protector: the woman, being little capable of reasoning, feeble and timid, requires protection. Under such circumstances, the man naturally governs: the woman as naturally obeys*'.

Surprisingly even some women were opposed to the idea of equality for women. Sarah Stickney Ellis, a clergyman's wife who was a popular writer in the 1830's, advised women that *'The first thing of importance is to be content to be inferior to men, inferior in mental power in the same proportion that you are inferior in bodily strength'*

However, women did have their champions. Sydney Smith, the well-known writer, in an 1810 essay on *'Female Education'* asked *'Why should the disproportion in knowledge between the two sexes be so great, when the inequality in natural talents is so small; or why the understanding of women should be lavished upon trifles, when nature has made it capable of better and higher things'*.

It is astonishing today to think that most women - half the human race - were thought of in this manner and were therefore condemned, in most cases, to a life devoid of a decent education and prevented from reaching anything like their full potential.

It's not surprising, therefore, that the education of girls was so inadequate and their education was far inferior to that experienced by boys. Boys from wealthy or upper class homes would normally be sent to board at Public Schools, such as Eton and Harrow, where they received an academic education and they would then probably go on to university. Girls from affluent homes attended boarding schools while girls from even wealthier backgrounds, were often taught by governesses at home. Usually the curriculum for girls was not academic. It consisted of basic literacy lessons and some arithmetic and possibly French. However, a great deal of the time was occupied in genteel activities such as needlework, art, dancing, and playing the piano - all with a view to attracting a husband and making a good marriage.

In the eighteenth and nineteenth centuries most middle class girls who were not wealthy viewed marriage as the only means of providing a secure future. If they did not marry and had no money of their own they would find themselves dependent on a male member of the family. It was a sad situation for a poor female, as a young woman's chances of matrimony were greatly increased if she or her family were wealthy in the first place. Jane Austen in her letters to her sister Cassandra in the early 1800s expresses her concern about the lives of a number of impoverished unmarried women she knew. In one of her letters she wrote *'Single women have a dreadful propensity for being poor, which is one very strong argument in favour of matrimony'*. However, in another letter she wrote *'Anything is to be preferred or endured rather than marrying without affection'*.

This unhappy female plight was illustrated by Jane in her book *"Pride and Prejudice"*. Mr Collins, who was described as a conceited, pompous, narrow-minded silly man, had originally asked Elizabeth Bennet to marry him and having been refused had become engaged to Elizabeth's friend Charlotte. Jane Austen wrote that Charlotte thought Mr Collins was neither sensible nor agreeable, his society was irksome, and his attachment to her must be imaginary. But still he would be her husband. Jane writes that *'without thinking highly either of men or of matrimony, marriage had always been Charlotte's object; it was the only honourable provision for well-educated young women of small fortune and, however uncertain of giving happiness, must be their pleasantest preservative from want. This preservative she had now obtained, and at the age of twenty seven, without having ever been handsome, she felt all the good luck of it.'*

During this period very few women worked outside the home. There were, of course, female domestic servants and as the industrial revolution progressed women would find work in the mills, but for middle class women there were few opportunities except perhaps that of a governess, and even this position did not provide sufficient salary to save for old age.

DROYLSDEN

Not only was it a surprising time to establish a girls' boarding school but the place itself was quite unpretentious. Droylsden in 1796 was a village of just over one hundred houses situated four miles directly east of Manchester. Like hundreds of other villages in the country there was nothing about it that was in any way significant. It had no old church and no "famous son" or wealthy landowners forming a social class which was set apart from the rest of the community. However, it has to be said that this situation did lead to a certain sense of individual worth and independence amongst the people of Droylsden as is shown in their support of the Independent Church Movement and an interest in education which would lead to the building of schools and the Mechanics and Educational Institute well before the 1870 Education Act. [3]

The fact that the place had little importance was partly due to it having no direct road to Manchester and having quite a barren soil that needed very hard work to make it productive. Droylsden at the time boasted a rule without exception – all its roads were in a dreadful condition. One length of road was so bad in the late 1700's and early 1800's that people took off their shoes and stockings and waded through barefoot. The surface of the roads in some places was so uneven that pedestrians fifty yards in advance of fellow travellers frequently appeared to disappear. One large rut or cavity was nicknamed Jack Holland Hole and sometimes called the 'slough of despond'.[4]

A story has been handed down which shows the unsophistication of the villagers. Tea was a very expensive commodity but when a woman living in Greenside (a hamlet to the north west of Droylsden) received a present of a whole pound of it, she, on the advice of her neighbours, cooked it like cabbage. Her husband was none too pleased with this new delicacy and ordered it to be 'thrown into the midden.'[5]

As in many other villages, educational provision in the last quarter of the eighteenth century was minimal and inadequate. In 1774 Jonathan Grimshaw taught a few pupils for one shilling and sixpence a quarter. This teaching took place in his cottage in Far Lane where he carried on his work as a weaver at the same time. In 1775 Sarah Hibbert taught about half a dozen young children who, in between their lessons, picked out the seeds from cotton ready for Mrs Hibbert to carry on the process of spinning.[6]

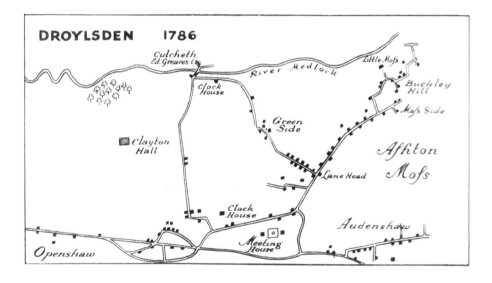

Droylsden from Wm. Yates Survey

THE MORAVIANS

Into this rather unsophisticated village came a group of deeply religious people belonging to the Moravian church. They came in 1783 and bought land to the south of the centre of Droylsden on which they could build a Settlement or small village. They gave the name Fairfield to this Settlement. The Moravians had come over from the neighbouring township of Dukinfield where they had established a Settlement in 1755. They had remained there for nearly thirty years until lack of room for expansion and problems with the lease had forced them to look elsewhere.

The Moravian church is one of the smaller Christian bodies in Britain. It has a long history and is the oldest free-church in Northern Europe having been founded in 1457, in what is now the Czech Republic. In 1732 they were the first Protestant church to venture out on foreign missions and it was this evangelical calling that brought the Moravian preachers to England.[7]

The Settlement

The Settlement at Fairfield was opened in 1785 and like other similar Moravian Settlements in England, it was planned and built by its own people. It was a self-contained and self-governed community with its own inn, shop, bakery, laundry and farm. It had a fire-engine, night watchman, inspector of weights and measures, an overseer of roads and a physician. The design of the Settlement was impressive and spacious. The main buildings were typical of the Georgian architecture of the time and compared to the cottage homes in Droylsden the buildings would have appeared sophisticated and modern.

The Settlement had the appearance of a little town and in many respects it remains unchanged to this day. The ground plot forms a large square with the chapel and some large dwelling houses built of brick forming the front. On each side of the Chapel are two deep rows of dwelling houses and on the back behind the chapel is a row of elegant large houses. One of the houses in the square was an inn with stabling. This provided accommodation for visitors whose journeys, even of relatively short distances, would take many hours of travelling on horseback or by coach.

Spinning and weaving of cotton was one of the main occupations and as well as the bakery and farm there were also tailors and shoemakers. The

Manchester, Ashton and Oldham canal which was completed nine years after the establishment of the Settlement was close by and carried goods to and from Manchester and Ashton.[8]

Fairfield Moravian Settlement founded at Droylsden, Manchester 1785

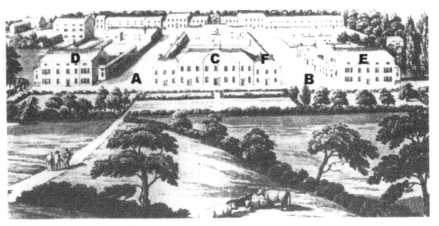

A	Brethren Street	**C**	Moravian Church	**E**	Sisters' House
B	Sisters' Street	**D**	Brethren's House	**F**	School from1815

In the Settlement there was a community house for single men (Brethren) and another for single women (Sisters), where they were engaged in a number of different occupations. Parents in the Settlement agreed to allow their children at the age of fourteen or fifteen to enter these community houses. In 1785 there were 22 single Brethren occupying the single Brethren's house and 45 single Sisters living in the Sisters' house. The Settlement was a hive of industrial and religious activity.[9] The single Brethren ran the bake house which was the only one in the area. Every week a single Brother rode out on horseback delivering bread through Ashton to Oldham and even as far as Lees and Saddleworth. As well as the bake house the only drapery and provision store in the area was to be found at Fairfield. It was to remain the principal shop of its kind in the district for many years.[10] The single sisters had a farm and a laundry and did fine needlework. They sent some to Queen Adelaide, wife of William IV, who was so pleased with it she ordered more. One of the sisters made long journeys to London and Edinburgh to sell their products. The Sisters also did a great deal of spinning and weaving. Although the main reason for all this activity was to survive and make money, it also presented the opportunity to spread their religious beliefs.[11]

The Settlement was the home of law and order, peace and quiet. No tradesmen were allowed to create a monopoly, no dogs were allowed to roam the streets, and no children played in the streets after 8 p.m. The spiritual side of life was not neglected. Each week night there was a service in the church.

The Moravians were committed to a life of Christian faith and love. Their care for the sick, the widow and the orphan was real and attentive and provision was made for the poor. They were also, at this time, pacifists. They believed that non-violence and non-resistance was the true Christian vocation. During the Napoleonic wars, they were given, under an Act of Parliament, exemption from military service.[12]

The Moravian church also had a long-standing commitment to education. Amos Comenius, a Moravian Bishop in the seventeenth century, is acknowledged by many educationalists to be the "Father of Modern Education". In 1654 he published the first textbook with pictures for teaching children and his scheme of educational stages was very similar to that in force today. Comenius visited England in 1641, at the invitation of both Houses of Parliament, to join a Commission looking into the reform of education. It is also claimed that he was asked to be the first President of Harvard College in America (now Harvard University). The Moravians' influence in education was far-reaching. The oldest girls' boarding school in America was established by them in 1746. This is Linden Hall in the small town of Lititz near Lancaster, Pennsylvania. The town was founded by members of the Moravian Church.

In 1791 the Moravians opened a Sunday school at Fairfield, Droylsden. This school was established in co-operation with the town's people who paid for the rent of the building. A paid teacher was provided and the children paid a very small sum for their tuition. The children who attended were those who either couldn't afford to go to day schools or were working during the week.

THE GIRLS' BOARDING SCHOOL

A year after the Fairfield Settlement opened, the Elders of the church started day schools for boys and girls. Some of the girls attending the day school lived quite a distance away and had to stay either in the Single Sisters' House or in the home of a Church member. This situation was discussed at the Elders' Conference (the governing body of the Settlement) on 14th March 1795 and the following entry is listed in the Minutes of the Meeting: *"On account of the number of applications from different places for children to come to our school the Conference is of the opinion that we should think of beginning a Boarding School"*. The next year the following entry was made in the Congregation Diary for the 27th June 1796 *"in the course of this week the Girls' Boarding School was opened."*[13]

Sister Mary Tyrell started the school in the Sisters' House with seven boarders. The fact that Religion was a great influence when the school was first established can be seen from the words Sister Tyrell wrote in her Memoire *'At the opening of the School the Minister, Brother Swertner, addressed the children in a very affectionate manner, explaining to them the true motives which induce us to begin schools and prayed Our Saviour to lay his blessing upon us. My prayer was that through their education the girls might get a feeling of the Saviour's love in their hearts'.*[14]

To girls of today the school regime would seem restrictive and rather solemn. However, the girls came from Christian Moravian homes and were familiar with the religious observance and restraints that were expected of them. On the positive side they were being cared for and taught in a loving, secure environment, which, as can be seen from contemporary literature, was not always the case in other schools. It also has to be said, that Fairfield, set among fields and orchards, must have been an extremely pleasant place in which to live.

In many ways, this first group of Fairfield Girls was extremely fortunate. Their parents must have been wealthy enough to pay for their education and board and their experience would have been in sharp contrast to that of the great majority of children at the end of the eighteenth century. The girls also benefited from the Moravian views on education and the serious curriculum that was offered in their schools.

Sampler – 1811

Two Moravian Women wearing the typical, plain Moravian dress of the early 1800s

This is illustrated by a textbook on arithmetic, written by a woman in 1804 and found at Fairfield. It included an arithmetic problem which asked the pupil to calculate how much to charge in order to make a profit on the import of a boatload of Barbados sugar, bearing in mind the cost of purchase, shipping, and customs duty. Such practical exercises were rarely given to girls elsewhere at the time.[15]

The school day started at 8.30 and after morning prayers there were lessons. There are few details of the curriculum for the first ten to twenty years but it is assumed it would have been similar to that in other Moravian Girls' Boarding Schools. (There would eventually be about ten Moravian schools in England – the first was established in 1753 at Fulneck, near Pudsey in Yorkshire. This school and the Moravian school at Ockbrook in Derbyshire which was started in 1799 are still maintained by the Moravian Church). Evidence available shows that girls at Moravian schools were taught not only basic reading, writing and arithmetic but also literature, geography, history, French and German.[16] There would, of course, have been lessons in needlework and there are a number of samplers worked by pupils which are still in existence. The one illustrated is by Martha Shawcross aged twelve. It was made in 1811 and shows the Sisters' House and the Moravian emblem of the Lamb and Flag. Music would also have been part of the curriculum.

The Moravian dictum, "Vicit Agnus Noster Eum Sequamur", ("Our Lamb has conquered, let us follow Him"), was adopted as the School motto together with the emblem of the Lamb and Flag. Clothes were plain, as fashionable dress was frowned upon, and when it was suggested in 1803 that French should be taught by an émigré, the idea was rejected as 'unseemly'.[17] Perhaps the fact that Britain was at war with France at the time had something to do with this and the decision was changed a few years later.

The experiences of poor children living in Droylsden and in the growing industrial cotton town of Manchester just four miles away were very different. Many poor working class men and women lived in dreadful conditions and their children suffered greatly and had very little or no education. Not only was there a lack of educational provision, but many children were working from a very young age. Robert Southey in "*Letters from England*" published in 1807 wrote of his conversation with a Manchester businessman. The employer told him that the demand for child labour was such that in the new manufacturing towns the only method of keeping up the supply was to send people round the country to get children from their parents.

Some children, if they were lucky, might be able to attend schools established by the Society for Promoting Christian Knowledge (SPCK), which was an organisation closely connected to the Church of England. The girls in these schools were taught to read, write a little and to sew and knit; in contrast to the boys who were taught to read and write and do accounts. The main reason for the founding of these schools was to promote the Christian Religion and to teach children 'to know their station in life and to be humble and submissive'.[18] Charity schools were also founded by the Roman Catholics and Non-conformists. During the 1780s the first Sunday schools were set up in England and they provided a little education for those children who were working during the week. They were taught to read and sometimes to write.

MORAVIAN INFLUENCE

Although Fairfield girls were fortunate in that they lived in a protective and loving environment, did they think of themselves as inferior second-class citizens because they were women or did their schooling help them to have confidence in their abilities? They were, of course, very much influenced by their teachers and their Headmistress.

From the information in the Moravian records, Sister Mary Tyrell was a skilled administrator and organiser. She was Headmistress for eleven years until she moved back into the Sisters' House to take up the post of Warden. She then became a full member of the Elders' Conference taking her share in the work of administration and thus demonstrating that women alongside men played their part in the running of the Settlement.[19]

The girls would also have been influenced by the lives of the single Sisters in the Settlement. The Sisters lived and worked together in the large Single Sisters' House in which the school was placed.

For the girls at Fairfield to see a group of single women successfully manage a farm, a laundry and run a spinning and weaving establishment as well as doing fine needlework which was recognised in royal circles, all in a 'secure for life' environment, must have influenced their perception of women's worth and position. The sense of satisfaction and security that could be gained from belonging to a hardworking and thriving community would surely have been noticed by the girls at the school.

The girls must also have been influenced by the news and stories which came from all over the world from the Moravian missionaries. The Settlement received many letters but it was also visited by the missionaries. They heard about work in the West Indies, Labrador, Russia, South Africa, Greenland, North America, and the Indian Ocean. In 1805 Mary Jackson who was a missionary's daughter and a Mrs Russell who accompanied her, came to Fairfield from Jamaica. They told how their ship was seized by a Spanish privateer, and taken to Cuba. Mrs Russell, a widow, succeeded in getting the ransom money required for their release and secured a passage to England via North America. [20]

A number of the Single Sisters married Brethren who went abroad as missionaries. They either went out to marry them at their missionary station or married their husbands in England and they then went abroad together. Some of the girls at Fairfield were the children of missionaries and were sent back home to England to be educated.

The girls would also be aware of the journeys made by the Single Sisters. They frequently travelled to London and Edinburgh to sell their lace work and in 1818 Sister Mary Tyrell attended the Synod (international meeting of the Church) at their headquarters at Herrnhut, which is about thirty miles east of Dresden in Germany. All this travelling was before the introduction of the railways and entailed long arduous journeys by coach and sailing ship. The Conference Diaries mention the spirit of travel and adventure that the Sisters experienced. Comment is made about two Sisters who rode from Dukinfield on horseback to a church service at Fairfield when, on their return journey, they were thrown from their horse, but were mercifully unhurt and arrived home shaken but safe. Also in the Diaries it was noted that "*Some Sisters wished to bathe in the seas for the benefit of their Health: the Conference wished them to go to Blackpool rather than Liverpool.*" However the entry a month later reads "*Some Single Sisters wish to go to bathe in the sea at Liverpool, if a proper [married] Sister can be found to go with them.*"[21]

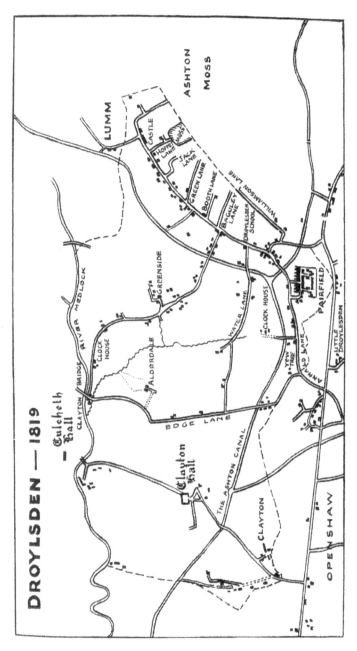

Johnson's 1819 Survey

Not only were the housing and other facilities at Fairfield superior in many ways to that in the surrounding area, but the lifestyle of the Moravians with their knowledge of and contacts with people in "foreign parts" made them more cultured and "worldly wise". In contrast, many of the people in Droylsden would have done very little travelling. Only those who were wealthy enough to own a horse or a horse and carriage or who could afford the cost of travelling by coach were able to go on journeys of any distance. The majority of people were restricted to travelling on foot; so many rarely left their immediate neighbourhood. This meant that the great majority led restricted and insular lives and had very little knowledge or experience of the wider world.

Fairfield's girl boarders, by leaving home and travelling to board at school, were gaining a wider experience and a sense of independence which was unobtainable by most girls. They gained knowledge and a wider view of the world from living in a Moravian environment.

MISSIONARY WIFE AND MOTHER

One girl who attended the school in the early years of the nineteenth century and who was influenced by her time at Fairfield showed by her courage and fortitude that she was not going to be an "inferior" female. Mary Smith married the celebrated African Missionary, Robert Moffat, and spent fifty years in Africa supporting her husband. Mary was born in 1795, just one year before the Moravian School was established. Her father was John Smith, a prosperous market gardener of Plantation Farm, Dukinfield. The market garden business was a large thriving concern – at one point more than fifteen labourers were employed, many of whom slept in the loft of the large Georgian house which had been built in 1790 and still exists.[22]

John Moffat in his biography of his parents tells us that Mary often spoke to her children about the happy time she had at school in Fairfield and it was there that she first became interested in missionary work . He wrote that the faith which was nurtured at Fairfield helped to carry her through many hardships and enabled her to be a great help and support to her husband. It was the custom at the school for each of the youngest children to be placed under the special care of one of the elder girls who was called her 'little mother'. When John came to write his parents' biography he met a Mrs Buckley of Ashton under Lyne who told him that Mary was her 'little mother' and she had many happy memories of that time.

Robert Moffat came to work for Mary's father on 1st January 1816. He was introduced to Mary's father by the Rev. William Roby, a Director of the London Missionary Society, who was helping Robert in his endeavours to become a missionary. Soon after arriving at Plantation Farm Robert's and Mary's joint Christian faith and missionary zeal led to a deep affection. Robert had joined the London Missionary Society in 1814 and after undergoing a part-tine study course he was ordained in London in September 1816. At the end of October, only ten months after he and Mary had first met, he sailed for South Africa and travelled to Namaqualand on the Orange River leaving Mary behind. They corresponded for three years and in one of Robert's letters to his family he wrote that the letters he had just received from Miss Smith made him believe that she would soon be joining him. He wrote *'This I trust will be soon, for a missionary in this country without a wife is like a boat without an oar'.*[23]

In September 1819 Mary, having overcome her parents' opposition, left for South Africa, chaperoned by a couple who were going out to the Dutch Church in Southern Africa. It was a sad farewell. Mary and her parents knew it was likely that they would never see each other again. In fact, Mr Smith was still alive when Mary and Robert came to England on leave twenty years later and was ninety when he died, but Mary never saw her mother again. They corresponded frequently over the years but letters took months to arrive.

During the voyage Mary kept a journal and from this we learn how very different travel in 1819 was compared to today. The voyage by sailing ship was delayed and it wasn't until two weeks later that the Captain decided he could wait no longer for the wind to change and they set sail on a voyage which would last three months. The conditions on board were, to modern eyes and ears, unbelievable. It was noisy – pigs squeaking, geese gabbling, ducks quacking and sailors bellowing. Her mattress was full of bugs. She took it off and made up a bed with books, linen and blankets. Mary's cabin was tiny and the heat and the constant drenching by sea water if the porthole was left open made life below decks very miserable. When they neared the equator the weather worsened. Lightning flashed, and the wind and rain beat down, confining the passengers to their cabins below decks, which were hot and airless. Mary opened her porthole and she became soaked along with her possessions. She shut the porthole and the heat was unbearable. The whole ship stank with the smell of people, animals and rotting food in the tropical heat and her hands and feet became raw with bug bites. Throughout these hardships she endeavoured to think of this voyage as a training-ground for the life she might have to face in Africa and was glad that she had been able to withstand it.

On December 6th she disembarked to meet the man she hadn't seen for three years and with whom she was to spend the next fifty one years in a loving relationship which became a true working partnership. In Cape Town on the 27th December 1819, thousands of miles away from family and friends, Mary and Robert were married. Mary then cut off her curls and tucked her hair under a matron's cap, as was the custom for the wife of a missionary.[24]

They then embarked on a seven week journey by ox-wagon beyond the Orange River to Latakoo, a mission station 600 miles north of Cape Town. The early years were extremely harsh. They grew their own food, built their own living quarters and learned to communicate with the Bechuana tribe amongst whom they were living. By 1828 they had learned the Sechuana language and had built a new mission station at Kuruman with a school, church and dwelling houses. Robert at this time began translating the New Testament into Sechuana. They came back to England for a visit from 1839 to 1842. Robert was received as a celebrity and addressed meetings all over the country and was influential in David Livingstone deciding to devote himself to work in Africa. David went out to Kuruman in 1841 and when Mary and Robert Moffat arrived back in Africa he travelled 150 miles to meet them and help them on their onward journey. Kuruman was the mother station, from which were drawn supplies of books and other commodities. Livingstone travelled out from Kuruman to Chonwane. During this time he was mauled by a lion and while recovering stayed some time at Kuruman and became attached to the Moffat's eldest daughter, also Mary. They were married in 1845.

During her time in Africa, Mary Moffat (senior) had ten children. She also went on a number of journeys unaccompanied by her husband. While her daughter and son-in-law were at Chonwane, she went out to visit them. This involved a journey of about nine to ten days, travelling seven to eight hours a day. In 1847 she went to Cape Town with three of her younger children in connection with their education. The two girls boarded a ship to England, (a friendly minister of the church offered to take care of them during the journey), and her son stayed behind at school in Cape Town. This journey by wagons pulled by oxen from Kuruman took two months[25].

The Moffat Mission at Karuman in 1839

The Moffats spent over fifty years in Africa. During that time Mary was wife, mother, housekeeper, teacher, nurse and administrator under the most difficult and arduous conditions, conditions which the modern girl of today would find it hard to envisage.

Unlike many middle class wives in England, Mary was able to support her husband in his work. When he frequently went off in search of new converts, Mary had to manage the mission station. Theirs was surely a "*marriage of true minds*".

In 1870 the Moffats returned to England after fifty years in Africa. Robert Moffat addressed the General Assembly of the Free Church of Scotland and he was able to speak of churches and missions scattered over the whole of the Bechuana country from Zululand in the east to Demeraraland in the west, having forty thousand communicants and forty five thousand pupils. Sadly, Mary died only five months after arriving back from Africa in 1871. She was seventy six.

Two years after Mary's death, Dr Robert Moffat paid a visit to Plantation Farm in Dukinfield where he met the Rev. William Glover of Crescent Road Congregational Church. The Rev. Glover wrote *'I shall never forget the dear old man when he went over the distant past, and talked about the old days with the beautiful woodland scenery which beautified this district, and when he talked about the time he used to walk out with Mary Smith and of serving his apprenticeship as gardener to Mr Smith; when he talked about the time and what he had seen in South Africa and in other parts, and how Mary Smith was such a great help and inspiration to him, the big tears rolled down his face, until his heart was almost melting through his eyes.'* [26]

EARLY NINETEENTH CENTURY LIFE

Viewed from today's standpoint, there are many aspects of life in the first decades of the school that are difficult to imagine. One of the main differences was the lack of good artificial light. Then, the main means of lighting was by candles. Anybody who has experienced an electricity power cut when they have had to depend on a few flickering candles, will know the eerie and difficult situation that it causes and the welcome relief when the lights come on again. We complain about the cost of electricity, but in the early nineteenth century candles were expensive commodities. Night-time outside the home was even more bleak. Unless there was a moon it would be completely dark. Our girls at Fairfield would no doubt have spent their winter evenings reading or sewing by candlelight. Maybe they would sing and perhaps some would play the piano. But they would no doubt have gone to bed early..

The advances in communication over the last two centuries have been tremendous. However, until the mid-nineteenth century, when the telegraph came into use, the only means of communication was by letter. The slowness in communication is illustrated by the death at sea of two Moravian Sisters.

The packet ship they were travelling on ran onto rocks in the bay of Holyhead, Anglesey, very near to the town, on 18th December 1790. The news wasn't received in Fairfield until thirteen days later.[27] Communication, therefore, was very slow and until the railways came into operation, was completely dependent on the speed of a horse or a sailing ship. Journeys of any real length involved many hours of uncomfortable travel by coach or even more dangerous voyages by sea.

There were no labour-saving devices and much time was spent on everyday tasks. Clothes were made and laundered by hand and carpets beaten. Meals were made from locally available and seasonal ingredients and cooked on an open fire or, in a more affluent home, in and on a kitchen range. It wasn't until 1851 that a gas cooker was first exhibited.

Pure water at the turning of a tap is something we take for granted today. The water at Fairfield was first supplied from the wells at the bottom of Fairfield Avenue. There were two paths down to these wells and it was a long walk with heavy buckets suspended from a yoke across the shoulders. It is also thought that there was another supply of water from a pond at the front of the School.[28]

Two hundred years ago the lack of pure water was the cause of many fatal illnesses. Medical knowledge and provision was meagre and the death rate, especially amongst children, was high. Mary Tyrell, the school's headmistress, writing in 1807 stated that '*the number of children educated as boarders since the school opened in 1796 is 127; of this number nine have departed this life, but only one of them at Fairfield*'.[29] The death rate was therefore over 7 per cent over an eleven year period. But these mortality figures were low compared to those of children in poorer circumstances, many of whom died before they were five years old. Sometime between 1809 and 1815 there was a serious epidemic in the Settlement. According to the *Moravian Messenger Magazine* it seems that '*a most fatal fever entered the Settlement and the Schools and carried off several – both teachers and pupils.*'[30]

As the Girls' Boarding School settled into the nineteenth century they were joined in the Settlement by the Boys' Boarding School which was opened in 1803. (It is interesting to note that the Girls' School opened before the Boys' School). The number of girl boarders soon increased to thirty. The girls came from many different places including Cheshire, the Midlands and

Ireland. Some pupils, mainly the children of missionaries, came from as far afield as the West Indies.

School wasn't without its treats. The Boys' Boarding School opened a tuck-shop for its students in a house (now demolished) near to the present day post box in the Square. In 1810 the Girls' Boarding School Conference, which had been formed to assist with management, discovered to its dismay that the shop was a meeting place for pupils from both schools. This was, of course, frowned upon by the teachers at the 'Moravian School for Young Ladies' and they decided in future that fruits and sweets should be brought to the school and the pupils prevented as much as possible from visiting the shop. [31]

Mary Smith, our intrepid, would-be missionary, was also not averse to a bit of frivolity. In later life she told one of her daughters about winning a beauty competition whilst she was at the school. Apparently one day the young ladies of the Moravian School had an argument about who had the most perfectly shaped leg. The girls pulled up their long skirts to check and measure their legs and then paraded up and down. Mary's legs were chosen as the most perfect.

During the first decades of the nineteenth century, life in the Settlement and the school changed very little. The school grew and in 1815 moved from the Sisters' House across Sister Street to the building (today Nos. 30 and 15A) attached to the east side of the Church. The school dormitories were above the church. Four rooms were in the East and two in the West. On Wednesday evenings there was a church service so the boarders had to go to bed very quietly in order not to disturb the Service in the Church. They would each have had to carry a candle up a dark narrow staircase so it's no wonder that there was a rumour of a ghost and every one dreaded going near Room 4.[32]

Soon life outside the Settlement and, to a certain extent, inside it, would begin to change as the Industrial Revolution gathered momentum. Great developments in science and technology would bring tremendous changes to people's lives. However, the changes in women's lives were less dramatic and society's views and expectations of women were still very different from what they are today. Women had hardly started on the road to equality and it was going to be a very long and slow struggle before they were considered in any way equal to their husbands and brothers.

CHAPTER TWO

GREAT INDUSTRIAL PROGRESS
1825-1870

"Love, not knowledge, was the Victorian Heroine's fate.
Science, like industry, was the province of men"

Jenny Uglow

THE INDUSTRIAL REVOLUTION

By the second quarter of the nineteenth century the changes brought about by the industrial revolution were affecting people all over the world. Droylsden like many other small townships would never be the same again.

The manufacture of cotton cloth in Droylsden had been a domestic industry and the spinning of yarn on a spinning wheel had taken place in the cottages, one good weaver keeping three women spinners at work.[1] Gradually the spinning jenny and the power loom were introduced and in 1831 an Ashton-under-Lyne family built the first factory in Droylsden on a twelve acre site on Edge Lane. It used steam power to work both spinning and weaving.[2] Over the next twenty years, six further mills and factories were built and by the mid 1850's Droylsden was no longer a sleepy village but had become a small town of industrial workers who were not only employed in the cotton mills but also in factories devoted to hat making, dyeing, patent leather manufacture and chemicals.[3]

All this industrial activity meant that the town expanded to house the workers. By 1851 the population had quadrupled from 1552 in 1801, to 6280. This increase in the population automatically led to the provision of a whole range of shops, inns and other services. In fact by 1852 there were 9 inns and

public houses, 23 beer shops, and 52 provision and other shops.[4] Droylsden
had come a long way since the only bake house in the district was the one in
the Fairfield Settlement and a Brother went out every week on horseback to
deliver bread as far afield as Saddleworth.

Droylsden, therefore, was gradually transformed from a rural village four
miles from Manchester into a small industrial town with its attendant
problems of poor sanitation and housing.

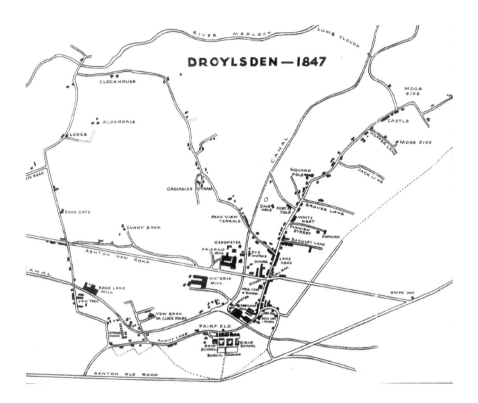

Droylsden, from the Ordnance Survey and Tithes maps

The Moravian Settlement

Life in the Settlement was also changing but at a more gradual pace. It was
still the same quiet place and would always remain an enclave of tranquillity
surrounded by the noise and bustle of a growing town. The Night Watchman
still did his rounds of the Settlement every hour from 10 p.m. to 3 a.m. and

anybody needing the doctor or other assistance still placed a candle in a downstairs window to attract his attention. There were also peg-clocks on the doors of the houses and the Watchman, as he did his circuit of the Settlement, moved the peg on for each of the hours of the night, to show that he was fulfilling his duties.[5]

However, by the 1820s some members had begun to leave the Settlement. Times were hard and a life outside the Settlement that was not based on cottage industries had its attractions. Although the Single Sisters' House was still working successfully, the Single Brethren's House was not viable and was closed. It was clear that community life and worship as organised in the Settlement was failing to keep a hold on the second generation. In 1828 fifteen houses were left vacant by members who had gone to seek work elsewhere. However, the Fairfield Settlement was an attractive place to live and people who were not members of the Moravian Church now began to apply to live there. The Elders eventually allowed outsiders, but let it be known that only those of the Christian faith and practice would be welcome.[6]

There was a severe drought in 1824 and plans were drawn up to convey water from the Ashton – Manchester Canal which ran about one hundred yards away around the north and east sides of the Settlement. The work involved digging and the laying of pipes to convey the water to a central cistern from which the inhabitants would draw the water. The work was paid for by money from the Inn, the shop, the Boys' School, the Girls' School and the Single Sisters' House. All the domestic users paid a yearly sum.[7] The water from the canal needed to be purified and the Moravians built a filter composed of stones, river sand and charcoal. In coming years water pipes were laid to most of the houses [8] and sewers were constructed complete with settling tanks.[9]

This piped supply of water was the first of its kind in Droylsden. A supply of pure water was very important but even thirty five years later there was no water supply in the township other than a few pump springs and surface wells and stale water was sold from water carts calling twice a week at a half penny a bucket[10]. The lack of water also gave rise to a serious situation in case of fire and the Moravians owned the only fire engine in the township.[11]

The girls boarding at the Moravian school came from many parts of the country and their journeys were much improved when the Railways were built. The world's first passenger railway service, hauled by steam locomotive from Manchester to Liverpool, was inaugurated in 1830 and by 1841 the Manchester, Sheffield and Lincolnshire Railway Line was running through and stopping at Fairfield Railway Station, about a five minutes' walk away from the school.[12]

WOMEN'S LIVES

Although the Industrial Revolution brought many changes, the lives of most middle class women remained virtually unchanged until the later years of the century.

However, a woman living as a member of the Moravian Community would probably have felt more secure than many other women. Married women in England had few legal rights and only wealthy single or widowed women were able to lead independent lives. The property of a married woman, whether earned or inherited, legally belonged to her husband and she had no legal right to her children. A man, without the consent of a court, was able to forbid his wife seeing their children. It wasn't until 1839 that Caroline Norton, who was well connected, and who had suffered greatly at the hands of her husband, managed to work for the passing of the Custody of Infants Act. This Act allowed a judge to make an order allowing mothers, against whom adultery was not proved, to have the custody of their children under seven, and access to older children at stated times. It wasn't until the Guardianship of Infants Act of 1925 that full and equal guardianship of their children was granted to English women.

An indication of how women were viewed is the fact that during the nineteenth century there were a number of instances of husbands selling their wives and in May 1851 it was reported that a Droylsden man had attempted to sell his wife in Stockport market-place. A fellow weaver from Droylsden Mill started the bidding at seven pence, which was soon advanced up to ten shillings; but the police dispersed the competitors "ere she was knocked down"![13] This incident seems unbelievable, but in the eighteenth and nineteenth centuries wife-selling was not unusual and according to the historian James Bryce, the custom persisted in England in some form until the early twentieth century.[14] Divorce was practically unheard of and with no financial resources, and no skills on which to trade, some women found that a sale was the only way out of an unhappy marriage. In most recorded cases the intent was to end a marriage in a way that gave it the legitimacy of divorce. Sometimes the Poor Law Authorities stepped in as in the case in 1814 when they forced the husband to sell his wife rather than have to maintain her and her child in the Effingham Workhouse. She was taken to Croydon market and sold for one shilling, the Parish paying for the cost of the journey and a "wedding dinner"![15]

Influential Women

There was a growing movement, composed of intelligent, affluent and influential women, who were gradually striving for at least an acknowledgement that women deserved something more. Some of these women were writers who expressed their criticism and gave vent to their frustrations in their written work. Others were brave enough to challenge the superiority of men in their working lives and some worked hard to secure improvements in girls' education. These women were at the forefront of a movement that would eventually open up a world of opportunity undreamed of by Fairfield girls in the first half of the nineteenth century.

Charlotte Brontë (1816 – 1855)

Writing was one of the few occupations in which an intelligent, gifted woman could excel and pursue a career with very little male opposition. (Although Charlotte and her sisters Emily and Anne had to write under a male nom de plume when they first started writing). Charlotte in her novel *"Jane Eyre,"* published in 1847, has Jane arguing in Chapter Twelve that '*Women are supposed to be very calm generally, but women feel just as men feel; they need exercise for their faculties, and a field for their efforts as much as their brothers do; they suffer from too rigid a restraint, too absolute a stagnation, precisely as men would suffer*'. Jane Eyre also comments that '*It is narrow-minded to say that they ought to confine themselves to making puddings and knitting stockings, to playing on the piano and embroidering bags. It is thoughtless to condemn them or laugh at them, if they seek to do more than custom has pronounced necessary for their sex'*. We are surely right in thinking that Jane is echoing Charlotte's feelings of frustration. Jane Eyre was portrayed as a very independently minded woman who, nevertheless, was restricted by her class, her poverty and her single status. She had to support herself and to do this she had no choice but to join the ranks of the poorly paid governesses - much the same as Charlotte, herself, had done. However, for Charlotte, marriage was important and this feeling is reflected in the words which she wrote at the beginning of the concluding chapter of *"Jane Eyre"*: '*Reader, I married him'*.

The hardship of a governess's life and other aspects of her life are described by Charlotte in the five hundred or so letters which she wrote to her dearest, life-long friend, Ellen Nussey. These letters form an important part of Barbara Whitehead's book *"Charlotte Brontë and Her Dearest Nell"*. The two girls first met at Roe Head House, a small boarding school at Mirfield, in the West Riding of Yorkshire on the 25th January 1831. Charlotte's previous experience of boarding school life had not been a happy one. She was eight when she went with three of her sisters to the Cowan Bridge School for the daughters of clergymen. Two of her sisters died after contracting tuberculosis there and Charlotte used her unhappy time at the school as a basis for her description of the infamous Lowood School in *"Jane Eyre"*. The fourteen year old Charlotte had been at Roe Head School for about a week when Ellen arrived, aged thirteen. Of particular interest to us, is the fact that Ellen moved in Moravian circles and in 1826 she had entered the Moravian Ladies' Academy at Gomersal, West Yorkshire. Barbara Whitehead tells us that the pupils came to the school from all over the world and the curriculum was unusually wide.

Before Ellen was born, two of her sisters had become involved in the local Moravian community at Gomersal and in 1817, the year that Ellen was born, her sister Mary joined the Single Sisters' House at Fairfield, Droylsden. She took the religious name of Mercy and Charlotte Brontë always called her by this name. Mercy was not a Moravian Sister all her life and by 1831 she was living at home. Barbara Whitehead goes on to say that the Moravians influenced the Brontës, particularly Anne, and they also had a lifelong influence on Ellen.

Charlotte's letters and Barbara Whitehead's research help us to understand Charlotte's marriage relationship. Charlotte had been married to Arthur Nicholls for only nine months when she died. (It is thought that her death was caused by the severe morning sickness illness, hyperemesis gravidarum). Although Ellen Nussey recounted that Charlotte was extremely happy at the beginning of her married life, she, Ellen, feared that such happiness could not last. Many years after Charlotte's death, Ellen is reported as saying that when she asked Charlotte if she would be writing anything more, Charlotte had replied '*I have got a story in my head, but Arthur does not wish me to write it. He thinks I should attend to other things now*'. When Ellen argued with Nicholls about his idea that a clergyman's wife should not engage in literary work, he replied "*I married Charlotte Brontë not Currer Bell*". (Currer Bell was Charlotte's literary pseudonym). Arthur Nicholls also wanted Ellen to burn her letters from Charlotte and if she didn't promise to do so he said he would censor them. Ellen did promise to do this but, of course, the promise was never kept, mainly because Ellen suspected that he had already censored them. Barbara Whitehead suggests that Arthur Nicholls' voice seemed to have held an unpleasant harsh note of command, as if Charlotte was a chattel or a being inferior to him.[16]

Elizabeth Gaskell (1810 – 1865)

Elizabeth was born in 1810 and published her first important book in 1848. This book - "Mary Barton" - was, and still is, of particular interest to the people of Manchester because in it Elizabeth Gaskell described in detail the dreadful poverty and housing conditions in which the Manchester mill workers lived and contrasted this with descriptions of the wealthy mill owners' homes. The book shocked many middle-class readers - they had no idea about the conditions in which the working class lived. It also, of course, described in detail the lives of people living only a few miles from Fairfield.

Given the improvements in communication and travel in the mid nineteenth century, we can only assume that the people of Fairfield were very much aware of the burgeoning city on their doorstep. What was happening four miles west of Fairfield was quite phenomenal. Nothing like the rapid growth of Manchester had ever been seen before.

One of the main roads going from Droylsden into Manchester passed through Beswick and Ancoats on the east side of Manchester city centre. These two areas formed part of the main mill area and it is here that the greatest poverty could be seen. In 1842, six years before "Mary Barton" was published, a Report by the Town Mission described many appalling cases. Some families had gone for days without food and lived in damp cellars without bedclothes or furniture.

Elizabeth Gaskell came from an intellectual and wealthy family. Her mother had died when she was a year old and she went to live with her Aunt in Knutsford. She attended a boarding school near Stratford upon Avon for five years until she was sixteen.

Elizabeth's spirit of independence was encouraged by her father. He wrote many published articles and in the Westminster Review of 5 January 1826 he wrote that *'women should be seen as companions and co-operators with men in intellectual pursuits. Women, therefore, ought to discountenance every kind of treatment and behaviour which, proceeding on the supposition that they are helpless, dependent and frivolous in their thought and pursuits, renders them so, and bestow their approbation only on those men who regard and trust them as equal to themselves in their capacity for knowledge and usefulness.*

Elizabeth was well aware that this opinion held by her father was not the norm. In her last book "Wives and Daughters" she describes the heroine, Molly's, early years in the 1830s and expresses the prevalent view of girls' schooling, while stressing the desire for a better education. Molly's father in Chapter three tells her Governess, Miss Eyre *'Don't teach Molly too much - she must sew and read and write and do her sums. After all, I'm not sure that reading or writing is necessary. Many a good woman gets married with only a cross instead of her name; it's rather a diluting of mother-wit to my fancy; but, however, we must yield to the prejudices of society, Miss Eyre, and so you may teach the child to read.'* Molly does manage to persuade her father to allow her to learn French, and although her father is opposed to any other intellectual pursuits, she is determined to learn even more and reads everything she can.

Elizabeth never thought of herself as the obedient subordinate wife. She always signed herself Elizabeth Gaskell, never Mrs William Gaskell as was expected then. She was, however, completely aware that in the majority of marriages the husband was the powerful one and marriage was not a union of equals. It was fortunate that she married a Unitarian minister. The Unitarians thought that marriage was a partnership between equals.[17]

It was a time of great developments in science and engineering and also of political ideas and agitation. Through family and friends Elizabeth had connections with industry, railway development, the anti-slavery campaign and the movement for the extension of the franchise. Although she was influenced by these things, in her novels she wrote of the norm not the exception and showed that '*love, not knowledge, was the Victorian heroine's fate. Science, like industry, was the province of men.*'[18]

Harriet Martineau (1802 – 1876)

Another important and influential woman writer at the time was Harriet Martineau. Her story "A Manchester Strike" of 1832, which was published in Illustrations of Political Economy, was the forerunner of some of the ideas expressed in Gaskell's "Mary Barton". She was well-known as a journalist and novelist on both sides of the Atlantic. Harriet was one of the best-informed and most intelligent writers of her time and was intensely aware of the conditions of the poor. It is thought that Charles Dickens when writing Oliver Twist may have been influenced by the details in her book "*Poor Law and Paupers Illustrated (1833)*". Her articles dealt with controversial issues such as female and working class education and trade unionism.

Florence Nightingale (1820 – 1910)

Florence Nightingale's efforts helped to change the way women were viewed in society. Details of how she developed nursing as a profession are well known but perhaps what is not so well known is her background and her early struggles against the restrictions of women generally and in particular women of her social class. Born in 1820, she came from a very privileged background but because she was a woman, even wealth could not bring her freedom from the restraints imposed upon her because of her sex. From an early age she loved learning and she was much influenced by her father who was educated at Cambridge. Under her father's tuition she studied French, German, Italian, Latin and Greek and also history and philosophy. Florence thrived in this academic atmosphere. She desperately wanted to put the knowledge she had gained to good use. Unfortunately, that was not what a young lady in society was expected to do - and in any case at that time there were no careers or professions open to ladies - and so, in 1839 she was presented at court.

She felt completely stifled by the life she led at home which consisted of unimportant domestic duties such as flower arranging, needlework and visiting friends and acquaintances. To lessen the boredom she began to take up charitable work and it was from this that her interest in nursing grew. In the 1840's, it was unheard of that a woman of her status should become a nurse. Nursing was work done by uneducated, working-class women. She faced great opposition from her family. However, she moved in the higher ranks of society and became friendly with Sidney Herbert who was Secretary to the Admiralty and through him she met other influential people who, like her, were interested in hospital reform. She made it her business to study the Blue Books. These were Government Reports which were used as a basis for the reforms of the dreadful social conditions of the time. These Reports made a great impression on Florence as she learned of the awful, perilous lives that many people led. She became an expert on Government Social Statistics and her opinion was sought by Sidney Herbert and his friends.

It wasn't until she was thirty in 1850 that she was offered the position of Superintendent of the Institute for Sick Gentlewomen in Distressed Circumstances. She accepted the position and her father then made her an allowance of £500 a year which meant that she would be completely independent. £500 a year was a tremendous amount of money. Even by the 1930's a working man usually earned less than £200 a year. Four years later, when a Cholera epidemic broke out she went to the Middlesex Hospital as a volunteer where she supervised the nursing of cholera patients. She established an excellent standard of nursing at the hospital and shortly afterwards she was invited by the Government to go out to Scutari to supervise a party of nurses in an attempt to ease the suffering of the soldiers in the Crimea. After the War, she devoted herself to the development of nursing as a career, which would eventually become recognised as a skilled profession.

Florence was also a gifted mathematician and a pioneer in the visual presentation of information and statistical graphics. In 1859 she was elected as the first female member of the Royal Statistical Society.

Florence's early life must have been similar to that of many thousands of women at that time, however, the great majority would not have had the opportunity to reach anything like their full potential in the way that Florence did. Florence achieved this mainly, but not solely, because of her tremendous intellect and determination. The other main contributors were her family's social position and wealth and the presence of important friends.

Elizabeth Garrett Anderson (1836 - 1917)

Florence Nightingale's work, in setting up a school for nurses, most likely encouraged the ambitions of the girl who was to become the first Englishwoman to qualify as a doctor. Elizabeth Garrett Anderson enrolled as a nursing student at the Middlesex Hospital in 1860 and attended classes for male doctors, but was barred after complaints from them. However, the Society of Apothecaries did not forbid women from taking their examinations and in 1865 Elizabeth passed their exams and gained a certificate which enabled her to become a doctor. The Society then changed its rules, preventing other women entering the profession in this way. Elizabeth had to study at the University of Paris to earn her degree and even then the British Medical Register refused to recognise her qualification.

In 1866 she established a dispensary for women in London and in 1870 she was made a visiting physician to the East London Hospital. She married in 1871 and went on to have three children. This did not prevent her continuing with her career. In 1872 she founded the New Hospital for Women in London staffed entirely by women. Elizabeth's actions paved the way for other women and in 1876 an Act was passed permitting women to enter the medical profession. She founded the London School of Medicine for Women in 1874 and was appointed Dean of the School in 1883.

EDUCATION

Working Class Education

Education was still thought to be the province of the well-to-do. The scientist, David Gilbert, had argued in the House of Commons in 1807 that giving education to the labouring classes would in effect be prejudicial to their morals and happiness. It would teach them to despise their lot in life, instead of making them good servants to agriculture and other laborious employments, to which their rank in society had destined them. While our Fairfield girls were receiving a full-time education, the children in the surrounding areas were less fortunate. Industrialisation was having a harmful effect on literacy. In Ashton-under-Lyne, four miles from Fairfield, those able to read and write fell from 48 per cent to 9 per cent between 1823 and 1843. In the 1860s, at a Manchester sewing school, only 21per cent of the girls could read and write.

However, education in Droylsden gradually improved. A juvenile and infant day school was built by the mill owner William Miller Christy in 1838 which became part of the British Schools system (an organisation attached to the non-Conformist churches). A day school for girls had been opened in Fairfield as early as 1809 which was incorporated into the system of the National Society (an establishment run by the Church of England) in 1854, when it became a mixed day school.[20] Education in Droylsden, especially for men, was greatly improved by the opening of the Droylsden Educational Institute in 1858.

It was not until the Education Act of 1870 that it was made the right of every child to have an education and not until 1880 was education made compulsory for five to ten year olds. During the first half of the century many children did not attend school because they were working, firstly at home and later on, in the mills, and many parents couldn't even afford the few pence which a school education cost. In Droylsden in 1845 only 167 children out of 1,352 attended the day schools and 633 attended the Sunday Schools.[21]

Education at Fairfield

It became evident that new schools in Manchester and, of course, the long established Manchester Grammar School, were presenting a challenge to the Boys' Boarding School at Fairfield and there were, indeed, going to be difficult times ahead. However, the Girls' Boarding School, which now also took day pupils, continued to meet a growing need for the education of girls.[19] Unlike the Boys' School, the Girls' School was faced with little competition. It wasn't until the second half of the nineteenth century that the education of most girls from affluent homes progressed beyond an elementary standard and only then because of the agitation, hard work and farsightedness of a few dedicated women.

During the first half of the nineteenth century, the teachers in the schools for middle class girls were untrained poor gentlewomen. The only teacher-training available was that set up for teachers in the National and British schools and no gentlewoman would consider such a training or teaching in the schools for the 'lower classes".

It has to be assumed, that the teaching at Fairfield was better than that experienced in many other girls' boarding schools around the country. The teachers at Fairfield were drawn from the Moravian community and were sincere dedicated women concerned about the moral as well as the educational development of their pupils and the girls were fortunate in that they were living in a loving Christian community.

In the 1830s and early 1840s there were as many as fifty boarders and twenty day pupils studying at the school. Journals and Accounts Books in the Fairfield Moravian Church archive show that fees started at about £25 per year, but there seemed to be many extras. For something called a "tea or coffee breakfast" an annual charge of £2.2s.0d was made (one shilling is five pence in today's money and there were twenty shillings in a pound and twelve old-pennies in a shilling). The same annual fee of £2.2s.0d was charged for both music and drawing lessons. Apart from these two subjects, there was a charge for extra lessons in French and in the accounts for 1839 there is an item headed "Sundries from Boarders' Bills" which included amounts for copy books, new music, use of musical instrument (e.g. use of pianoforte), drawing materials, hair cutting, Chapel seats, millinery, shoe bills, pocket money, medicines, collections, stationery, washing and doctor's bills. There must, therefore, have been a considerable sum added to the basic school fee and the likely total cost would probably have been at least £40 per year. This was at a time when £40 could represent a year's wages for an ordinary working man.

In the accounts there were details of books for sale. These books give a clear idea of the education the girls received. The subjects covered were English, Poetry, Grammar, Spelling, French, Geography, History, Scripture, and Arithmetic. There was also a book entitled *"Magnall's Questions"*. This particular book was prominent in the education of English girls in the first half of the nineteenth century. It was written by Richmal Magnall, a Yorkshire Headmistress and is mentioned in Elizabeth Gaskell's novel *"Wives and Daughters"* in which it is described as 'ubiquitous'.

As in other girls' schools, considerable time was given to needlework, or "Fancy Work" as it was called. Each year the materials used for this work were listed in the school's accounts - and it was a long list comprised of the following:- embroidery silks, silk braid, silk satin, chenille, hand screens, baskets, cards, silk canvas, souvenirs and spill cases, watch pockets, satin, sampler canvas, tassels, floss silk, crepe, pug canvas, Berlin wool, picture for embroidery, worsted, beads, ribbons and lambswool.[22]

In the first half of the nineteenth century, as was to be expected, the education at the school in many ways did follow that experienced in many other girls' schools. There seems, to a certain extent, to have been some emphasis on the accomplishments that a young middle class lady should learn, namely a knowledge of music and the playing of an instrument, drawing and painting and needlework. However the study of more academic subjects gave the girls a good education which was far better than in many other girls' schools and certainly set them apart from the working class child who received a very elementary education.

A close examination of the school's accounts gives an indication of the difference in lifestyle compared to today. Items which were purchased in 1833 included a tea caddy, a high fire guard, candles, dips, bush lights, mantel candles, steel snuffers (for candles), bedsteads and bed ticks, coal and quills. The cost of quills for 1830 was £4.11s.3d which was a considerable sum. Money was paid to a blacksmith to carry out repairs and the services of joiners, stonemasons, clock repairers, painters and paper changers, (presumably what we would call decorators), were sought.

The kitchen accounts listed payments to butchers, bakers, and grocers and payments for milk, potatoes and malt.

The stock of provisions was listed. In 1830 this included hams, bacon, cheese, preserves, pickles, wine (foreign), spirits, ginger and currant wine, loaf sugar, soap, and white soap and two pigs! It's amusing to note that the total value of these provisions was £25.19s.0d which included the cost of £4.6s.0d. for foreign wines and spirits - a sixth of the total cost. The Sisters perhaps made these wines and spirits last because by 1841 the stock of wine and sherry was listed as having a value of ten shillings. However, the list of provisions for 1840 notes a stock of sixty bottles of homemade wine at a value of £2.6s.0d. The accounts for the years following 1841 are extremely brief, so there is no way of telling whether the sixty bottles were disposed of in that year or were made to last for a few years.[23] It seems that the life of a schoolmistress had its compensations!

There were usually at least five teachers plus the headmistress and given that during this time the school usually had no more than seventy pupils (boarding and day), the class size would be less than fifteen. This would make for a very pleasant atmosphere and one conducive to quiet learning.

The girls who boarded at the school had to bring sufficient clothing and other personal items to last them a complete term and before the introduction of the railway line in 1841, they would have had to travel to school by coach. Depending on the length of the journey, it would be quite likely that the adults travelling with them would have stayed overnight at the inn in the Settlement. Recently the Old Girls' Association was given a copy of a letter written by a Boarding School pupil dated the 28th November 1837. In it the girl, Elizabeth Shaw, writes in a very formal manner to advise her mother that the school vacation would commence on the 21st December and that her uncle had kindly promised to fetch her.

Her uncle would have had to come for her by coach – it was another four years before the railway came to Fairfield. The letter was beautifully written, probably using a quill pen as there is no mention of metal nibs in the school's accounts and it wasn't until the 1850s that the use of the quill pen began to fade.

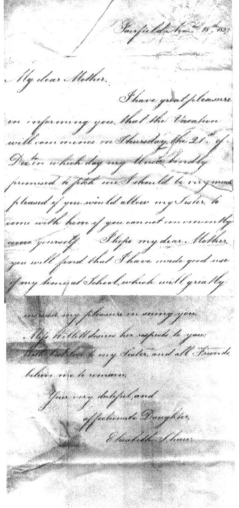

Fairfield Novbr 28th 1837

My dear Mother,

I have great pleasure in informing you that the Vacation will commence on Thursday the 21st of Decbr on which day my Uncle kindly promised to fetch me. I should be very much pleased if you would allow my Sister to come with him if you cannot conveniently come yourself. I hope my dear Mother you will find that I have made good use of my time at school which will greatly increase my pleasure in seeing you.

Miss Willett desires her respects to you.

With best love to my Sister and all Friends, believe me to remain,

Your very dutiful and
affectionate Daughter,

Elizabeth Shaw.

Above – An 1837 letter from a Fairfield pupil to her mother

Above – A transcription of the same letter

Women's Education

The change in the position of women had to start somewhere and education was the key. It was realised that women had to equip themselves with knowledge so that they could prove themselves equal to men. It would only be then that they would be in a position to grasp future opportunities.

However, the much-needed improvement in the education of middle-class girls was a gradual one and was dependent on the work of a few inspirational and dedicated individuals. In 1848 Queen's College, London was established. It had its origins in a series of lectures given by a lecturer from King's College for the Governesses' Benevolent Society. This Society had been set up to help unemployed and incapacitated Governesses. The plight of many Governesses was pretty dire. They were poorly paid, lacked any professional training, had no other source of income and little expectation of finding husbands to provide for them. The Society's funds were inadequate – in 1848 the Society could provide only three annuities for which there were ninety five applicants. It was realised that the status of a governess would be greatly improved by the introduction of qualifying examinations and certificates of proficiency which would then improve their bargaining power and a gift from a benefactor enabled premises for the Queen's College to be purchased. The lecturer, F. D. Maurice, felt that instruction was also needed for younger girls (over twelve) and so the school had preparatory day classes for these girls and evening classes for girls who were already governesses. Bedford College, a similar institution to Queen's, was opened in 1849. These colleges attracted intelligent middle-class girls living in London and were an important influence on the higher education of girls during the next decades. Both Frances Mary Buss, who went on to establish the North London Collegiate School, and Dorothea Beale, who was the first Head Mistress of Cheltenham Ladies' College, were among the early students at Queen's College.

It is interesting to note that Cheltenham Ladies' College was founded in 1854 by a group of men (women were involved later) who wanted a school which would stretch a girls' intellect sufficiently "*to fit her for the discharge of those responsibilities which devolve upon her as a wife, mother, mistress and friend, the natural companion and helpmate for men*" They did not want to train her for any greater responsibility nor in any way to undermine their own superior position.[24]

There was early opposition at the school to the academic curriculum. Dorothea Beale in her history of the school recalled one mother withdrawing her daughter saying *"It is all very well for my daughter to read Shakespeare, but don't you think it is more important for her to be able to sit down at the piano and amuse her friends.*[25]

Emily Davies (1830 – 1921)

The ambitions of girls to further their education was encouraged and inspired by Emily Davies, who, like Florence Nightingale, had felt stifled by the life she was expected to live as a Victorian Lady. She was astounded that working opportunities for women were so limited. She could see no reason why a woman was not capable both physically and mentally, of doing many of the jobs which were only open to men. By working, a woman would not become a burden on her family. She once pointed out that *"all over England large numbers of able-bodied girls are kept at home because of the assumption that indolence was feminine and refined. No man in his senses would keep two or three sons at home doing nothing".*[26] She felt that girls did so little in life because they were educated to do so little. If their education improved they would be qualified to gain employment in many different spheres. The problem was further exacerbated by a situation revealed by the 1851 census, which showed that there were half a million more women than men in England. Clearly, not all of them would be able to find husbands to support them and many would therefore have to support themselves.

Emily's greatest hope was for girls to be allowed to study at University but her initial attempts failed. She then decided to lower her sights and attempt to enable girls to sit the new Local Examinations set up by Oxford and Cambridge Universities. These examinations had been started in 1858 in an attempt to measure achievement in the middle class schools for boys because these schools were not covered by H.M. Inspectors as were the national elementary schools. Emily envisaged these examinations as stepping stones to getting entry to degree examinations.

Oxford at first refused to allow girls to sit their exam but Cambridge gave permission for copies of the boys' papers to be provided and the girls sat the exam in December 1863. The results were that the girls did very well in English and, in every other subject, except Arithmetic, their standard was just as good as the boys.

Because of the poor result in Arithmetic, it was suggested that the Arithmetic exam should be 'lightened' for the girls. Emily insisted that the exam for girls should be the same as for the boys. The problem with Arithmetic, she said, was caused by the poor teaching of the subject. Because of Emily's persistence, girls were soon achieving similar results to the boys and sometimes even better.

Moravian Education

A perusal of the Moravian monthly magazine *"The Messenger"* helps to show the attitude of the Moravian Church. They wrote that they regarded education as one of the most important "fields of usefulness" that a religious community could have. They were very much aware that knowledge was advancing rapidly and they hoped that their institutions would keep pace with the "advancing intelligence of the times". They stated that "there is nothing antagonistic to Christianity in knowledge which is based upon well ascertained and demonstrated facts".

They also welcomed the extension of knowledge to the lower classes of society and suggested that the establishment of Mechanics Institutes, Free Libraries and Sunday Schools were no longer viewed by the wealthy with prejudice and suspicion[27]

The Messenger Magazine contained a series of articles entitled "The Aims and Nature of Education". In 1866 the writer listed the qualities that a Christian teacher needed - the child should be treated with respect, love and patience and the writer took it for granted that no one would be accepted as a teacher in a Moravian school who was not knowledgeable and talented.[28]

It was stated that if a teacher really loved her charges, if she had their real welfare at heart, the children would notice it. She would win their confidence, which would not be easily disturbed. The spirit of the school must be one of love - love to one another, and love to the children.[29]

One interesting comment stated *"Every beginning is difficult. Much of life is spent surmounting difficulties, therefore it is folly to expect to make learning an amusement. Teachers should correct the false idea that everything must be entertaining".*

Teachers were advised not to use sarcasm and to be completely impartial. They were told that impatience was a very serious fault. They should never relinquish hope but should try to understand a child's bad behaviour and find the cause. They should let the child feel warm sympathy. Even though a child had to be punished he should still remain loved and the teacher's judgement should be mild not condemnatory.[30] Children being taught at Moravian schools were indeed fortunate to be studying in such a loving and sympathetic environment.

MORAVIAN WOMEN

What did the future hold for our Fairfield pupils? For a few it would have been a very different life from that experienced by the majority of middle-class English girls. The daughters of Moravian Missionaries, along with other Moravian girls, would sometimes marry missionaries and serve abroad. For others their lives would have followed the expected restricted path of a middle class lady, of marriage and children, or teaching or helping other needy members of their families. I found that even girls who had benefited from the broadening experience of living abroad, settled down to a life of domesticity or teaching.

The 1851 census shows that the school was composed of a cosmopolitan group of teachers and pupils; only the Headmistress was born locally. Two teachers had been born in Jamaica, probably born to Moravian missionary parents, one was born in Herrnhut, the place of the first Moravian "Settlement" in Saxony, and three were born in Ireland. Of the pupils, one girl was born on the island of Antigua, and others were born in Wales, Ireland, Scotland, Yorkshire, Gloucestershire, Northumberland and Cheshire. Of the twenty nine borders, only eight were born within ten miles of the school.

Ten year old Anna Willett who was born in Sheffield, was one of the youngest boarders. Anna must have been an intelligent pupil. Ten years later in 1861 she was a member of the teaching staff at the school. A fellow pupil was Mary Ann Blake who was fourteen in 1851. She was born on the island of Antigua and married an Army Sergeant and spent some time with him on the Island of Barbados where their son was born. They returned to England for a number of years and lived in Army accommodation at Aldershot.

Another girl who was well travelled was Ada Anne Lee who was born in Melbourne, Australia. Although there were Moravian missionaries in

Melbourne her parents were not among them. They must have been reasonably wealthy to afford to send their daughter to an English boarding school. Ada stayed in England after finishing her education and went to live in London where she worked as an embroiderer before marrying an architect, Arthur Breeds, in 1886. They went on to have two children and, like most middle-class families, they were always able to employ domestic servants.

One girl, Harriet Ford (née Hall), who became a day pupil at the school in 1861 when she was eight, wrote to the school in 1946, when she was ninety-three, congratulating the school on its 150th anniversary. She compared school life when she was a girl with the life in the present day. She said there was no hockey, tennis or netball and there were no cinemas to go to in their leisure time. (Harriet did not mention television because the BBC did not re-start its TV service after the War until June 1946, and only a very few homes had a television set). She went on to say that during her schooldays in the 1860s, the pupils from both the Girls' School and the Boys' School attended the Moravian Church. The girls had to sit on one side and the boys on the other.[31] Harriet's father, Robert Hall, was a brick manufacturer. She had three sisters and three brothers. Her brother George was a boarding pupil at the Fairfield Moravian Boys School in 1861 when he was thirteen. Her parents must have been quite wealthy - they were able to privately educate seven children and employ a live-in general servant and a nursemaid. Harriet married Palmer Crucifer Ford, a cotton goods merchant, in 1874 when she was twenty one. They had seven children, two of whom died before 1911. The Ford family usually employed one or two live-in servants. Harriet's youngest son, Charles Musgrave Ford had a distinguished naval career. As a very young man he served in the First World War and was awarded the Russian Order of St Anne. During the Second World War he was a Commodore of Ocean Convoys and during that time he was ADC to the King (Aide de Camp or Personal Assistant). After the war, he was Captain of the liner Queen Elizabeth and awarded the CBE in 1946. In 1949 he became Commodore of the Cunard Fleet and was made USA Commander of the Legion of Merit.

Her other sons all followed professional careers and one can safely assume that they would all have been encouraged and supported by a well-educated mother - the sort of mother and wife of a busy member of the "commercial class" that Mr James Bryce, in his Report for the Schools Enquiry Commission of 1868, suggested would be a great influence for good.

It is interesting to note that there is no evidence of Harriet's two daughters continuing their education or pursuing any kind of career. In 1901 Mary aged sixteen and Laura aged twenty two, were living at home in South Manchester. The census gave no details of their occupation so one can only presume that Mary had left school and neither girl was working. Mary married in 1908 and sadly Laura died in 1910.

Children of Moravian Missionaries were usually sent back to England to continue their education in Moravian Boarding Schools. One little girl who was born in Antigua came to live in the Settlement at Fairfield under very tragic circumstances. Her father, James La Trobe Harvey who was a member of a prominent Moravian family was a missionary in the West Indies. James' father, Bennett Harvey was the church minister at Fairfield from 1858 to 1865 and he remained at Fairfield in his retirement. James Harvey was a missionary in the West Indies for twenty nine years. He had come back to England after ten years to marry and he and his wife (Ernestine Meyer) returned to the West Indies and raised four children. James became extremely ill in 1879 and was advised to return to England for treatment. Two of his children, Edgar aged nine and Amy aged six, travelled with him. Tragically, James died aboard ship, the same day that it docked at Southampton. (James's wife had died earlier and his two oldest children were already at school in England). All four children came under the care of their grandfather, the Rev. Bennett Harvey.[32] The eldest three children were educated at the Moravian boarding school at Fulneck in Yorkshire but Amy lived for a time with her grandparents in Fairfield and attended the Fairfield Moravian Girls School for at least the first few years of her education. In 1891 she was working as a mother's help for the wife of a Methodist Minister in Islington, London aged eighteen.

LIFE IN THE SETTLEMENT

During the second half of the 19th century life in the Settlement had become less insular. F H Mellowes in his History of the Moravian Church at Fairfield wrote that, *"… the sheer force and magnitude of the growing industrial scene and the growth of Science were all influential in bringing <u>to</u> an end the attempt to live a life preserved from the World and its evil ways. Up to one third of the houses were now occupied by tenants who were not members of the Church. The emphasis was now on serving the wider community and attending to the needs of men and women in a period of rapid social change"[33]*

Technical and scientific developments were having their effect on the life in the Settlement. Gas lighting was introduced there, in the 1850s, well before it was established in Droylsden. It was obtained first from Benson's Mill and then from the Droylsden Gas Company. The light given off from a gas lamp was far superior to that from candles. [34] There was no longer the need to fetch water as this was piped to every house in the Settlement. The train service between Fairfield and Manchester developed swiftly, after the opening of the railway station at Fairfield. People from Fairfield could now travel by rail in many directions.

We will see in the next chapter that improvements in girls' education, both nationally and at Fairfield, would be made during the following decades. It was a progress which was sorely needed if girls were eventually to step out from a life of domesticity and at last widen their horizons and become, as Charles Dickens wrote in 'Our Mutual Friend' *'something so much worthier than the doll in the doll's house.'*

CHAPTER THREE

IMPROVEMENT IN EDUCATION 1870-1905

Universities reluctantly open their doors to women.

THE SCHOOLS' ENQUIRY COMMISSION

The much needed improvement in girls' education was greatly helped by the recommendations of the Schools' Enquiry Commission (sometimes known as the Taunton Commission). This Enquiry was set up to look into the condition of middle-class schools but its remit at the time was to look into boys' not girls' schools unless specifically asked to do so. Emily Davies vigorously campaigned to get this decision changed and she was eventually successful in persuading the Commission to include the education of girls, and the means of improving it, as part of their Enquiry.

The conclusions reached when the Report by the Commission was published in 1868 were extremely critical of girls' education and included the following comments *"Want of thoroughness and foundation, want of system, slovenliness and showing superficiality, inattention to rudiments, and those not taught intelligently or in any scientific manner; want of organisation."*

The Commission also noted that *"We find, as a rule, a very small amount of professional skill, an inferior set of school books, a vast deal of dry, uninteresting task work, rules put into the memory with no explanation of their principles, no system of examination worthy of the name, a tendency to fill and adorn rather than to strengthen the mind"*.

Mr J. G. Fitch, who was responsible for the Commission's investigation in York and the West Riding, reported that he had found that girls were not even taught about any domestic subjects, which would have been of benefit to those women who would have the responsibility of running a home and looking after a family. Such subjects as, cooking, the supervision of servants, and family health were absent from the curriculum.[1]

Mr Fitch visited the Moravian Girls' School at Fulneck in Yorkshire and gave the School a favourable Report. He identified the School as being worthy of praise with particular emphasis on a feeling of unity among the teachers.[2]

Mr James Bryce, the Assistant Commissioner for Lancashire Schools, in his Report on Girls' Schools in the county, criticised the continued use of obsolete methods and incompetent teachers. He also wrote of his concern about the indifference of the commercial class to any education that was not of any pecuniary value. He suggested that an educated and cultured woman would have a great influence for good on this middle class society. However, before this could be achieved the education of girls had to improve.

As an indication of the present situation James Bryce cited comments made by parents to teachers. One teacher commented that it was put to her that *"Boys are educated for the world, girls for the drawing room."* Another parent said *"I'm anxious about the music but it really doesn't matter about her arithmetic, does it? Her husband will be able to do all her accounts for her, you know"*. One teacher commented that parents filled their daughters' minds with the notion that their education had not been of any use to them and they did not care whether or not they profited by it, so long as they possessed showy qualities which were supposed to command the admiration of the opposite sex.

Mr Bryce was extremely critical of the teaching he found in Lancashire schools. There was a great amount of money and time spent on the teaching of music - often two hours a day and very little or none spent on mathematics and science. Although he admitted that a considerable number of women of ability, energy and refinement could be found among the mistresses of girls' schools, there was a body of teachers who were not competent in their work. He reported that this incompetence appeared to be due to three causes.

Firstly, the teachers themselves had often not received an education of an acceptable standard, especially in Maths, Sciences and Languages; secondly, specific teacher training hardly existed and thirdly, many women teachers were isolated. This isolation meant that there was lack of contact with better teachers from whom they could learn and discuss subjects such as history and scientific advances. This lack of communication meant that they continued to use obsolete methods and text books and were possessed of antiquated notions which seriously impaired their efficiency as teachers.

Mr Bryce further reported that there was no external qualification and testimony of fitness (i.e. university degree grade). The teachers, themselves, had not been well taught and they did not know how to teach.[3]

Mr Bryce did not single out the Moravian Girls' School at Fairfield for comment, but it was likely that the standard there would be similar to that at Fulneck in Yorkshire and would be found to be good in many aspects. The teaching of French and German would have been of a high standard. There was much contact with the Church on the Continent and would-be teachers would sometimes go to study in the Moravian teacher training schools in Germany and France, which had been established by 1850. Some German teachers also came over to teach in Moravian Schools. There was, however, no Moravian teacher training college in England and many girls wishing to become teachers stayed on at school and became pupil/teachers. As far as the isolation of teachers was concerned, those in Moravian Girls' schools had certain advantages over teachers in many other girls' schools. They taught in a closely knit group of Boarding Schools and took part in regular conferences where teaching methods, text books and new developments in a variety of subjects were discussed.[4]

Mr Bryce stated that, in his opinion, it was from the advent of more highly educated teachers that the first improvements in the education of girls would come about, but such teachers could not be had until places were provided where they might obtain a training longer, more thorough and more stimulating than that which was at present available.

One very important conclusion that the Taunton Commission came to was that *"There is mighty evidence that the essential capacity for learning is the same or nearly the same in the two sexes"*. The Commission also recommended that schools should submit themselves to regular inspection and that boys and girls should be allowed to share examinations where "the subjects dealt with are the great fundamental ones of general knowledge".[5]

According to the National Archives website, the Commission found that there were only thirteen secondary schools for girls in the whole of the country and to rectify this the Commission proposed that girls' secondary schools, modelled on the North London Collegiate School, should be established in every town of four thousand or more inhabitants but no details of how this plan was to be carried out were suggested. It did, however, recommend that endowments should be distributed more fairly between boys' and girls' schools.

After the publication of the Report of the Schools' Enquiry Commission, there was a gradual improvement in the education of middle class girls. There were already a number of girls' schools offering an academic education similar to that at the North London Collegiate School and the Cheltenham Ladies' College. The Cambridge and Oxford Local Examinations had been opened up to girls by 1865 and eight years later Girton College, Cambridge, was founded to give girls a university education. This was followed a few years later by Newnham College, Cambridge and Somerville College and Lady Margaret Hall at Oxford.

Education at Fairfield

One of the problems at the Moravian girls' schools had been the lack of professional training for the women teachers. Until 1878 most teachers were trained within the schools as pupil/teachers and a few would have had some training at the Moravian schools in France and Germany. However, in 1878 arrangements were made for candidates for school service to be trained at the Home and Colonial Institute in London or in a similar establishment.[6] By 1878 The Home and Colonial College was well established. Frances Buss, the Headmistress of the North London Collegiate School, had inaugurated a teacher training course for secondary school teachers within the Home and Colonial College and many of her teachers were trained there.[7]

Two years earlier, in 1876, the School at Fairfield had moved back into the Sisters' House which was a large imposing Georgian house far more in keeping with the status of a boarding and day school than the buildings attached to the east side of the Church which had been the home of the School since 1815. This new accommodation coupled with a well- trained teaching staff, meant that the school would now be in a position to offer an even better education for its pupils. The School was also fortunate in that for half a century (from 1841 to 1892) it was served by just two devoted and dedicated Headmistresses. Mary Ann Willet was Headmistress until she retired aged seventy in 1871. She was succeeded by German born Pauline Kofler who was Headmistress until 1892. Having only two Headmistresses for a total of fifty years gave the school an ethos of stability and strength and a foundation on which to provide, in the years ahead, a sound education for its pupils.

From 1883 onwards the education at the school began to reach a higher standard. Only five years after the recommendation that teachers should be trained at the Home and Colonial College, Fairfield girls were successful in the Cambridge Local Examinations and in most years, from then on, a number of girls from the school passed these examinations.

By 1892 the Provincial Elders' Conference of the Moravian Church stated that it was desirable that the Moravian Ladies' Schools, as well as the Boys' Schools, should be encouraged to aim at the standard of the university middle class examinations and the teaching of Latin and mathematics in the advanced classes of the Ladies Schools should be encouraged.[9] These changes to the curriculum and the taking and passing of the Cambridge/Oxford Local Examinations, meant that the good education that the girls at Fairfield had been receiving for many years would now be recognised and would be the means, in the future, of enabling Fairfield girls to go on to a college or university education.

THE MORAVIAN ATTITUDE TOWARDS WOMEN

In 1883, an interesting article appeared in the *Moravian Messenger* magazine, which demonstrated the attitude which some male members of the Moravian Church still had regarding women's abilities. A Mrs Booth had written papers advocating that qualified Christian women should be allowed to speak at public meetings in front of men. The article in the *Moravian Messenger* discussed the question of whether or not public addresses by a woman to audiences consisting wholly or partly of men, were sanctioned by Holy Scripture or were in harmony with natural propriety.

The article commented that there were certain natural characteristics of the sexes which pre-eminently fitted the one for some duties and the other for other duties. It stated that '*when in individual cases the order of nature is reversed it is rarely a matter for congratulations.*'

The writer went on to state '*the prevalent sentiment, both amongst men and women, is and always will be, that public oratory belongs to the masculine rather than the feminine order of accomplishments and that, even when successfully undertaken by women before men, the feeling of admiration is leavened by a somewhat painful counter feeling of regret akin to that which is felt when a woman is found successfully exhibiting in public as a gymnast, or when a man is found distinguishing himself as a milliner!*'. The writer commented that '*surely if this feeling, in regard to public oratory by women, is so universally prevalent as we believe it to be, it goes far to prove that in this instance custom has not been confounded with nature*". The writer went on to say that "*nobody disputes women's ability to minister, only that speaking or preaching should be limited*'.

The writer concluded that '*when women do speak in public they should be careful not only to attire themselves in the more unobtrusive and modest manner but should also take pains to evince by their language and demeanour and consciousness that* **women are placed in the order of God's economy in a ranking subordinate to that of men**'.[10]

As late as1892 the inferior position of women was highlighted by the vote taken at the Provincial Synod of the Church on whether married women could exercise an independent vote i.e. '*that every communicant over 21 of either sex, married or single, have an independent vote at all congregation and council meetings.*' On division, only seven recorded in its favour. The motion was therefore lost. The reason given was that Christian teaching held that the wife was clearly commanded to be in subjection to her own husband.[11]

It has to be noted here that this religious belief, that women should be in subjection to their husbands, is one that is still held to be true today by some members of the clergy. As recently as February 2010 a Church of England Vicar caused outrage among his congregation after suggesting that women should be silent and submit to their husbands. These comments were included in a leaflet entitled 'The Role of Women in the Local Church' written by the rector of St. Nicholas Church in Sevenoaks, Kent. He said that women should not speak if asked a question that could be answered by their husbands and should *submit to their husbands in everything*'. The difference between 1892 and today is that the women expressed their outrage in no uncertain terms and were supported by the great majority of men. The reaction in the media against such an out-dated view was overwhelming.

Still on the subject of whether women should obey their husbands, it was interesting to note an article in the *Moravian Messenger* in 1894, which introduced the question of whether women ought to promise to obey their husbands. The writer of the article commented '*observation and experience both teach us that whether the promise is made or not, the general practice is for the husband to obey the wife and when they do so they find that they are generally in the right*''' I found this humorous, gentle comment particularly pleasant and far removed from the strident views expressed a few years earlier.[12]

UNIVERSITY EDUCATION FOR WOMEN

A milestone was reached when London University announced in 1879 that all scholarships, prizes and degrees (except for medicine) would be open to men and women equally and in 1882 the first women to graduate in England received their degrees from London University. London University was an examining body and teaching institutions with a high academic record could apply to London for the award of external degrees. It was in this way that Nottingham, Bristol, Reading and Sheffield became university colleges between 1881 and 1897. In 1881 the colleges in Manchester, Liverpool and Leeds formed their own degree-granting body named The Victoria University.

Male Opposition

The higher education of girls met with much opposition. Many critics used the old chestnut that using her brain could be extremely detrimental to her health. One of the main advocates of this theory was Dr Henry Maudsley (the Maudsley Psychiatric Hospital in London is named after him). In an article in the Fortnightly Review in 1874 he used menstruation as justification for his anti-feminism. He said women could never hope to match masculine accomplishments, because their physiology acted as a handicap; body and mind being, for one quarter of each month, more or less sick and unfit for hard work. He wrote that they ran the intellectual race at a cost to their strength and health and it even incapacitated them for the adequate performance of the natural functions of their sex. This brought a strong reaction in the next issue of the journal from Dr Elizabeth Garrett Anderson. Elizabeth had been the first woman in the country to qualify as a doctor in 1865 and now, as a practising doctor and mother, she was well placed to oppose his arguments. She stated that domestic servants and other manual workers managed perfectly and were not allowed to rest for a week each month.

The opposition on medical grounds eventually collapsed when it was realised that such fears were unfounded. However women were still subjected to many attempts to undermine their work and achievements. One Cambridge professor, faced with only a female audience closed the meeting stating that "*As there is nobody here, I shall not lecture today.*"[13] The Dean of Chichester Cathedral told an audience of women at Oxford in a sermon in 1884: "*Inferior to us God made you: and our inferiors to the end of time you will remain. But you are none the worse off for that*"[14] Well, that was all right then. Thankfully, his audience burst into laughter.

Three years later a Girton College student scored top marks in the classical tripos (the Cambridge degree exam). No man achieved higher than a second class degree that year.

During this time the much-read '*Girls' Own Paper*' tried to exert its influence. In 1886 it suggested the numerous ways in which a girl could occupy herself in the period of her life between school and marriage. She could join a reading or study club, a lecture or discussion group. She could consider charitable work and also become knowledgeable about house work - if only to set the servants a good example. Occupied in this way the writer suggested that '*she will be able to wait in dignified tranquillity until the right man comes to claim her*'![15]

MORAVIAN EDUCATION.

By 1896 the Moravian Church's view of women's capabilities was now more favourable. An article in favour of preaching by women was included in the *Moravian Messenger Magazine.* It also mentioned that women were beating senior wranglers in examinations (a wrangler was a student who gained first class honours in the third year of an undergraduate degree) and also winning the choicest appointments in the civil service, although there was no indication that girls from Moravian Schools were among these high achieving women. The magazine did, however, mention that prospects were encouraging for the Fairfield Ladies' School. Over one hundred pupils had enrolled in September and out of nineteen sent up for the Oxford Local Exam, twelve had passed. It was stated that this was satisfactory as it was only at the beginning of the previous term that the classes were arranged for the exam.

The School celebrated its centenary year in 1896 with a party to which old girls were invited. Fifty years later in 1946 when the school celebrated one hundred and fifty years, the school received a letter from a pupil who was at the school in 1896. The 'Old Girl' was Lucy Eagle and she commented on the rather Spartan mid-morning lunches which were comprised of a small piece of thick bread and a sip of water. The classrooms were heated by coal fires and the girls often surreptitiously toasted the pieces of bread on the end of slate pencils which, of course, was against the rules. At the Jubilee party Lucy recalled meeting two very old ladies who, as girls, had come to school by stage coach from Chester and who remembered, when they were boarders, having to go to bed by candlelight.[16]

Lucy and her elder sister Rachel lived in the Fairfield Settlement Square at number six and they and their family were part of the Moravian Community and both girls passed the Oxford Local examinations. Rachel married the Rev. Samuel Wilson, a Congregational Minster, and had three children and Lucy became a distinguished wood carver. An example of the work she did for the school can be seen today in the Lamb & Flag plaque carved on the panelling behind the hall platform. She was particularly noted for her wood carving in Moravian churches and she was also responsible for some of the restoration to the wood panelling in Manchester Cathedral which was badly damaged by enemy bombing during the Manchester blitz in December 1940.[17]

Although the lives of Fairfield girls had always been more comfortable and pleasant than that of poor working class women, they did experience the universal drawbacks of being female. Their lives followed the same pattern as the majority of middle-class girls in the Victorian Era. If they married, they were not expected to work and it wasn't until the last decades of the nineteenth century that even single women started to find employment in a more varied selection of work. As they became better educated they began to be employed in book-keeping, typewriting and telegraphy, and post-office and clerical work. By the late 1880s typewriters were being used and women were beginning to learn shorthand. Women also began working as shop-assistants, which until the 1870s was seen as man's work. Although it was going to be some time before highly educated and university qualified women could compete in male dominated professions, there was a gradual change in attitudes taking place. A lady's life was no longer regarded as being necessarily one of idleness and dependency on a man. There was a realisation that she could have a more independent existence with experience of life and work outside the home.

MANCHESTER UNIVERSITY

Three girls who entered the school in its Jubilee year were the first Fairfield girls to go to University. They began their university careers at Manchester in 1903 and graduated with B.A. degrees in 1906. When they began their studies, in 1903, they probably travelled into Manchester on the newly introduced electric tramcars. It would be another twenty years before the first Fairfield girls studied at universities other than Manchester and stayed in Halls of Residence.[18]

Manchester University had its origins in Owen's College which had been established only fifty years before in 1850 by a wealthy businessman - John Owen. From the late 1870s it was hoped that Owen's College would be converted into the University of Manchester but this was opposed and a compromise was reached by the establishment of the Victoria University in 1880 which, as mentioned earlier, was a degree granting body for the colleges in Manchester, Liverpool and Leeds. Of significance, was the fact that the Charter of the Victoria University fully recognised the equality of women students. Clause IV stated that '*the University has the power to grant and confer degrees and other distinctions on all persons, male or female, who shall have pursued a regular course of study in a College of the University and shall submit themselves for examination'.*

However, there was still at least one obstacle barring the way which had to be overcome. A necessary qualification for a degree was membership of a constituent college and Owen's College refused to open its doors to women. This refusal caused much agitation and a vigorous controversy in the Press. The weight of the argument was in favour of the women. The point at issue was no longer whether women should receive higher education but the advisability of common education with men.

Eventually, three years later, in April 1883 membership of the College was, by resolution of the University Court, opened to women students. However, there were conditions. Women were only to be admitted to classes held in Owen's College if they were in preparation for the final examinations, or for the final and intermediate examinations jointly. All other classes were to be held in the house in Brunswick Street which was the building that had been used by the Manchester and Salford College for Women since its foundation in 1877.

From 1888 women were admitted to any lecture class of higher than matriculation grade (a grade similar to GCSE A. Level). They were also admitted to laboratories but a special resolution had to be passed in these cases. Scholarships were thrown open unless definitely restricted to men. By 1897 all subjects were open to women with the exception of engineering and medicine but two years later in 1899 a decision was taken to allow women into the School of Medicine. Engineering had not been opened to women simply because it was not expected that any woman would wish to study it. As soon as such a woman did appear a few years later, she was admitted at once.[19]

The old worry, that too much intellectual study was harmful to women's health was still prevalent. In 1884 Dr John Thorburn who held the chair of obstetrics at the University, had delivered and published a lecture in which he argued that women were incapable of following an unbroken routine of work and of accepting the fixed times of examinations, without permanent injury to their health. He stated that to enter upon a degree course was, for women, to enter upon *'one of the dangerous occupations of life'*. *'No physician'*, he added, *'will deny this for a moment'*. Thankfully, Dr. Cullingworth, who succeeded to Thorburn's chair in 1885 disagreed with him. It was Dr Cullingworth's opinion that women suffered more harm from having nothing to do, than they ever did from overwork. However, the College authorities were still anxious about this situation and from 1884 until 1903 women students were required to furnish a written statement from parent or guardian that '*such course of study may be entered upon without the prospect of injury to her health.*'[20]

Until 1897 the headquarters of the Women's Department was housed in the old house in Brunswick Street and the girls studying for degrees went across to Owen's College to attend senior classes. A girl on her own had to be accompanied by the women's Tutor. Two or more girls together were allowed to go unaccompanied. By 1887 a little room in the University, under the roof and approached by a small staircase behind an iron gate was made available. This room was next to the museum and stuffed lions, tigers and gorillas lurked in the corridor outside. The girls managed to make this into a common room and each student contributed something towards its furniture and decoration.[21]

It seems that the girls were treated like a race apart and there were many rules which kept the men and women students separated. The authorities wanted to guarantee the safety and privacy of their women students but this created an isolated position. The women were not allowed to enter the main building by the principal door, but by a smaller one. Professors ushered them out of lecture theatres and might even escort them across the quadrangle.[22] They sat together in their own particular (usually front) rows of seats in classrooms and the male students chided them when they became confused if their seats were accidentally occupied by a man.[23] The rules for using the library were restrictive. One student wrote that '*it would have been the height of impropriety to enter the library and demand a book in the hardened manner now usual. No, we had to 'fill up a voucher', and a dear little maid-of-all-work, aged about thirteen, went to the library with it. If we were not quite sure of the volume required, she might have to make the journey ten times, but it was never suggested that she should be chaperoned.*'[24]. There was far greater freedom at Liverpool University and it was only after a group of women students had visited there that they plucked up the courage to remove their hats and jackets.[25]

The women for some years felt that they were only just about tolerated.

A Dr Ward was quoted in the Manchester Guardian in October 1899 as saying *'The governing body had always to bear in mind the obligation, in their case explicit as well as implicit, that the interests of their men students should not be prejudiced, the College having been founded for men in the first instance'.*[26] The women, themselves, showed no sign of resentment at their unequal status and their main concern was to succeed as students and were grateful for the friendly unstinted help they received from the teaching staff.[27]

The women's accommodation gradually improved. In 1888 they were offered a small common room and two dressing rooms and in 1898 following an extension of the University's premises, the spacious professors' common room became the women's common room.[28]

The women's common room in 1901

Even by 1900 girls at university were still met with opposition and much criticism and discrimination from within the universities. It is an understatement to say that women weren't made particularly welcome at most universities. Some colleges lacked adequate toilet facilities for women and their lecture rooms were often cramped and uncomfortable. At the Royal Holloway College for Women they were able to study for science degrees but they didn't have any laboratories.

When women were allowed into the Manchester University medical school in 1899 they were given one small room which served as a dissecting room and cloakroom and on some occasions they had to take their lunch there.[29]

An article published in the Durham University Journal in 1899 stated that *'Woman acts within her natural rights when she demands opportunity at least of increased scholastic freedom; the mistake she makes is in imagining - as so many seem to do - that she can surpass or even equal the intellectual achievements of man. All history, all experience, goes to prove how great is the delusion'.*[30]

One of the main social activities for the women students at Manchester was provided by membership of the Social Debating Society. A perusal of the topics discussed gives an interesting idea of the prevailing attitudes and opinions at the time. Socialism was admired but declared impracticable. Old age pensions and the payment of Members of Parliament were rejected. The disestablishment and disendowment of the Church of England was finally carried after a lively debate. The motion that "Women should have equal rights with Men", organised by a future organiser of the women's suffragette movement, (this was likely to have been Christobel Pankhurst who entered the University the same month as our Fairfield girls), was only carried by the casting vote of the President. In 1894 they debated the entry of women into Parliament but again the motion was only carried by one vote. Five years later, at a debate to which the public were invited, the motion "That it is desirable to extend the Parliamentary franchise to duly qualified women" was passed, only two men and no women opposing it.[31]

Manchester University circa 1905

By the time our Fairfield Girls began their studies at the University in 1903 the Women's Department had overcome many obstacles. In 1889 the first science degree had been awarded to a woman. In 1897 a woman student secured a degree in zoology and in 1898 two women graduated in chemistry.

In 1901 a woman student gained a degree in botany and in the same year a woman secured a first in mathematics. The first M.A. degrees were conferred upon three women in1892[32]. All these milestones had occurred only a very few years before the girls from Fairfield entered the University. They must surely have felt thrilled at being able to experience the satisfaction of being educated on an equal footing with the men. One can only imagine the joy and confidence they would have felt on graduation day.

One of the Fairfield girls was Gwladys Evans who stayed on at the University and gained her M.A. degree in 1908. Her father, the Rev. George Evans, was the Minister of Brookfield Unitarian Chapel on Hyde Road, Gorton, not far from the School. They lived at Brookfield Parsonage on Hyde Road, just across the road from the Chapel. It was a middle-class household and in 1901 the Rev Evans employed two servants to look after himself and his three children. The Rev Evans had a Master's Degree and Gwladys' elder brother, Walter, who was eighteen in 1901, was a theological student. Her other brother, George, was thirteen. It seems that she was brought up in a family which understood and appreciated academic endeavour.

After gaining her M.A degree in 1908 Gwladys went on to teach History and Geography at Manchester High School for Girls, commencing in January 1909. She gave up her teaching position when she married in 1915. It was generally expected that a woman would give up her work when she married and this attitude generally prevailed until the 2nd World War. However Manchester High School was unusual in not requiring staff to leave when they married. This was a deliberate policy which had been in place since the foundation of the school, although, of course, many staff , like Gwladys, did leave. The fact that she married a Congregational minister would have influenced her decision. A fellow teacher at Manchester High School, who was also a graduate of Manchester University, was Gertrude Powicke whom Gwladys already knew.[33] Gwladys had been at boarding school with Gertrude's sister Agnes and had spent holidays with the Powicke family in Anglesey. It was Gertrude's brother, William, whom Gwladys married.[34]

However, in 1915 there were far more tumultuous events taking place than a proposal of marriage. The devastation and horror reaped by the First World War affected nearly everybody and Gwladys was soon to hear, from her sister-in-law Gertrude, a first- hand account of the suffering at the 'front'.

After War was declared in 1914, Gertrude decided to join the war effort and she trained as a nurse and learned to drive. In 1915 she joined the Friends Emergency and War Victims Relief Committee, which had been formed by the Society of Friends (Quakers). In a letter to Manchester High School she wrote '*Some of the things I see and hear are terrible, and there is an appalling amount of misery to combat - it is difficult to know where to begin or to end. We are at the nearest point to the battle line - in the war zone - under the Third Army; at night we can hear the guns sometimes very clearly. We have heard that the Germans intended to bombard us, but so far they have done nothing except drop a few bombs over the aviation sheds. It is very hot. I spent three days at Germaize, in the Marne department; there the whole town has been destroyed. Anything more desolate I cannot imagine. Fortunately the crops have grown up, so the country around does not show signs of the battle in so marked a way and the men are building wooden houses as fast as they can*'.[35]

After the war ended in November 1918 Gertrude, with twenty other members of the Friends' Relief Committee, was transferred to Poland to assist with a typhus epidemic. In December 1919 she was nursing in the Lemburg area when she herself contracted typhus and she died on the 20th December in Warsaw. Because she wasn't a Catholic she couldn't be buried in the Church cemetery so the local people arranged for her to be buried in land adjoining, on the other side of the fence. The next morning, the Friends discovered that the fence had been moved to include her grave within the cemetery's consecrated ground.

Gertrude Mary Powicke is believed to be the only woman commemorated on any war memorial in the Borough of Stockport. Her name is inscribed on those at Heaton Moor and the town's art gallery. Gertrude's relief work had been supported financially by the Women's Union of Manchester University and followed with great personal interest. As a memorial to her a plaque was placed in the Women's Union and £60 collected and sent, with gifts of clothing, to the Friends' War Victims' Relief Committee. Her name appears in the list of the fallen on the University War Memorial.[36]

I imagine that Gwladys and the whole Powicke family were deeply affected by the loss of Gertrude. Gwladys and William went on to have four children. A girl, Helen, in 1916 followed by two boys, John and Michael in 1918 and 1920 and then a girl, Gertrude Mary, named after her aunt, in 1923.

Gwladys was 38 when Gertrude Mary was born and, as a mother of four children and the wife of a Congregational Minister, it was not possible for her to continue her teaching career. However, her educational achievements, I suspect, would have inspired her children. Both her sons achieved academic success. John published work on economics and Michael on mediaeval military history.

For her daughters it was a slightly different story. Rosalind, Gwladys granddaughter, recalls her mother, Gertrude Mary, telling her that she remembered her mother, Gwladys, weeping because she and her husband could not afford to send their daughters to university as well as their sons. Gertrude Mary would have liked to have studied English at University but both she and her sister Helen received a grant to study for a teaching certificate as long as they both agreed to become teachers once they qualified. Rosalind says that her mother found the teaching certificate course very undemanding academically.[37]

Girls it seems, even by the 1940s, were still not quite equal to their brothers.

CHAPTER FOUR

YEARS OF PEACE AND WAR
1906 – 1918

"How can you send your daughter to college?
Don't you want her ever to get married?"

Vera Brittain *"Testament of Youth"*

SCHOOL LIFE

By 1906 the school had occupied the attractive Georgian Sisters' House to the east of the Church, for thirty years but it was inadequate for the educational needs of a twentieth century girls' school. In 1871 the Brothers' House to the west of the Church had been rebuilt to house the Moravian Boys' School but twenty years later the school closed and the building was taken over by the Moravian Theological College. In 1906 the Theological College moved into the Sisters' House and the Girls' School moved over to what had been the Boys' School.

At the annual concert and prize distribution that year, the Headmistress, Miss Hull, described their new accommodation as large and commodious. Extensive alterations and improvements had taken place and the building now answered all modern requirements. Miss Hull went on to say '*the class-rooms are all of adequate size, lofty, well lighted and ventilated. The physical and chemical laboratory is fitted up with all requisites for experiments and practical work in connection with instruction in science. Comfortable sitting-rooms, apart from the class-rooms, are provided for boarders, so that in their free time they can enjoy far more home comforts than was formerly the case. The playground, a full-sized hockey field, and three tennis courts are not yet completed, but it is hoped they will be ready for the summer term. It is also intended to have part of the new ground laid out in gardens for the use of the girls'.*

The Girls' School moved to this building in 1906

The girls' sitting room

The dining hall

In the school grounds

The Headmistress neglected to mention, however, that the school was still heated by coal fires and lighted by gas and it would remain so for at least another fifteen years.

Miss Hull also reported that following a recent inspection by His Majesty's Inspector, the Board of Education recognised the Fairfield Moravian Girls' School as an efficient secondary school. Pupils had been successful in public examinations and at the recent Oxford Local examinations all the candidates had passed.[1] The fact that the school had a laboratory would have singled it out as a girls' school that was ahead of its time.

Four years later at the School's annual Prize Day a rather 'interesting' speech was given by Professor Alexander of Manchester University. If given today, the speech would, I think, be thought of as somewhat provocative. After praising the modern girl and describing her as one who was better able to stand up for herself, form and maintain her own opinions, who was more confident, and physically more capable than the older type of girl produced by the older system of education, he went on to say that domestic training ought to form part of a girl's education. Girls, he said, should be given the knowledge and training which was necessary for them to carry out their work as citizens. He said he was not speaking in a political sense. Apart from whether or not women should have political rights, there was no doubt they had a duty as citizens.[2] One wonders how many supporters of the Women's Suffrage and Suffragette Movements were in the audience - 1910 was a year when they were gathering some of their greatest support.

Shortly after the school had moved to its new premises a new School Prospectus was issued. The situation of the school was described as pleasant and healthy and with convenient access to Manchester and the surrounding districts, Fairfield Railway Station being only a few minutes' walk from the school.

The subjects studied were listed as: Reading, Writing, English Language and Literature, Composition, History, Geography, Arithmetic and Mathematics, Latin, French and German, Elementary Science, Botany, Nature Study and Hygiene, Class Singing, Drawing, Needlework and Drill. Classes for Cookery and Dressmaking were held when there were sufficient applicants.[3] A perusal of the School Timetable of 1908 reveals that the actual curriculum was even more extensive and also included Political Economics for Sixth Form pupils, Scripture and Mathematics which included Algebra, and Geometry. As well as

'Drill' the girls had physical exercise and games, which included Hockey, Cricket and Tennis. There was a Preparatory and Kindergarten Department, to which boys under nine years of age were admitted. Pupils were prepared for the Local and Matriculation Examinations of the Universities, the Associated Board of the Royal Academy and the Royal College of Music and others if desired.[4]

This education was far superior to the basic education which the majority of children received in the Elementary schools where they were educated until they were twelve and it would also compare favourably with the country's best secondary schools for girls.

The school hours ran from 9 to 12.15 in the morning and from 2 to 4 in the afternoon. Saturday was a whole holiday.   Fees were listed per term. To the basic fee for boarders of 11 guineas (£11.55p) plus one guinea (£1.5p) for laundry, quite a number of optional extras could to be added; these included one guinea each for music, painting and elocution, half a guinea each for Gymnastics, Advanced Drawing, Cookery and Dressmaking, one and a half guineas for 'music with master', and two guineas for violin lessons. For a child who chose all the extras the cost would have been just under £22 a term or £66 a year. Bearing in mind that at this time the majority of working men probably earned no more than £2 a week, education at Fairfield would only have been available to children of middle class parents. The fees for weekly boarders and day pupils were proportionately lower.

The Prospectus requested that each boarder bring two pairs of sheets, three pillow cases, three towels and two bath towels, three serviettes, two spoons and two forks; all articles to be clearly marked with the owner's name.

More than sixty years later, in 1969, when the Old Girls' Association celebrated fifty years since its foundation, a number of former pupils reminisced in the Old Girls' News Letter about their time at the school during this period. The school was known as the Moravian School for Girls or the Moravian Ladies School and it was described as a genteel establishment very much in the old tradition which produced shy young ladies. Discipline was strict but there was much fun. Many of the boarders had parents who were living abroad. The girls wore long dark skirts, and white high necked blouses with full sleeves and a patent leather belt encircling the waist. The young boys used to mischievously tie the belt of the girl seated in front to the back of her chair resulting in many snapped belts and tearful girls. For Prize Day the girls wore white party dresses and black hair ribbons. The bigger the bow the smarter a girl was considered. The summer school hat was a large straw boater around which there was a broad green ribbon with badge and motto embroidered on it. The straw was extremely stiff which made the hats very uncomfortable, particularly so if a boy pupil jerked it forward on to the girl's nose, which was a very common prank.[5] One Old Girl later wrote that one of her lasting memories of school was walking down the stairs with books on her head to improve her deportment. [6]

Much was made of slight misdemeanours which were described as letting down the school's tradition. One mistress, Miss Waugh, visited each form room at the end of every afternoon with her pince-nez spectacles and register. Five good conduct marks were recorded in this register for every pupil except any who had been so careless as to lose one. In turn the pupils answered "five please Miss Waugh". Keeping these five marks intact was a matter of honour and woe betide the one who had to admit to "four please Miss Waugh" or even worse "three please". Off came the pince-nez and beating the air with them Miss Waugh would duly emphasise the gravity of the situation. The writer recalled one occasion when a small girl, indulging in conversation behind raised desk lids with a small boy, did not observe the arrival of the Register. Miss Waugh unbelievably enraged, personally ordered girl and boy each to take five marks. Translated it meant 'nought please, Miss Waugh.' That made school history. Reminiscing in 1970, another old girl commented that "dear old Miss Hull (the Headmistress) called us all "darlings"; she could afford to, so austere was the treatment meted out by lesser members of the staff!"[7]

One girl wrote that the normal introduction of a new girl was a visit to the school with her mother one afternoon prior to the commencement of term. A "Victorian" maid would usher mother and child into the Visitors' Room. This also served as a sickroom and it was hoped it wouldn't be required for both purposes at the same time. The maid put a match to the fire which was always left laid. Soon after this Miss Hull in a silk or satin dress would 'swish' into the room. She was a woman of great charm and motherly understanding and she and her small dog, Crab, were loved by all the girls.[8]

The writer went on to say that they had two grass tennis courts, a croquet lawn, a 'giant stride' and see-saws and the girls were taught gymnastics, eurythmics and country dancing.

The gymnasium

The Giant Stride at the North London Collegiate School

The giant stride was described as a tall strong 'telegraph pole' firmly set into the ground, with eight stout ropes attached from the revolving top. Each rope had a hand-hold at the bottom (shaped wooden bars of strong smooth wood) which the eight girls took hold of with both hands. They then ran clockwise all together in rhythm – 1, 2, 3, jump, in an effort to make themselves airborne. This was achieved in a limited way but it was better if half the team were bigger, fifth or sixth formers – then they soared![9] The illustration of a giant stride shows girls of the North London Collegiate School in their Gymnasium and it is interesting to note that their 'Gym' uniforms were similar to those worn by Fairfield girls in the school's gymnasium. The 'giant stride' was a popular piece of Victorian and Edwardian gymnastic equipment.

Hockey was played at first with 'shinty' sticks but they were discarded for proper hockey sticks when a coach was engaged. The girls played in ankle length dark skirts and bright red woollen pullovers with MHC emblazoned on them. The goalkeeper and the full backs often stooped to stop the ball with their long skirts.[10] Tennis was a more sedate and well-mannered game. One girl remembered playing in a long white dress and a 'boater' hat

As the education of the girls improved so did their prospects for a more interesting life after school. Employment in many new spheres was opening up for women. A Report as early as 1886 on the 'Occupations of Women, other than teaching' had listed such work as prison officers, medical practitioners, dispensers, masseuses (later called physiotherapists), draughtswomen, clerical workers and nurses as well as sales assistants, typists and telephonists. [11] It has to be said, however, that the number of women employed in such work as medicine and dispensing was still small and in many other professions they were still practically non-existent. It wasn't easy to find interesting work in the business world other than in the routine jobs of basic clerical work or typing. Women who had ambitions to do more than this were considered quite extraordinary and often when they had the necessary qualifications they would be told that the company could not employ a woman. Each year there was a gradual increase in the number of Fairfield girls gaining good results in the Oxford Local Examinations and the Matriculation Examinations for Manchester University but the number was still a small percentage of the girls.[12]

Vera Brittain

In her book *"Testament of Youth"*, Vera Brittain writes about this particular period, just a few years before the start of the 1st World War, and her experiences as a fifteen year old girl in a private girls' school. She wrote that *'almost every girl left school with only two ambitions - to return at the first possible moment to impress her school-fellows with the glory of a grown-up 'toilette' and to get engaged before everybody else'*. She went on to say that most parents had little intention of ensuring that their daughters were trained for exacting careers or even useful occupations. Vera Brittain, although she had been brought up, as were nearly all middle class girls of that period, to look upon marriage as her ultimate goal, was determined to go to college and at least to prepare for a type of life more independent than that of a Buxton young lady. [13] She was much inspired by Olive Schreiner's book "Women and Labour", known as the "Bible of the Woman's Movement", from which she quotes *'We take all labour for our province, from the judge's seat to the legislator's chair, from the statesman's closet to the merchant's office; from the chemist's laboratory to the astronomer's tower, there is no post or form of toil for which it is not our intention to attempt to fit ourselves; and there is no closed door we do not intend to force open; and there is no fruit in the garden of knowledge it is not our determination to eat'[14]* .

Vera wrote that her wish to study English Literature at Oxford caused her to be labelled "ridiculous", "eccentric" and "a strong-minded woman" and that acquaintances told her mother they thought her plans were deplorable and would lead to the abandonment of all hope of finding a husband. One woman said to her mother *"How can you send your daughter to college, Mrs Brittain! Don't you want her ever to get married?"*[15]

We can only assume that many of our Fairfield girls would have met with the same opposition. The above quotes only help to highlight the fact that those Fairfield girls who had already gone on to University were certainly brave and deserving of our admiration.

1913 brought changes in public examinations. Instead of the Oxford Local Examinations the school decided to take what the Headmistress in her Speech Day Report called the "Manchester University" exam, but later in her Speech she referred to it as the School Certificate. This was the forerunner of the GCE 'O' Level examination. To gain the Certificate passes in at least six subjects were needed. The acceptable subjects were English,

History, Geography and Arithmetic with Elementary Maths (these four subjects were compulsory) together with a foreign language and a science.

FIRST WORLD WAR

Life for everyone was about to change. The 1st World War which began on the 4th of August 1914 brought tragedy and devastation to millions. It would last until the 11th of November 1918 - four years in which nearly a whole generation of young men was wiped out. It also brought immense changes to ordinary people's lives and society's attitude to women. At first people thought it would be short lived but it became obvious by 1915 that it was going to last longer than predicted. More and more fighting men were needed as well as an increase in armament production. Women were now required to replace the working men who were fighting, to work in the munitions factories and to nurse the wounded. It would provide women with the opportunity to show what they could do.

However there is little evidence, in the available archive material, that the School was greatly affected. There is no mention in the Headmistress' Reports to Speech Day of any of the girls' fathers or brothers being killed or wounded but it would have been quite remarkable if none of the girls had lost a relative over those four years. There was no mention of the three quarters of a million British soldiers killed or the effect this would have on the present generation of girls who would face a life where they would outnumber men by one and three quarter million. They were spared the stark truth which was given to the sixth form girls at Bournemouth High School for Girls by a senior mistress when she made this statement: '*I have come to tell you a terrible fact. Only one out of ten of you girls can ever hope to marry. This is not a guess of mine. It is a statistical fact. Nearly all of the men who might have married you have been killed. You will have to make your way in the world as best you can. The war has made more openings for women than there were before. But there will still be a lot of prejudice. You will have to fight. You will have to struggle.* One girl who remembered this speech wrote years later "*How right she was. Only one out of every ten of my friends has ever married. Quite simply, there was no one available.*"[16]

During the War current affairs were discussed extensively, the difference between news and propaganda was recognised and the girls were encouraged to think things through.[17] Hilda Hughes (née Chatterton), reminiscing in 1970, wrote about 'meatless' days when they had to make-do with dark bread and watery soup and exercise-books, which were as rough as coconut matting, on which algebraic symbols were impossible to read.[18]

The Head Mistress, in her speech on Prize Day at the end of 1916, reported that the pupils were endeavouring to help in the country's needs. They had raised money to be sent to the Red Cross and a subscription had been sent to the Girls' Patriotic Union for Secondary Schools, which had been passed on to the Star and Garter Hospital for disabled soldiers for the ward provided by the Girls' Schools of the Nation. A large box of comforts had been sent to the Lancashire Soldiers' Christmas Fund and another to the Sailors' Society.[19]

Miss Hull spoke again in December at the 1917 Prize Day about the girls' contribution to the War effort and she also reported that she had been pleased to hear from many Old Girls who were doing their part either in hospitals or in helping to fill the places of the men who were at the front. One girl she had heard from was Gwendoline Hughes who was now an Acting Matron at a Military Hospital in Cairo. She had recently been awarded the Royal Red Cross Medal.[20]

Gwendoline Hughes

Gwendoline was born in London in 1880 and was a pupil at the school during the 1890's. When she was twenty three in 1903 she enrolled to be trained as a nurse at the David Lewis Northern Hospital in Liverpool. Gwendoline was at the "Northern" for four years and at the end of this time she was appointed as a Staff Nurse.

When she was twenty eight, she applied for a position with the Queen Alexandra's Imperial Military Nursing Service. On her application form she stated that she had been educated at the Moravian Ladies' School, Fairfield, near Manchester. Her application was accepted and she joined the QAIMNS on the 16th January 1908.[21]

QAs (as they became known) were expected to serve wherever the British Army was stationed and qualifications for entry were strict. Applicants had to have at least three years training in a civil hospital before being accepted. In choosing candidates, their character, education and social standing were carefully considered as well as their training and experience. The fact that Gwendoline had been educated at the "Moravian Ladies School" and her father was a civil engineer would have meant that her education and social standing were acceptable.

Many nurses who applied to join the QAs were rejected. The reasons given for their rejection included candidates having an 'unsuitable appearance', being an unsuitable age (not being between twenty five and thirty five) and several were considered to be of 'unsatisfactory social status'. QAs gradually came to be regarded as members of an exclusive service and by the time of the First World War they were thought of as the *elite* among the thousands of nurses who served in the War. Gwendoline's uniform consisted of a ground-length grey dress and white apron with a square bib and a short scarlet cape on the right side of which she would pin her badge. Off-duty she would have worn a thicker cape under a long cloak and a grey bonnet tied with a big bow under the chin. The badge was designed by Queen Alexandra and had only been approved as the insignia of the QA's three years previously in 1905. For many nurses the badge would become one of their most treasured possessions and, like Gwendoline, many would ask that they might retain the badge when they retired.[22]

Queen Alexandra's Royal Army Nursing Corps Uniform during World War One

Gwendoline was first posted to the Royal Victoria Hospital at Netley which was twelve miles from Portsmouth and six from Southampton. The hospital had been specially designed to accommodate sick and wounded soldiers who were brought off ships docking at these two ports. The hospital which was opened in 1863, was extremely grand and it looked over Southampton Water. The building was dressed with Portland stone and had a dome in the centre, between two wings. However, the design of the hospital met with criticism, especially from Florence Nightingale. She was concerned that no sunlight came into the wards which faced north-east and overlooked the coal heaps and hothouses behind the hospital. It measured nearly 1,500 feet in length and had corridors on the three floors extending from one end to the other. At the time it was built the hospital was reputed to be the largest military hospital in the world. When Gwendoline was issued with a Railway Warrant for her to travel to Netley she would have found that the Hospital had its own railway station with a line connecting it to Southampton Central Station.[23]

Gwendoline stayed at Netley for three and a half years and she was then moved in July 1911 to the new Military Hospital on Millbank alongside the Thames. This Hospital had been opened six years previously in July 1905 by Queen Alexandra and was named after her. It was far more modern in design than the Netley Hospital and was constructed on the 'Nightingale' pattern. This was a design that Florence Nightingale had advocated at the time the Netley Hospital was built and meant that, unlike those at Netley, the airy wards had plenty of sunshine. Gwendoline was thirty one when she was posted to the Queen Alexandra Hospital. She was by then a very experienced and independent young woman and I would like to think that she felt some excitement in working in such a great city and pride when walking out in her very distinctive uniform. From 1902 nurses in the QAIMNS were regarded as having officer status. In 1926 a Sister or Staff Nurse was granted the equivalent rank of Lieutenant and a Matron that of Major.

Gwendoline had been at the Queen Alexandra for nearly two years when she was warned that she was likely to be needed for service abroad and at the beginning of June 1914 she left for Egypt aboard the P & O ship Mongolia.[24]

Gwendoline arrived in Egypt just two months before the outbreak of the 1st World War. At that time there were only a few QAs stationed in Egypt. However, during the Gallipoli campaign the following year, hundreds of sick and wounded were taken to Egypt and the original small group were regularly joined by reinforcements.

The wounded and sick at Gallipoli were not treated on the peninsular - there was no room for hospital tents. They were taken to the port of Mudros on the Island of Lemnos by hospital ships. The hospitals at Mudros were often full and frequently the hospital ships could not take any more on board. When this happened the soldiers were taken by sea to Egypt. The conditions on board were horrendous. The men were either suffering from wounds which often became gangrenous or were suffering from fever and dysentery. There was little medicine and very little nourishment, very few pillows or blankets and one bedpan to thirty or forty men.[25]

A nurse serving in one of the receiving hospitals in Egypt described the condition of the men suffering from dysentery as brutal and terrible. Although they were kept clean, were given an appropriate diet, were able to rest and were given injections of Emertine, many soon became emaciated. In a very short time strong young men looked like old men lying in agony and often dying within forty eight hours.[26]

There was worse to come. By November 1915 the weather had become cold and stormy with snow blizzards which were so bad that the troops who had no shelter were frozen where they stood. The weather prevented the ships from evacuating the sick and injured. By the time the men were reached there were more than 16,000 cases of frostbite. When they reached hospital their fingers and toes were already dropping off and their bodies were filled with a creeping poison because their uniforms which had been frozen like boards had stuck to the sores on their bodies and turned them gangrenous.[27] By the time the Gallipoli campaign ended in January 1916 over 117,000 soldiers had been wounded or killed and 100,000 had been evacuated sick. Nearly half of the sick had died.

The above details help us to appreciate the work and stress that Gwendoline experienced during the War. At the time of the Gallipoli Campaign she had become Acting Matron at the Helmieh Military Hospital in Cairo. She was mentioned, along with a number of other nurses, three times in Despatches during the War. Of particular interest is the Despatch in the London Gazette of 1 December 1916 which gave the following Officer's Report *'I wish to call attention to the admirable work that has been performed by the Nursing Services in the hospitals in Egypt. Not only have they had to deal with a very* large number of wounded and sick from Gallipoli, Salonica and Egypt itself, but also from other theatres of war. The devotion to duty, zeal and skill of the Nursing Services has been beyond praise and I have great pleasure in bringing to your notice in a subsequent despatch the names of a number of these ladies for specially distinguished service.'

On the 1st of January 1917 Gwendoline was awarded the Royal Red Cross Medal.[29] This Medal was instituted by Queen Victoria in 1883 and is awarded to army nurses for exceptional services, devotion to duty, professional competence and special exertions in providing for the nursing of sick and wounded men of the armed forces.

Gwendoline Hughes' Record Card detailing her Royal Red Cross Medal and the mention in Despatches on three occasions

One note of particular poignancy is that many Droylsden men were wounded or lost their lives at Gallipoli. They belonged to the Manchester Regiment. Most of them were in the 1/19th Battalion, Manchester Regiment (Ashton Territorials) but some were in the 8th Manchester Regiment which was composed of Ardwick Territorials.[28] It is deeply moving to think that, far away in Egypt, they may have been nursed by someone who was familiar with their own home town.

Gwendoline finally left Egypt in March 1919 and was granted five weeks' leave and reported to the Royal Herbert Military Hospital in Woolwich on the 22nd April. By then her uniform had been updated, the bonnet had been replaced by a grey felt hat and the long cloak by a coat.

For ten years after the War she served in a number of Military Hospitals in England and Ireland. Then, in 1929, she was informed that she was to be posted to China. She boarded the 'City of Marseilles' at Southampton on the 6th January 1930 and disembarked in Shanghai over a month later and commenced duty as Acting Matron in the No. 7 General Hospital. She was promoted to Matron in July 1931 and by August 1932 she had become the Senior Supervising Matron.[29]

In August 1932 she was moved to Hong Kong and seven months later she sailed for home and arrived in Southampton on the 4th May 1933 after a voyage of five weeks. She was then posted to the Queen Alexandra's Military Hospital on Millbank - the hospital where she had worked before the War as a staff nurse - she was now returning as a Matron.[30]

Just a few weeks after she returned Gwendoline became ill with what was called 'Renal Colic' and she spent three weeks in hospital and two weeks on sick leave. She was now fifty three and she retired in January 1935 when she was fifty five. She was able to retire on a pension of £158 a year which was gradually increased over the years to £223 in 1952 - the year before she died aged 73. This pension seems very small but it compares well with the five or six pounds a week that a working man earned. Gwendoline was fortunate in that she had a home base. Her younger sister, Frances, who was single, lived in Torquay and it is likely that they shared this home. Gwendoline always gave the Torquay address as her home for any communications during holidays or sick leave[31] and because of this Gwendoline was able to enjoy a happy retirement in one of England's most beautiful resorts.

CHAPTER FIVE

THE BEGINNING OF THE MODERN ERA 1919 -1929

"Don't be prevented from following your star because you are girls and not boys"
Lady Simon of Wythenshawe

The War finally came to an end. On the morning of the 11th November 1918 the Head Mistress, Miss Hull, entered each classroom to tell the pupils that hostilities had ended and pointed out from some of the classrooms, the Union Jack which had just been hoisted on a local church. The girls were then given a half-day's holiday.[1]

Although the War had brought restrictions in the supply of food and educational equipment, such as books and paper, the school had survived and the girls' education had not suffered. One particular girl did exceptionally well. Marguerite (Greta) Johnstone went to Manchester University and graduated with the M.B. medical degree in 1921. She was awarded the very first John Henry Agnew Fellowship from Manchester University which enabled her to go to the Orthopaedic Institute in Bologna, Italy to carry out research into children's diseases.[2] She worked as an orthopaedic consultant for Lancashire County Council Clinics for a number of years. She did feel, however, that her career as a consultant was held back by the fact that she was a woman and she later practised as a G.P. in the Didsbury area of Manchester for about twenty years until she retired.[3]

LOCAL AUTHORITY HIGH SCHOOL

In the year after the war ended the school experienced the greatest change in its long history. It had become evident that the school was encountering financial difficulties and that it would be difficult for the school to provide the increased salaries, expensive equipment and alterations needed to enable the school to meet the demands of a modern High School education. A sale was agreed and the School was purchased by the Lancashire Education Authority who began work to bring the School up to the required Government standard. In future it was no longer to be known as the Moravian School for Girls - from September 1919 its new title was Fairfield High School for Girls. Miss Hull who had been Head Mistress for twenty eight years retired but stayed on for the first term to help Miss Edwards, the new Head Mistress and there was an amicable official hand-over of duties at the School Prize Day at the end of November.

The Moravians generously left behind some beautiful antique pieces of furniture that had been at the school for many years. These included a set of chairs, a Czechoslovakian oak chest, a rosewood bookcase, several tables, a bureau with a secret drawer, and two Grandfather clocks. [4]

The school, until then, had been a private, fee-paying boarding and day school. From September 1919 when the Lancashire Education Committee took it over, it became a day school for pupils over ten years old and the Kindergarten department for younger children was gradually given up in the following years. The young boys in the Kindergarten had to leave but the girls were allowed to grow up into the school. Fees still had to be paid but about 25 per cent of the pupils were from the local elementary schools and had gained free places by passing "The Scholarship" Exam. One girl, who was one of the first 'Scholarship' girls to enter the school in September 1919, remembered passing the former dormitories which still contained the beds.[5]

Another girl, who started at the school when it was still the Moravian establishment, fondly remembered sleeping in these dormitories and being tucked into bed by Miss Appleyard, who was the chief 'tucker-upper'. Miss Appleyard was alleged to be double-jointed and was able to bend over backwards and touch the ground with her hands. She would display this particular talent just before lights out and it was greeted with much appreciation. A number of years later Miss Appleyard also delighted the girls by sweeping into school driving an Austin Seven motor car accompanied by a fellow teacher. The writer commented '*how modern we thought they were and how dashing*'.[6]

A number of teachers of the Moravian School were invited to remain under the new regime but Miss Edwards also appointed new mistresses. One of these new teachers, Miss Brooks, reminiscing years later, recalled the school being lit by gas. Her first sight of Fairfield was at the Staff Meeting held on a January evening in 1920. The room where they met was very dimly lit, but she soon found out that the rest of the school was a good deal worse. On one particularly foggy afternoon, when the girls were sent home early at 3 p.m., she remembered one of the other teachers helping the girls to find their coats in the junior cloakroom by the light of a taper. Miss Brooks went on to say that the Chairman of the Governors had to make strong appeals to the County to have electric light installed to replace the gas.[7]

The summer holidays in 1919 were extended by three days to enable some extensive alterations to be finished, and for the next three years a succession of workmen were in and out of the buildings. The teaching took place under very difficult and noisy conditions. The upstairs dormitories were converted into laboratories. This took a long time, and the unfortunate Science staff had to carry around elementary pieces of apparatus and manage as best they could in a small classroom. Attics on the same floor were turned into a dining room, and a Cookery Room emerged at the end of the corridor opposite the Head Mistress's room. Miss Edwards was able to report to Speech Day at the end of 1921, that a central heating system had been installed to replace the fireplaces, the school had been painted and whitewashed and electric light had been installed - the last perhaps the most valuable of the improvements which made the working of the school so much easier and more satisfactory.[8] It would be 1925 before the new building, consisting of the Hall/Gym., a small cloakroom, a classroom and the library was opened.

The laboratory in the 1920s

The sixth form of the new school consisted of five girls, all of whom had been educated in the Moravian School. They had all passed the School Certificate and were now working towards the Higher Certificate of the Northern Universities and hoped to go on to University in two years' time. Connie Davey was the Head Girl and she had the dubious pleasure of ringing the hand bell for the end of lessons.

Miss Hull had kept hens at the bottom of the garden for a number of years (the gardens and lawns were delightfully laid out in front of the School) and now Miss Edwards found herself going out to feed the hens every dinner time. One year the hens were joined by a turkey. Apparently this bird was quite fearsome and escaped into the playground one dinner hour and spread alarm among the more timid girls until a teacher quelled it with a well-aimed cardigan. [9]

Art had been taught by a male teacher, but always with a mistress in the room as chaperone. However, it wasn't long before an art mistress was employed and after that, for many, many years, Fairfield remained an all-female establishment except for the caretaker. [10]

It was only a very small percentage of the girls at Fairfield who stayed on until they were eighteen. By 1921 the school had 293 pupils of whom, during the next seven years, only twenty five would stay on at school after they were sixteen.

In 1922 Mr Gater, Director of Education for Lancashire, was the invited guest at the school's Speech Day and in his address he did little to boost the self-confidence of our 'elite' girls. He said he was considering girls' education more thoroughly and he thought that people over-estimated a girl's power for work. He thought that **a girl could not do as much work in a fixed time as a boy could!** I can imagine the disbelief and deadly silence with which those remarks were met. All the girls in the audience disagreed with him – especially those who had brothers. He then went on to remark on the improvements in girls' education during the last century. It's doubtful that he was ever asked back again.[12]

Speech Day, the next year, was addressed by a far more supportive guest. Mrs Simon, the Mayoress of Manchester who later became Lady Simon of Wythenshawe, and who was a well-known educationalist and feminist as well as a City Councillor, urged the girls to *"take an interest in politics, to read the newspapers, to find anything of benefit in their city and to help its progress"*. She told them *"… don't be prevented from following your star because of the fact that you are girls and not boys"*. She spoke of the value of women to the country and looked forward to the time when the Chancellor of the Exchequer would be a woman.[13]

Life at Fairfield in the 1920s did not solely revolve around academic studies. The teaching staff helped to widen the girls' horizons by introducing them to cultural activities and encouraging an interest in current affairs.

In the Spring of 1924, two mistresses took a party of thirteen girls on a visit to France. They travelled by train and boat to Le Havre (using the Underground to get across London). They then went by the French 'Rapide' train to Rouen. They described visiting lovely little French towns and stopping for "cafe-au-lait" and "petit pain" in French cafes. They went on to Paris and saw the motor vehicle which had been the first to cross the Sahara Desert in 1923 and the train dining car in which the Armistice Agreement was signed in 1918. [14]

As well as foreign travel, other school activities during the 1920's helped the girls to become less narrow and provincial minded. An important School Society which was set up at the beginning of 1924 was a school branch of the League of Nations Union. This organisation was formed to promote international justice and a permanent peace between nations based on the ideals of the League of Nations which was established as part of the international settlement following the First World War. During the next few years many important topics were discussed including the economic conditions of various countries, child labour, refugees and disarmament.[15]

Other extra-curricular activities included Literary and Science Societies. Fairfield hosted a visit to School of the famous poet Walter de la Mare. Fairfield was chosen as the venue for his talk to the older pupils of Ashton Secondary School, Stretford Secondary School, Stretford High School and Fairfield. The talk took place in Fairfield's newly completed Assembly Hall.

The school hall was also used for the girls' Christmas parties which took place in the evening. One Old Girl, reminiscing in 1992 wrote that she was always amazed how everyone managed to get there *"Hardly anybody had their own car in those days, so they travelled on foot, train or tram. I was specially favoured because my friend's family were taxi proprietors (taxi in the singular) and her brother took us to Speech Day and parties. It was a taxi such as you might see now on the Brighton Run and it even had acetylene lamps."*[16]

The Science Society had some rather interesting and novel talks. These included one on fireworks (with practical experiments), another on coal gas and its manufacture. This was demonstrated by the use of various tubes representing a gasometer and several people were noticed hurriedly leaving the room when the gas escaped. No "Health and Safety" rules and regulations there then![17]

During the 1920's the school changed in a great many ways. A glance at the photographs of pupils in Chapter Four taken in 1908 and those of the girls in the gym in this chapter during the 1920s shows that the girls' appearances had altered as well. The 1908 pupils of the Moravian School for Girls looked very ladylike - wearing long skirts, high-necked, long-sleeved blouses, patent leather belts round their waists and their long hair tied with a ribbon. In contrast, the 1920s girls of Fairfield High School looked every inch the school girl. They had short cropped hair in the new twenty's fashion and wore gym slips and square necked blouses.[18]

The school gymnasium in the 1920s

The school had gone through a process of modernisation and in 1924 the Headmistress was able to report that Fairfield was now one of the largest Girls' Secondary Schools in Lancashire. By 1927 the new Assembly Hall and gymnasium had been completed as well as a music room. Although the Hall was light and spacious the Education Authority could not spend money on its decoration due to the economic hardships the country was going through. Because of this, the parents and pupils set about organising money-raising activities and managed to raise £226 to provide the fine carved oak panelling at the back of the raised stage.[19] This was a substantial sum of money – it represented nearly the cost of a small house. It's on this wall that the plaque of the Lamb and Flag that Lucy Eagle carved is placed. (This panelling and the plaque can be seen in the colour photograph taken at the time of the Duchess of Gloucester's visit during the school's bi-centenary celebrations).

There were some things that weren't so up to date. One Old Girl reminiscing in the 1990s recalled that in the late 1920s the cookery room only had a coal-fired oven and two gas cookers. She remembered astonishing the teacher, Miss Holt, by telling her that they were completely out of date and that her mother had an electric cooker. Miss Holt was invited to her home to see it and sample scones made using this new modern device.

Life outside the school during 1926 was particularly fraught, as the General Strike affected many aspects of society. There is no way of knowing how many children came from families who were supportive of the strikers' aims; all we have is evidence of how the school coped under difficult conditions. At the annual Speech Day early in the following year, the Headmistress thanked the parents and others for the way in which the children were helped to come to school during the Strike. Fairfield served a wide area, extending into parts of Yorkshire and Cheshire and although attendance was small on the first day of the Strike, the next day attendance was nearly back to normal. The girls had begun the long walk to school under the well founded conviction that they would be offered lifts of transport once they were on their way. One father had brought as many as eleven girls to and from Mottram every day in his car.[20]

Before the end of the decade the girls had abandoned the motto "Our Lamb has Conquered let us follow Him" and had chosen a new motto "The Utmost for the Highest". Miss Edwards commenting on this said *"Of course we do not yet realise what "utmost" really means and we can spend all our lives without complete success in searching for the "highest", but the aim is before us and it is for us to live up to it."*[21]

It appears that eighty years ago the worries about teenagers were very similar to that of today. Miss Edwards mentioned her concern that the girls' work was hindered by lack of sleep caused by the attendance at cinemas and parties during the week (The new 'talkie' films were introduced in 1928). She went on to say that *"Life for us all in the present day goes at such a feverish pace and sleep is necessary to restore the energies and foster the growth of a generation which is certainly feeling the effects of the War."* She then went on to point out to fathers that the effects of very long motor rides are both fatiguing and demoralising and cause bilious attacks and fatigue on a Monday morning![22]

THE MODERN GIRL

The five girls who were in the Upper Sixth Form in 1921 and hoped to go to Manchester University were successful and all graduated. Frances Lotte Stephens who studied biology was awarded the Manchester University Grisedale Scholarship for Advanced Research. She was awarded her M.Sc. degree in Botany in 1928 and then went on to do very interesting work at the Natural History Museum into the study of fungi, or mycology.[23]

Frances must have been an independent, confident woman. Although no member of her family had an academic background, her family was wealthy and her father owned a leather works. Her two sisters, Frieda and Margot, both suffered from diabetes, which until the discovery of insulin and its use in the treatment of the disease, was incurable. Frieda was fifteen when she died in 1922, the year that insulin was discovered. She had been a pupil at Fairfield and a note in the School Register mentions that she left school when she was fourteen due to ill health. Margot developed the disease when she was twenty two, but by that time insulin treatment was available and she enjoyed a long and reasonably fit life. The School Register notes that she left school at sixteen but did not go to work and stayed at home.[24]

Frances remained at the Natural History Museum all her working life and became an expert in her chosen field and a Principal Scientific Officer. However, her life was not without adventure and romance.

She lived in a flat in South Kensington and had a full and interesting social life, going to concerts, operas, plays, ballets and films in the city. She also took up English and Scottish country dancing and tap dancing and studied emergency first aid nursing for the Red Cross. Up until 1939 she took part in many field trips, and attended meetings of the Mycological Society. She also attended most of the annual meetings of the British Association for the Advancement of Science. In 1938 she was appointed as a "Scientific Assistant". This was a permanent appointment and was confirmed by letters signed by the Trustees, the Archbishop of Canterbury, the Lord Chancellor and the Speaker of the House of Commons. It appears that many of the Museum workers were not permanent members of the

Staff during the whole of their working lives and were classified as "unofficial workers".

Frances was very much the modern independent single woman and in August 1939 she sailed for America on the luxury liner Aquitania with a colleague. (Trans-Atlantic air travel was still very much in its infancy). They enjoyed a tour by train across America, visiting Niagara, New Mexico, the Grand Canyon, Los Angeles and San Francisco, before attending the Third International Congress for Microbiology in New York. The Congress finished on the 8th September, five days after war had been declared and they had considerable difficulty organising a return passage, eventually managing to travel on SS Manhattan. This ship, being American, was a non-combatant vessel and they arrived safely back in Southampton on the 16th September.

Frances was in London during all the war years. Because of her Red Cross first-aid training she was given an extra job as one of the first-aiders for the Museum. In September 1940 bombs fell on the Museum's Department of Botany. This was in the very early hours of the morning so no lives were lost but considerable damage was caused and the Department had to move to another part of the building. Further bombs fell on and around the Museum buildings in September, October and November of that year.

In 1944 three V1 flying bombs fell very close to the Museum causing much damage and injuries to fifteen members of staff. One of these members was John Balfour-Browne who was injured as he was working at his desk. He was knocked unconscious by flying glass and debris. It was Frances who treated his initial injuries and visited him during his recuperation. The Museum had quite a large staff and although Frances and John had seen each other on a few occasions before, they worked in quite separate departments, in different parts of the building, and hardly knew each other. When John was moved to Stoke Mandeville Hospital where he was treated for a number of weeks, Frances visited him on a number of occasions and they wrote to each other often. It soon became apparent that their relationship was more than just friendship and the couple were married at the beginning of October 1944. John had two small children from a previous marriage, having divorced his first wife in 1942.

Frances Stephens with her sisters Frieda and Margot

Frances, looking very stylish in a 1940's hat and veil. This was her husband's favourite photograph

Unusually for the time, Frances, as a wife and stepmother, was able to continue her work at the Museum. They employed domestic help and later on Simon, Frances's stepson, went to boarding school. Frances did, however, have to have permission to stay on at work. The Director of the Museum had to apply to the Treasury and a letter dated the 27th November 1944 from the Director to the Keeper of the Department of Botany states *"The Treasury have considered Miss Stephens's case in response to our application and, though they think it a borderline one, they are prepared, in view of her highly specialised function and her years of service, to approve her retention in an established capacity after her marriage"*. The wheels of change were still moving very slowly. The bar on married women serving in the Civil Service was eventually lifted in 1947 but an extract from the Civil Service National Whitley Council Committee Report "Against the Removal of the Marriage Bar" stated that *"The married woman's place is in the home and home-making is a full time job."*

Frances was two months off forty when she married and the rest of her life was spent in a happy marriage with loving step-children. She continued to work at the Museum where she wrote a number of scientific papers. She was promoted to Senior Scientific Officer in 1949 and Principal Scientific Officer in1955. She retired on her sixty third birthday in 1967.[25]

LIFE IN THE 1920S

In life outside the school, significant changes were taking place. Just before the end of the First World War, women who were over thirty and householders, or married to a householder, at last won the right to vote and in 1919 "The Sex Disqualification (Removal) Act" allowed women to take up any civic or judicial posts that were open to men, such as MPs, magistrates or barristers. In 1928 all women were given the vote on the same terms as men. These important changes to the status of women would surely have influenced the girls at Fairfield and would have helped to strengthen their ambitions. Women were slowly becoming more independent. It was, however, for most women, a very gradual process involving the breaking down of long-held prejudices, but many realised that the main 'weapon', in their fight for equality, was education.

The importance of education was stressed by Virginia Woolfe in her book "A Room of One's Own". The book which was published in 1929 was based on a series of lectures which she gave to Cambridge students at the Newnham and Girton women's colleges. It is mainly concerned with women writers and their need to be financially independent and to have a space or a room of their own if they were to succeed in a world dominated by men. Virginia's father believed that only boys of the family should be sent to school and he did not believe in investing in the education of his daughters. In her book, Virginia Woolfe illustrates through the life of her fictional character, Judith Shakespeare, how it was impossible for most women to have any creative life. Judith was not allowed to go to school and was pressed into marriage. The restrictions and expectations affecting women meant that they were treated unequally in society. Virginia expressed the opinion that until this changed women would remain second class citizens.

Every year, in the School Magazine, there would be news of former pupils' marriages and these would be listed by giving the girl's Christian name followed by her maiden name. It was then stated that she was now Mrs (this was followed by her husband's initials or first name and his surname.) This was standard practice at the time; it seemed that a woman's former identity was not acknowledged - not only had she lost her original surname but from then on she was to be known by her husband's initials or first name as well. The only time she would revert back to her own initials or first name was when her husband died.

Ninety years ago people were gradually experiencing the beginning of the "modern" age. By the late 1920's the aspirations of a small number of people included the ownership of a motorcar, many now listened in wonder to the new "wireless" transmissions from the BBC, electricity was beginning to reach quite a number of homes and those households who could afford it, delighted in the use of the new vacuum cleaner. Many of the girls who were at school then, would have been born before or during the 1st World War, and for them it must have felt quite wonderful to be part of this new 'modern' world - even if they did have to contend with having to be known by their husband's name.

EDUCATIONAL STANDARDS

When the school was taken over by the Lancashire Education Committee in September 1919 a Register of all the pupils was started.[26] Each girl was allocated a numbered page. The first few pages were for the top form (6th Form) and then the next pages were taken by those in the 5th Form, and subsequent pages continued in the order of form year; so when the Register was started, it contained all the information on the girls who were there in 1919. It gave details of the girls' exam results, future occupations, as well as their fathers' work and whether they had received a grant towards their education. As they went through the school their exam achievements and future careers were noted on their personal pages. Each huge Register contained three hundred pages and the two registers that I have examined contained information about the six hundred girls who were at the school between 1919 and 1933. By the end of 1921 there were details for 293 girls, which meant by that year the first book of three hundred pages was almost full.

When the Register was started in 1919, it was composed of all the fee-paying girls who were former pupils of the Moravian Girls School plus the new intake for the first form of the newly-named Fairfield High School for Girls. Between 20 to 25 per cent of these new pupils were clever girls from working class homes who had been pupils at the local elementary schools and had passed the Scholarship exam. Their school fees were paid by the Local Authority.

The chronological way, in which the Registers were arranged, allows us to examine the development and achievements of the school in a period when women's education was becoming more important. There was also a gradual realisation that a secondary education was something which should be available to all those who were able to benefit from it. By examining the records of these six hundred girls, we are able to see what actually happened to a group of girls who were from very varied home backgrounds - some had parents who were professional people, such as Doctors and business people who owned factories, but some came from homes where their fathers worked as cotton mill operatives and general labourers. We need to remember that before the school came under the Local Education Committee, and made free places available for Scholarship girls, there was little chance of a

Droylsden girl from an ordinary working class background receiving a secondary school education.

So what happened to all those three hundred girls who were already at the school in 1919, or entered it from 1919 until the end of 1921, the youngest leaving in 1928? Only twenty five girls (just over 8 per cent) stayed on after sixteen. Of these twenty five, twelve went on to University. Only one of them was a Scholarship girl, although four other girls were given grants to enable them to stay on into the 6th form. The remaining thirteen studied for the Higher School Certificate most going on to teacher training or commercial colleges, although one went to work in a pharmacy and another in a bank and one girl became a policewoman. Six of these thirteen girls studying for the Higher School Certificate were Scholarship girls.

A further thirty girls passed the School Certificate exam but left at sixteen. Of the thirteen Scholarship girls who passed, four stayed on at the school as student teachers, two went on to Commercial College and the rest went to work in offices and shops. Many of the seventeen fee-paying pupils who passed the School Certificate followed a similar path, although three went to Domestic Science College, one went to work in a Hospital Dispensary and another girl went into nursing.

Out of the three hundred pupils in the first Register, only fifty five left school with a qualification – just over 18 per cent. This percentage should be a little higher because 28 of the three hundred left to attend other high schools.

There were thirty Scholarship girls who left without passing the School Certificate. The majority of these pupils didn't complete the five year course; some leaving after three or four years. The statutory school leaving age was fourteen and many would have felt it necessary to leave and to contribute to the family income. The fact that they had experienced a few years of Secondary High School education, achieved by passing the Scholarship exam, would help them to find work in the 'office rather than the mill'. It has to be borne in mind that during the 1920s, in the Manchester area, only one in thirty pupils received a secondary education beyond fourteen.

Eva Bates

Eva Bates née Dunks was one of the thirty Scholarship girls who had to leave before she was sixteen. She was part of the first group of Scholarship girls who entered the school in 1919, having gained a Junior County Exhibition. Tragically Eva's mother died and Eva had to leave Fairfield in July 1922. Her elder sister had to stay at home to keep house and Eva got a job at the Gib Mill in Haughton Green. Eva was a very clever girl – if she had been able to stay on at school she would have liked to have trained as a teacher. Her reference from the school, signed by Miss Edwards, the Headmistress, stated *"Her record of work and conduct has been uniformly good, and her mathematics especially was really promising. I am sure that if she had gone forward in her studies she would have been one of the best pupils of her year".*

Eva Dunks' Letter from the Headmistress

Soon after she left Fairfield Eva enrolled for evening classes at Denton Technical School where she studied Commercial Arithmetic and Accounts and her reference from there is also very complimentary. The Headmaster stated *"Her written exercises were of a very high standard and gained for her the premier position in the class."* Having completed the course at Denton Technical School Eva took up a position in the offices of Oldham Batteries where her knowledge of mathematics was put to good use. She was responsible for wage analysis, stores records and other statistical work. When Eva married she had to leave her job at 'Oldham's' as it was the company's policy not to employ married women. Eva and her husband then moved to Bredbury, South Manchester, where, until the Second World War began, she worked for a company manufacturing hats and also for Bredbury Council.

At the beginning of the War in 1939 Eva joined the St John Ambulance and was on duty in the underground shelters in Stockport. These shelters extended for nearly a mile and could accommodate up to eight thousand people. Eva then joined the ATS (the Auxiliary Territorial Service) stationed at Sittingbourne and worked her way through the ranks to become a Sergeant.

One evening she had a lucky escape. She had set off with a group to go into town when the air raid siren was sounded. Eva and some of the group turned back to camp, but the rest continued into town and were killed in the raid. She was well on her way to becoming an Officer when in 1944 she became pregnant and had to leave the service. She returned to Denton and was able to go back to work at Oldham Batteries. She eventually became their Export Manager and remained there until her retirement.

Eva Dunks in her ATS Sergeant's uniform

Eva was an example of a very clever girl who, with very little help except her short-lived secondary education and evening classes, managed to achieve a responsible position in the commercial world. One wonders what she might have been able to accomplish if she had been given the opportunity to continue her education. Eva's story was told to me by her son. An indication of how important her education had been to her, was the fact that she had, all her life, safely kept and treasured her Scholarship Certificate and her reference letter from Fairfield's Headmistress and the Headmaster of Denton Technical School.[27] Eva's situation at that particular time would have been similar to many other bright young people – boys as well as girls.

The biggest group of girls, in this first register, was the group of fee-paying pupils who left before they were sixteen or with no certificates. These girls numbered over two hundred although it must be noted that sixty of them left the school to go on to other secondary schools or colleges. Twenty six pupils were listed as being "at home" either in a leisure, or "mother's help", capacity. For some, presumably, there was no necessity for them to have paid employment. For the remaining girls, clerical and shop assistant work was most popular followed by millinery, (it was still a time when ladies wouldn't be seen without a hat), dressmaking and tailoring. One girl became a librarian and another went into the Civil Service. Post Office work and floristry attracted two other pupils. There were four pupils who gave poor health as a reason for leaving.

When analysing the details in the first register it has to be noted that the percentage of scholarship pupils was small. In 1919 only the first year form was made up of 25 per cent scholarship girls. All the pupils in the other five forms were fee paying.

The second Register of three hundred girls gives information on pupils entering between 1922 and 1926 and leaving by 1933. A comparison between the two Registers helps us to analyse the progress which was made.

Eight girls went on to university from this Register– four less than the girls from the first Register, (the first register was helped by the fact that it started with the five girls in the sixth form who all went on to university). Two of these eight girls were Scholarship pupils. However, there were a further thirty three girls who stayed on to take Higher School Certificate, making the number in the 6th Form up to forty-one, compared with twenty-five pupils in the first Register. As well as the two going on to University, twenty of the girls in the 6th Form were Scholarship girls or had received Local Authority grants for their final years at the school. This meant that more than half the sixth form girls were non-fee paying. The majority of the girls went on to teacher training college, domestic science college or commercial college. The occupations of the fathers' of the sixth form girls ranged from a surgeon, bone specialist, dentist, and engineer to cotton operator, labourer and motor-wagon driver.

There was a similar success for the School Certificate. Sixty left school having gained the School Certificate, including thirty scholarship girls. These exam successes meant that 101 girls (one third) in the second Register left school with a qualification and this was a marked improvement on earlier years. It still meant, of course, that two thirds left without any qualifications.

There were some interesting additions to the usual after-school occupations. Secretarial Work made its first appearance, although it is probable that many of the girls who went on to Commercial Colleges would learn secretarial skills there. Another new occupation was training as a Masseuse at a hospital School of Massage - the forerunner of Physiotherapy. Quite a number of girls went on to work in the laboratories at the Aniline Dye Works in nearby Clayton and Fairfield High School employed a laboratory assistant. One girl became an Electrical Showroom Demonstrator. She left school in 1931 just as electricity was becoming a really important part of many people's lives. The Central Electricity board was set up in 1926 and in 1933 a series of regional grids began operating and the grid was operating on a national system by 1938. By the end of the 1930s two thirds of homes in England had an electricity supply.

Of the seventy eight girls who took the School Certificate, eighteen failed. The School Certificate would eventually be replaced and even by the late 1930's it was being criticised by Heads of Schools, for its unfairness. Many pupils who achieved exceptional high marks in all subjects except one, sometimes didn't pass because of only just failing in this one subject. It was sometimes the case that somebody who had failed had a much higher average mark than somebody who had passed.[28] Employers were gradually becoming aware of this situation and when interviewing certain applicants it was nearly as important that they were educated up to the standard of the exam, and had sat the exam, as it was for them to have passed it and more notice was then taken of the pupils' school reports.

50 per cent of the scholarship girls did not take any exams, more than 25 per cent of them leaving school before they were sixteen. Three girls who left at fourteen went to work in local factories making hats, leather and the well-known Robertson's Jam. Their fathers' occupations were listed as a tanner, a grocer and a wagon lifter. Two of these parents were released from their Agreement with the Local Authority because of their financial circumstances. One girl became a machinist - her notes state that she was released from the Scholarship Agreement when she was fourteen because of her mother's poverty. Her mother who worked as a clerk was shown as her sole parent. Another scholarship girl left at fourteen because "her parents were unable to maintain her at school". No details of her employment were given.

As in the first register, the largest group was composed of the 137 fee-paying pupils who left without any qualifications, although 73 had stayed on until they were sixteen and of these 22 continued their education at Commercial Colleges, eight went to work in offices and eight became shop assistants. Once again some girls were needed to help at home but in these years the total was only seven compared with 26 previously. The work taken up included millinery, tailoring, fashion and print designing, confectionery, hairdressing, nursing and laboratory work. Two girls went to work for the Post Office and one went into the Civil Service.

From the wealth of information contained in these two Registers, certain circumstances stand out. By the end of the 1920's, far more girls were staying on into the 6th Form and gaining the Higher School Certificate and a greater number were remaining at school until they were sixteen and taking, and passing, the School Certificate. However, surprisingly, during the years covered by the Registers, there wasn't any increase in the number of girls going on to University. It seems the girls were still likely to be influenced by society's attitude to women and their social and family background could also hinder their progress. One girl who entered the school in 1921 gained her Higher School Certificate and was awarded a Manchester City University Scholarship but was unable to accept this and go to college because of family circumstances.[29] Of the twenty girls going to university only three were scholarship girls. Their father's occupations were that of clerk, railway store superintendent and hatter. For girls from this background to continue their education at university until they were twenty one was an exceptional achievement. Many girls would have been prevented from staying on at school until they were sixteen or eighteen because they were needed to go out to work to help with the family's finances. It must also be remembered that those scholarship girls who were successful in gaining University places, Higher School Certificates, entry into colleges or passing the School Certificate, would have finished their education at the age of fourteen if it hadn't been for the 'free places' made possible in 1919 by the Local Education Committee. Before then, these Droylsden girls would not have been able to reach anything like their full potential.

Even after gaining the Scholarship for entrance to the school, some very bright girls would not have been in a position to take it up, because of various family reasons, mainly financial. William Woodruff, the Oxford educated and renowned economic historian, was brought up in extreme poverty in Northern England and left school at thirteen. In his wonderful biography *"The Road to Nab End"* he poignantly describes how his eleven year old sister who had topped the state scholarship examinations in the county was denied a secondary education because of the cost of a pair of shoes. With permission from William Woodruff's widow, Helga Woodruff, I quote the following moving paragraph from his book.

'Well, we can borrow money to buy shoes, or we can leave her where she is', father said finally. 'We might be making a fuss about nothing It's not good to put big ideas into young people's heads. What use is there in this learning when she could be doing real work?' Although I was very young I knew that something was wrong. I wanted to shout through the cracks beneath my bed, 'Benda's name was in the paper! You can't stop her going to Preston because she hasn't got shoes.' But I didn't shout. Nobody did… ..Somebody, somewhere would surely have paid for the shoes had he gone and asked, but he was too proud to beg….The truth is he wasn't interested in education for his children – The mills were our destiny. There was nothing dishonourable in that. What had been good enough for him, and for his father and grandfather, was good enough for us. It's where we belonged….Instead of going on to higher education, Brenda entered the mill at twelve as a half-timer and became an assistant to a spinner.[30]

It is more than likely that there were a number of Droylsden girls who experienced the same disadvantages as William Woodruff's sister.

During the period covered by the second registers, there was a substantial increase in the number of pupils leaving school with qualifications - nearly twice as many girls gained the Higher and Ordinary School Certificates. However, it has to be pointed out that the number gaining certificates would have been far less without the contribution of the Scholarship pupils.

The number of fee-paying pupils who left before they were sixteen, or with no qualifications, had decreased over the years but it was still just over 50 per cent. One possible reason for this might have been that any entrance exam which the fee-paying girls had to pass was not particularly difficult. This would result in many of the girls not really being able to cope with an academic education. It is interesting to note that one pupil who entered the school in 1941 said that she couldn't remember her and her three sisters ever taking an entrance exam, but she remembers having to take £16 into school on the first day of each term.[31]

It has to be admitted that the statistics show that the school's academic progress in its early years as a local authority High School, was not particularly outstanding. To have two thirds of the girls leaving without any formal qualification would be seen, by today's standards, as being extremely unsuccessful. This situation was probably a reflection of how most of society viewed the education of girls at that particular time. However, the school was definitely making progress and gradually developing into what would eventually become a thriving and hardworking modern high school.

The education at Fairfield has also to be compared with the schooling available at the time for the rest of the girls in Droylsden. It would be many years before **they** received a good quality secondary education.

CHAPTER SIX

A DECADE OF SOCIAL CONTRASTS, 1930-1939

"One *of the outstanding social workers of the twentieth century.*"

By 1930 the school had been a Lancashire Education High School for just over ten years. It still, however, treasured, and in many ways retained, the Christian traditions of the Moravian School. The School met each morning for an assembly when hymns were sung and readings from scripture were read. There was an acknowledgement that the Christian faith was still part of the ethos of the school. It wasn't surprising, therefore, that Miss Edwards, the Headmistress, in her letter to pupils in the 1928 School Magazine, stated *"We now have a well-equipped and beautifully decorated school. Perhaps the most direct result of this is our new interest in the work of the Ancoats University Settlement. Because we have almost everything that we could possibly want in our school, we feel that we have been talking long enough, we must now begin to give to others who are less fortunate".*

Manchester University Settlement

The Manchester University Settlement at Ancoats was established in 1895. It was originally set up in a wing of Ancoats Hall, the old home of the Mosley family. Railway yards and slum dwellings inhabited by cotton workers surrounded the property. Many of the houses at the time were built back to back with no passage of air between them, and often three or four families would occupy a four roomed house. By the 1930's the back to back houses were being either demolished or altered but it was still a very poor place to live and during the 1930's there was much unemployment in the area. The

Manchester University Settlement took over a chapel, which was known as the 'Round House', and this was used as a place for the children in the area to play and in which to have a little entertainment.

For many years to come, the girls at Fairfield would give support of gifts, clothing, time and money to the Settlement. At Christmas time they collected old and new toys for the children's Christmas trees. On one occasion Miss Edwards had to make two journeys with her car to get all the toys to the Settlement. They held dances and parties to raise money and the proceeds of School's Sports Days were often sent to Ancoats.

SOCIAL WORKER

There would probably be many Fairfield girls over the years who would be deeply affected by the experience they gained working with the children at the Ancoats Settlement who were far less fortunate than themselves, but the story of one girl in particular needs to be told. Many years later she would be described as one of the outstanding social workers of the twentieth century. Until the end of her life she kept in touch with Fairfield Old Girls' Association and in one of her last letters in 1996 she wrote *"I have to thank school for encouraging my choice of career to the extent of promoting me as a volunteer on two evenings a week at the Ancoats Settlement, to the detriment of my homework but to the development of my life's work".*[1]

Joan Cooper was born in 1914 in the Moravian Settlement at 38 The Square. Her parents were Moravians and both her mother and great aunt were educated at the School and her mother also taught French there. Joan stayed at the school until she was eighteen, in 1932, and then went on to Manchester University where she gained a degree in Art and History and qualified as a teacher.

She spent some time teaching in Cornwall and then joined Derbyshire Education Department in an administrative capacity and then became Assistant Director of Education. She was responsible for overseeing the evacuation of children from London during the 2nd World War[2] and saw the same effects of poverty and deplorable conditions on these children as she had witnessed years before in Ancoats, Manchester.

Even before the War ended, people were beginning to stress the need for a change in social conditions and improvements in the lives of many people and after the War education was reformed and the National Health Service was established alongside national insurance and social security. The welfare of children was also of great concern. Until that time the help given to children in need was mainly through Industrial Schools, the Poor Law, Public Assistance provision and Charities. The Curtis Committee Report on the Care of Children in 1946 had found that children living in residential homes were not recognised as individuals with their own rights and possessions. They were merely one of a large crowd, playing and eating with the rest without any quiet room to which they could retreat. They were without the feeling that there was anyone to whom they could turn who was interested in their welfare or who cared for them as a person.[3] The Report described the appalling conditions of the homes and concern was expressed about the lack of good quality foster homes, the neglect of education and the low expectations and limited career choices. The Report was very enlightened for its time and even suggested that children in care should have the opportunity to go on to further education or university. The most important recommendation of the Curtis Report was that every local authority should set up a Children's Department, headed by a highly qualified Children's Officer, who would *'know, and keep in personal touch, with all the children under her care'*. This Report formed the basis for the 1948 Children Act. [4]

In 1948 Joan Cooper was appointed as the first Children's Officer for East Sussex and set about creating the Children's Department there. She described her first days there *"I started on July 5 1948, the day the Children Act came into being. I was thirty four years old, very young. At the top of County Hall was a large room which housed two boarding- out officers and a clerk. I joined them. I didn't know what to do. There was a copy of the 1948 Children Act placed before me and there were these people who didn't seem to want anything to do with me. There was a lot of resistance to 'new-fangled' ideas. One of the council members kept proposing to send all the children to Australia or New Zealand where there were 'wonderful opportunities in farming'".[5]*

Joan was strongly opposed to the emigration of children and only two East Sussex children in care were sent abroad. This emigration was still happening widely elsewhere until the 1960s.[6]

There was probably also some resistance to the fact that she was a woman as many were still opposed to women in positions of authority and the toilet facilities were for men only!"

Joan's experience was not quite as bad as a girl (not from Fairfield), called Emmerson Price, who became the first woman architectural assistant for London County Council in 1934. She was banished to a room under the roof of County Hall to renovate old workhouses and fever hospitals, away from the rest of the team. When she was eventually moved to the Design Section she was confronted by a boss who complained *"I have had some of the greatest idiots, fools and drunkards in this office and now for my sins I am to be landed with a woman.*[7]

Over the next sixteen years things improved as Joan endeavoured to meet the needs of the vulnerable and deprived children who were in care and for whom her department was responsible. Joan developed small residential homes and foster care and introduced training for staff. She looked abroad for ideas both on the continent and in America. In the Netherlands she studied how they educated and cared for disabled children and those with special educational needs and in France she saw and was impressed by their use of psychologists rather than social workers in the running of fostering services.[8] In 1952 she broadcast to France, in French, about Child Welfare.[9]

Sonia Jackson OBE, Professor of Social Care and Education at the University of London, in the third "Joan Cooper Memorial Lecture" at the University of Sussex in 2008, said that one of the main functions of her department, as Joan saw it, was to recognise talent and help individual children develop it, as well as to maintain links with their families. Joan had told Professor Bob Holman: *"We encouraged the education of our children, we wanted them to stay on at school and when I left we had six children at university. That does not sound very many but a comparative study with Birmingham found that it had only two amongst a much bigger population".*

The new Children's Departments helped to improve the lives of children *in care*. It wasn't until 1963 that the Children and Young Persons Act provided, for the first time, for children who were *not in care*, by providing preventive and rehabilitative social work.[10] However, Joan wrote, years later, that *"what seemed a breakthrough in preventive work for Children's Departments was sometimes seen by local authority health departments as trespassing on their territory".* It seems that various professions and services had different approaches to children's well-being and this created problems. This situation had worried Joan for many years and as a result of her lobbying and committee work the National Bureau for Co-operation in Child Care was established (later to be known as the National Children's Bureau) which brought together the range of professions and services involved with child welfare. This organisation celebrated its fortieth birthday in 2003. Joan was on the Executive Committee from the beginning and was a Vice President from 1966 until she died in 1999.[11]

In 1964 she was made Chief Inspector of the Children's Department at the Home Office. In this post she was responsible for the inspection of all child care services in the country and influenced important policies such as the White Papers leading to the Children's and Young Persons' Act of 1969 and the Local Authority Social Services Act of 1970.

The 1970 Local Authority Social Services Act centralised all social services into one department in each local authority. These changes were accompanied by similar changes in central government where responsibility for all social services passed to the Department of Health and Social Security and Joan became Director of the new Social Work Services. This meant that she was the Government's Chief Professional Adviser on all Social Work Services. It was a huge assignment to bring together all social services into one unified new service and Joan worked hard to provide the professional guidance and support which was needed during five years of change and local government reorganisation.

Professor Sonia Jackson OBE, when she gave the third Joan Cooper Memorial Lecture, said that she met Joan when they were on the Executive Committee of the National Children's Bureau. She said that Joan was not at all like most civil servants at the time. Instead of pointing out why things couldn't be done, like Sir Humphrey in "Yes Minister", she was always looking for a way forward. She was absolutely committed to improving the lives of children, especially those who were most disadvantaged. She had a sense of mission and she never lost it.

Before she retired in 1976 she was to see yet another Children's Act put into place. This Act of 1975 was the result of the Inquiry Report into the death of Maria Colwell in 1973. Maria had been killed by her step-father after being removed from her foster carers and put into the care of her birth mother. This 1975 Act meant that children at risk could be rapidly removed from their birth families into residential or foster care with the aim of permanent placement or adoption. The work of the Social Services became not only one of child-care but also of child protection.[12]

Joan Cooper retired from her work as a senior civil servant in 1976. She became a C.B. (Companion of the Order of the Bath) in 1972 and wrote to the Old Girls Association saying that she now felt she had joined the Establishment at last.[13] Her brother, Sir Frank Cooper who was the Ministry of Defence's Permanent under Secretary during the Falkland crisis, had been appointed the MoD's most senior official in 1976, just as Joan was retiring, so the Cooper family of Fairfield were well represented in the higher echelons of government. For someone of her background this was quite an achievement. Professor Jackson stated that *"Her background was quite unusual for someone who was to become a senior civil servant. She wasn't educated at a public school or Oxford or Cambridge: she went to Fairfield High School and then the University of Manchester"*. Being a woman would have made it even more unusual. Even by April 2011 women made up only 35.9 per cent of the senior civil service. Of the top management positions (Permanent Secretary or Director level) women made up only 29.5 per cent.

It is difficult in just a short summary to give justice to a life which was dedicated to helping those less fortunate than herself. It might seem that Joan's work was mainly concerned with administration but we can look to the tribute paid to her in the inaugural lecture to her memory by Professor Peter Wedge to see that there was much more. Among a great many other tributes he said that *"Along with her considerable intellect she was warm and generous in her friendships, encouraging to younger colleagues and maintained contact to the end of her life with children who had been in her care as a Children's Officer."* Professor Wedge went on to say that *"in short, she was a femme formidable, resolute and highly intellectual - but with a soft heart, a tremendous advocate for children, for families and for social work services for them."* Professor Sonia Jackson said, at the beginning of her lecture *"I feel extremely honoured to have been invited to give this lecture, in memory of one of the outstanding social workers of the twentieth century."*

ECONOMIC SITUATION

Joan Cooper left Fairfield High School in July 1932. During her last year she was Head Girl and seconded the vote of thanks to the Guest of Honour at Speech Day. All the speakers on that day showed their concern about the dreadful economic situation the country was going through. Joan herself wrote in the School Magazine that *"This year has been one of the most fateful years through which the country has passed."* She went on to say that the school had done its best to raise money to help to alleviate the distress in the local area.[14]

The same edition of the School Magazine contained an article by the mistress responsible for the School's contact with the Ancoats University Settlement . In it she states that *"amidst the general depression, the Settlement has suffered badly, not only owing to the unemployment and poverty in the immediate district, but also owing to the inability of subscribers to keep up or to increase their customary donations."* An appeal went out each year for summer frocks for the Ancoats Settlement girls. Over a hundred children usually went to a Holiday School in Didsbury in South Manchester and others went to a holiday camp. Many of the children lacked the clothing that they needed even for such a simple holiday. Used clothing was always wanted at the Settlement and was one of the main things that Fairfield Girls frequently gave.

The world economic crisis had started with the Wall Street Banking crash in America in October 1929 and had led to mass unemployment in Britain. By the end of 1930 there were 2,300,000 people registered as unemployed and the North of England was one of the main black spots, but the people affected by this situation numbered far more. If the unemployeds' dependants were added, the figure probably reached more than six million.

What added to the distress were the stringent cuts in public expenditure which were put in place to tackle the problem of the Budget deficit for 1932. Cuts were made in the pay of civil servants, teachers and other public employees including the Armed Forces. Unemployment Benefit was severely cut. A single man's benefit was reduced from eighteen shillings a week (90p) to fifteen shillings and three pence (77p). At the beginning of September that year, the Means Test came into force and thousands were struck off Benefit. Many middle class people were also affected. As companies closed, managers, accountants and clerks lost their jobs.

This situation was, in fact, reflected in the statistics in the School Registers which we looked at in chapter five. Unemployment and financial distress were the reason for many girls leaving school before they were sixteen and for preventing others from staying on into the 6th Form.[15]

Lena Slack (née Johnstone)

One Scholarship girl whose father was frequently unemployed during her time at Fairfield came from a very loving home and was able to stay on into the 6th form and then go on to teacher training college. Two years after starting at the school, her sister died, leaving Lena an only child. Her mother was a strong, capable woman and a great influence in encouraging Lena with her education. Years later, Lena Slack wrote about her early years and gave a detailed description of working class life.[16]

They lived in Audenshaw, a district adjoining Droylsden, in a small terraced house. Audenshaw still had some farms and fields and the house was away from the rows of closely-packed houses which made up much of that area, to the east of Manchester. The house had no bath or hot water but it had a nice flagged yard, an outdoor W.C. and a pleasant 'front room', as well as the living room cum kitchen.

In an attempt to earn some money, her mother turned her hand to a number of activities. She made frocks, trousers, coats and underwear and at one time the front room of the house was turned into a hardware shop and then for a few months a 'chip shop'. Although they had very little, there was always just enough and they never went hungry, although they had few luxuries.

Lena was born in February 1921 and memories of the War years were still fresh. Her father was in Germany until 1919, with the army of occupation, and became ill with rheumatic fever just a few months after he came home. His memories of the War made a deep impression on him and he would talk about being in the trenches and being heavily shelled by the enemy. He spoke of gas attacks and of running a candle up the seams of his uniform to kill the lice. Lena's father was one of four brothers, two of whom were killed in the War, one being only eighteen.

There was, of course, no National Health Service until 1948, so unless you were a working man "on the panel" the services of a doctor had to be paid for. The 'panel' was an arrangement under the National Insurance Act of 1911 whereby a man earning less than £160 a year contributed four pence a week into the scheme and was placed on a doctor's 'panel' which entitled him to 'free medical care'. Homely remedies were widely used. Lena remembered a square of camphor sewn into a little cotton bag which would hang round her neck to guard against colds and she would wriggle her chin inside the neck of her woolly jumper and draw up a warm, comforting wave of camphorated air into her nose. Goose grease spread on a flannel was applied to the chest if one had a cold or sore throat.

A doctor would be called only if you were really ill and if you were told to stay in bed a fire would be lit in the bedroom. On cold winter nights Lena's mother would wrap a hot oven shelf in an old piece of blanket and when it was put in the bed it would retain its heat for hours. If a doctor had been needed he would send an invoice stating the amount owed and this would be collected weekly by the "doctor's man". The weekly amount was usually about sixpence, in "old money".

Lena states that there was little contact with hospitals - to be admitted to hospital almost suggested that there was "no hope" and they looked on hospitals and ambulances with awe and horror. The death-rate, among children and young people, was much higher then. She remembers several children dying whilst she was at Primary School. She also commented on the fact that sick people, especially old people, took to their beds at home, sometimes for months or even years. It was a common sight to see a bed downstairs in the front room in many terraced houses. It was unusual for old people to die in hospital, much more common for them to die in the familiar surroundings of home. Lena comments that in those days to live to sixty five was considered a long life and very few reached their eighties. All four of her grandparents had died before she was born but today four generations in a family is not unusual. When I was researching my own family history I found that when my grandfather and grandmother married in 1901 both their fathers had already died and when my great grandmother married my great grandfather, in 1873, both their fathers were dead. Not to live long enough to see your children marry seems particularly sad.

When Lena passed the Scholarship examination in 1931 she was the only child in her year at her primary school to do so. She was a very clever girl and for years she had dreamed of going to Fairfield. Her father was unemployed at the time but there was no question about her not accepting the place. Her mother said *"She's going, we'll manage somehow"*. Her mother made her school gymslip and three square-necked short-sleeved blouses. She walked the mile to school and also walked one way in the lunch hour although the tram cost only a half-penny fare.

Lena says that she never felt at a disadvantage at school, but she did wish they had a bathroom, when she took her school friends home. Nearly all of them lived in modern semis or bungalows, with neat gardens; some lived in fine, large houses, to which she was invited to splendid parties. She reminisces about one of these fine houses where the family employed a maid who answered the door wearing a uniform of a black dress, and white cap and apron. She was invited there one Christmas and she remembers the lovely elegant rooms decorated for Christmas with a warm rosy glow provided by pink-shaded electric lights which she thought were like something out of another world. However, she was always happy to go back to her own living-kitchen with the black-leaded kitchen-range, a pan of broth on the hob, and the white gas-light from the incandescent "mantle" which had to be lit so carefully.

Lena described the teachers at the school. She said that many of the staff had strong connections with the Moravian Church. All of them were outstanding personalities and gentlewomen and Lena stated that they would have to be, because at that time it was mainly only women from wealthy families who would be able to continue their education at university. She describes them as speaking beautifully, in soft tones, and carrying themselves so regally. They wore unfashionable, but expensive clothes, real Macclesfield-silk shirt-blouses and good leather shoes. They were all religious women who were strongly dedicated to the task of teaching. Lena remembers them not only teaching the girls the usual subjects but much more of things 'true, lovely and of good report'.

Lena had a very successful school career and gained her School Certificate and then Higher School Certificate and in her last year in the 6th Form she was chosen as Head Girl. During the early years of the 2nd World War she was at teacher training college and she married shortly after she qualified. She was very accomplished. She played the piano extremely well and had a natural ability for composing poems and musical lyrics.

Lena Slack (née Johnstone) as head girl in 1938-1939, near the 'New Extension', which
was being built onto the original building at Fairfield High School for Girls.

She was greatly influenced by her mother. In the last paragraph of the story
of her early life she mentions that whenever her mother came to school, she
was received as if she had been a duchess. Though her clothes may have been
shabby, they would be brushed and pressed, and her old shoes polished till
they shone, and she would have trimmed her old hat with ribbon or a flower,
and finally she quotes her mother's frequent saying " *You've got to make the best
of it*".

Lena was clever and deep-thinking, as was shown by the following poem
which she wrote for the Old Girls' Section of the School Magazine. In it she
expresses her views on the great dilemma which even today is perplexing the
female population. Its title is "Fulfilment".

I was a schoolgirl, young and keen,
And when I was, perhaps, fifteen,
Adventure called and hopes ran high -
(In youth one's dreams and fancies fly)
I'd travel far, I'd rise to fame,
I'd soon become a famous name;
I'd write a book on noble themes

(All things are possible in dreams).
I'd act in Shaw, in films appear,
I'd be a queen in my own sphere;
The trivial round's a thing too mean,
How could a housewife be a queen?
The book's unwritten, the song unsung,
Creative work I planned when young,,
The picture, sculpture, of my brain
Ne'er came to aught, here I remain.
Yes, here I am, my name's unknown,
No worldly riches do I own,
A housewife merely, not a queen;
Yet not quite idle have I been,
Two perfect children I possess,
Two impish scraps of loveliness,
Flesh of my flesh, bone of my bone,
And brain - if any, of my own.
Their creature wants, my life supplies,
My whole existence justifies.
My every moment serves their need,
I wash, I scrub, I cook, I feed;
Could anything less glamorous be?
And yet I know it is for me,
The only life that I would choose,
In which I all my talents use.
For in the end when dreams may scatter,
Homes are the things that really matter,
Where lives are moulded, infants trained,
Where love is taught and wisdom gained.
Improve all homes and we progress
Along the road to happiness,
So in this thought I rest content,
I feel I do as I was meant.
I build a home, a family,
And so fulfil my destiny [17]

This poem was written in 1950 and Lena, contrary to the feelings expressed in the poem, didn't stay at home for ever. She was a well-educated young woman and in 1957, when her children were in full time education, she returned to teaching - at Audenshaw County Primary School, the school she attended in the 1920's. Teaching, of course, provided the ideal occupation for a woman with a family. In 1952 Lena broadcast on Woman's Hour on the art of occupying children in the home.

Her musical and poetic abilities did not diminish. From an early age she had played the piano – before she was four years old she was able to play 'by ear' and later she received professional piano lessons. In the early sixties she appeared in the Northern Talent Spot of ITV's television programme 'Scene at 6.30' where she recited 'Holiday Fever' a poem she had written, in Lancashire dialect. She became a county Magistrate in the late 1960's and was very supportive of her local church and was in great demand in the district to entertain local groups with evenings of monologues and verses.

Lena's life would have been entirely different if she had not passed the Scholarship. There would have been no secondary education, no teacher training and she would not have reached anything like her full potential.

SOCIAL CONTRASTS

By 1930 the school must have been one of contrasts - girls from affluent middle-class homes studying and playing alongside girls from poor working class families whose fathers were often unemployed.

One girl, reminiscing years later, spoke about only ever having had one family holiday. This was when she was five and went with her family for a week to Blackpool and stayed in a newly built house in an apartment which had an en-suite bathroom. They had to go out each morning to buy food for the day and then take it in for the landlady to cook. Not having a bathroom at home, they thought it was sheer luxury and had saved up all year for this one week's holiday.[18]

Blackpool Beach in the 1930s

In contrast to this Blackpool holiday, one Lower Sixth Form girl holidayed on the French Riviera in the summer of 1933. She and her family travelled by train and boat, leaving London at 9.30 in the morning and sailing from Newhaven to Dieppe and then by train to Paris. They left Paris on the 9pm night train to Nice, arriving there the following morning. From her description of the holiday it seemed that the long journey was worth it.

We are told that the family stayed at the Hotel Metropole and thoroughly enjoyed sun bathing on the beaches and swimming in the sea in glorious warm weather. At their favourite beach in Nice they were able to sit at sunshade-covered tables and to use the raft and diving board in the sea. The weather was so extremely hot that all excessive underwear had to be discarded and we are told that our Fairfield girl had to resort to a bathing costume or silk beach pyjamas *"which were acknowledged as being the most appropriate dress"*. These beach pyjamas had trousers which were widely flared and were an essential item for the fashion conscious Continental holidaymaker.

The family bathed at the four chief Riviera resorts - Monte Carlo, Cannes, Juan les Pins and Nice. They went to the Casino at Monte Carlo where unfortunately she was too young to go inside but enjoyed eating ice-cream on the terrace. Her father, although he didn't 'break the bank', managed to win enough to cover the day's expenses.

They travelled by car - we're not told whether it was Chauffeur driven or hired - along the Grand Corniche into Italy giving them beautiful views of the snow covered Alps. Their return journey was via San Remo along the Petite Corniche, arriving back in Nice in time for dinner.[19]

It wasn't only Fairfield pupils who went on continental holidays; members of staff also travelled abroad. Miss Holt, who was later to become Deputy Head Mistress, gave a vivid account, to the School Branch of the League of Nations, of her visit to Berlin in 1932 with emphasis on the political affairs of Germany and Berlin in particular. Unfortunately no record of her talk has survived but she did write an amusing article in the School Magazine on the use of a German phrase book. The phrases that the book gave were apparently not particularly polite, but she went on to describe her taxi-driver as the kind of man who accelerates at every corner and goes round on two wheels and she suggested that he was probably a **Nazi or a Communist!** It's interesting to find the word 'Nazi' used in such a pejorative way so early in Hitler's ascendancy. It was to be a few years yet before the threat of Hitler was taken really seriously.[20]

BROADCASTING

The early 1930s was a time when people were beginning to experience the pleasure of listening to the 'wireless' and to realise the future potential of long distance broadcasting.

On Christmas Day 1932 a ground breaking radio broadcast was transmitted. This was described by one pupil in the School Magazine in an article entitled "All the World Over". The broadcast consisted of messages sent from London to many parts of the world. In some places it was already Boxing Day and in others Christmas morning. A message was received from S.S. Majestic in Mid Atlantic and messages were sent to and received from New Zealand, Australia and South Africa; and from S.S. Empress of Britain, lying at anchor in Port Said. The captain of this ship said that most of the passengers were spending their Christmas Day visiting the Holy Land. The last greetings were sent to Gibraltar, to the men who guarded the entrance to the Mediterranean Sea. Finally listeners were taken over to Sandringham to hear King George V (the present Queen's grandfather) speak to all his subjects in the British Empire. It was the first time a King of England had been able to talk to his people in nearly every part of the British Empire and it was the King's first Christmas broadcast [21]

Christmas was perhaps one time when people tried their best to forget the difficult times the country was experiencing and the pupils and staff at Fairfield High School were no exception. From all accounts their Christmas parties were splendid occasions. One Scholarship girl remembers the beautiful dresses and opera-cloaks that the fee-paying girls wore. However, her mother always managed to make her a "best" dress and there was always a school friend whose father had a car and would pick her up to take her to the party in style.[22]

The staff and 6th formers joined forces to organise the Juniors' Parties. The Hall and the other rooms which were used were beautifully decorated and a delicious tea provided.[23] Every girl was given a small present and this event was usually performed with style. One year they had a silver ball that came down from the ceiling which opened when it reached the floor and the presents came spilling out. Another year Humpty Dumpty was sitting on his wall and when he fell off the presents came out of his broken shell. However, there was a near disaster one year as recounted in the School Magazine ... *"Father Christmas arrived with gifts for everyone, but he gave us all a fright when he let his scarlet cloak trail across the lighted candles on the big Christmas tree".*[24] Most Christmas tree lights in those days were in the form of candles which were similar to, but bigger than, the candles we now put on a birthday cake. They were put into metal holders which were clipped on to the branches.

CAREERS FOR THE HIGH SCHOOL GIRL

Although there was much unemployment it was hoped that the education the girls were receiving would help them obtain suitable work. The school magazine contained several articles on the various careers which were now opening up for women, including pharmacy and dispensing. Since the 1st World War women had gradually begun to take up analytical chemistry and research work in areas other than the medical profession. Many industries now had laboratories and employed trained chemists. However, one article mentioned that there still remained a good deal of prejudice against the woman analytical chemist.[25]

The Masseuse

Another article described the training and work of a hospital Masseuse which was the forerunner of today's physiotherapist and one former pupil described her work as a Masseuse in a school for disabled children.

There were 160 children in the school, all suffering from various diseases, the most common being infantile paralysis, rickets, spinal curvature and tubercular joints. The children were collected from within a radius of five miles and conveyed to school in two ancient buses. They remained at school for an excellent midday meal and in addition the children received milk and malt. There was a trained nurse in charge of the bathroom, and the children were given a much needed weekly bath, more often if necessary. The nurses also supervised the clothing and general health of each child and arranged for convalescent treatment and holidays. There was a Massage and Sunlight Department where the majority of the children received treatment three times a week throughout their school life and as a result most of them, on leaving the school, were able to work in the ordinary labour market. Everything possible was done to counteract the effects of an unnatural childhood, many of the children having come to them after prolonged restriction within the home or hospital and the writer pointed out how interesting it was to watch how soon in the new environment a child forgot its disabilities and was eager to join in work and play. She was always inspired by the Old Scholars' re-unions which proved how worthwhile the work was. The children started life with every drawback, poor slum homes, and physical disability and came back to the re-unions clean, happy and self-supporting.

Brief details were also given in the school magazine on a number of careers including accountancy and book-keeping, and it was interesting to note that training for all these careers involved quite expensive fees. This situation was verified by the Head Mistress at Speech Day in 1934 when she urged parents to keep children at school as long as possible and be prepared to spend money on training for many vocations. This situation created a further obstacle for the poorer girls at the school and would have resulted in many worthwhile careers being beyond their reach.

Woman Police Officer

Very few Fairfield girls became women police officers. However, there was at least one Fairfield girl who joined the police force in the late 1920's and she described her work in the School Magazine of 1930. Kathleen Raddin P.C. was stationed in Sheffield where, unlike in many other cities, the policewomen had full powers of arrest, and they were fortunate in belonging to a force whose Chief Constable believed in them and did his very utmost for their well-being. There were six policewomen working in Sheffield - five Constables and a Sergeant- and they had just been installed in a Section House together, so that they would be within call if required when off duty.

They did a great amount of plain clothes work - observations in the large stores for shoplifters, welfare of children and young girls, observations in Betting Houses and numerous enquiries accompanied by officers of the Criminal Investigation Department - but they also had a uniform. She mentioned that many cities did not allow their policewomen to wear any uniform, but in Sheffield patrolling of the parks and certain streets by a uniformed woman Police Constable was considered to be one of the most important branches of their work, and resulted in a great reduction of crime. Part of their work involved enquiries into the home conditions of juvenile offenders and bringing them before the Juvenile Court. All statements from women and young girls were taken by them and they escorted female prisoners to Strangeways Prison, in Manchester.

Kathleen described how the youngsters in the slum areas soon got to know the "Lady Policewoman" and were model citizens until she turned her back. They loved to get the "arm of the law" to bowl for them or wicket keep. She described the appalling conditions in some of the houses as almost unbelievable and said that *"one wonders how it is that crime is not increasing more rapidly than it is"*.

Kathleen indicated that because of her work she had gained invaluable experience and learned much that would otherwise have been denied to her. She said that, if she had followed any other profession, she would not have met with the same people, nor had to tackle the situations that confronted her daily.

She ended her letter by saying *"This can only be a very short account of the kind of things we do. A list of the jobs we tackle would be far too formidable for a School Magazine!"*

THE NEW SCHOOL BUILDING

During the 1930's the population of Droylsden greatly increased. Manchester had become overcrowded and between 1931 and 1939 large housing estates were built in Droylsden mainly to house Manchester's overflow population. The population of Droylsden doubled in those years.[26] Some of the houses were council houses but many estates were privately built on the surrounding farmland.

This increase in population caused an urgent need for Fairfield High School to expand and at the end of 1935 plans were put forward to the Education Committee. In 1938 the work commenced and was completed just as War was declared in September 1939.

Six and a half acres were added to the playing fields and the entrance to the school was now by a tree-lined driveway from Fairfield Avenue which replaced the need, for those girls coming from the direction of Ashton Old Road, to walk through the "ginnel" into Fairfield Square and then through the small gateway at the side of the school. [27]

The ginnel

THE SCHOOL BUILDINGS FROM 1796 UNTIL 1906

The Moravian Boarding School for Girls was housed in the Sisters' House
from 1796 to 1815 and from 1876 to1906

In 1815, the School moved into this house attached to the Church building

The school has been housed here since 1906. It was rebuilt on the site of the original Brethren's House in 1871

Plantation Farm, Dukinfield.
Mary Moffat lived here from 1795 to 1819.

The Duchess of Gloucester visited the school on the occasion of its bi-centenary. This picture shows the beautful wall panelling installed by the Parents' Association in the late 1920s.

2010/02/22

Edward Street, Audenshaw, Lena Slack's childhood home in the 1930s

THE CONTRASTING LIVES OF TWO 1960s FAIRFIELD GIRLS

Sister Scholastica enjoying a meal with a Palestinian, an Iraqi and a Jewish lady who were all attending one of her conferences.

Sister Scholastica (Christine McQueen) is a nun in the beautiful Benedictine Abbey of Frauenworth, on the island of Fraueninsel, Lake Chiemsee, Bavaria

Sharrnan Birtles née Newth wearing her Deputy Lieutenant of Greater Manchester badge of office.

THE NEW SPORTS HALL OPENED IN 2005

Olympic triple-jumper and holder of the world record since 1995, Jonathan Edwards visited
Fairfield in 2010 and met Georgia Taylor Brown, European Junior triathlon champion,
England junior volleyball player Julia Whalley and champion sailor Hannah Mitchell.
(photographed inside the new Sports Hall)

FAIRFIELD GIRLS AIMING HIGH

Flt. Lieut. (now Squadron Leader) Karen Lofthouse, in Afghanistan in 2009

Police Inspector Claire Galt presents school trophies to Fairfield girls as the Headmaster Mr John Hedley looks on.

VOLUNTARY WORKER IN SIERRA LEONE

Sarah Jones in Freetown, Sierra Leone

The Ola During Children's Hospital in Freetown, Sierra Leone on 27 April 2010, the day when healthcare for pregnant and lactating women and children under five became free.

FAIRFIELD GIRLS OF 2012

Head Girl Helena Rewko and Deputy Head Girl Tiarna Davidson photographed for a local
paper on the occasion of the school topping Tameside's GCSE league tables

Kelly Outhwaite – Chosen to carry
the Olympic Torch

The modern classroom.
Girls hard at work at their computer desks.

The school now had a large new building containing classrooms, up-to-date laboratories, a fine library and dining room accommodation. It also contained a modern gymnasium with showers and changing rooms, although the showers and changing rooms could not be used during war-time, owing to the risk of an air-raid.

THE THREAT OF WAR

The school's League of Nations' Branch gave particular attention to the effects of the World War (it wasn't, of course, referred to as the First World War until the commencement of the Second, although it was sometimes referred to as the Great War). Talks were given on the "Danger Spots in Europe" and the "Progress in Disarmament".[28] They watched a film entitled "The World War and After" which gave details of the destruction caused by the War and the changes made, in Europe, by the Peace Treaty of Versailles.

On Armistice Night in 1936 (which commemorated the ending of World War I on 11 November 1918) they attended a peace demonstration at the Free Trade Hall in Manchester. The following year the school took part in a Peace Pageant along with the Droylsden Elementary Schools, which, according to the editorial in the School Magazine, turned out to be a great success[29] - not successful enough, though, to prevent the 2nd World War two years later.

Earlier in the decade the School Branch of the League of Nations had heard a talk about Air and Chemical Warfare. The speaker warned that because of the advances made in the world's aircraft, any future war would involve the nations' civilians, and not just armies. Little did they realise how right he would prove to be.

Fairfield was fortunate that the new school building was finished just before World War II started. Other building projects in Droylsden were not so lucky. There had been few civic buildings and social amenities at the beginning of the twentieth century and the recent increase in the population meant that civic buildings, such as more schools, a swimming baths, library, public hall, public parks, community centre and municipal buildings, were urgently needed. However, in 1939, just as the new county library was built,

Britain again went to war and any plans for future building had to be abandoned.[30]

In the School Magazine, at the end of the school year in July 1939, the School Branch of the League of Nations issued this notice *'With the present state of the nations and events shifting from day to day, we cannot foretell the subject of our next meeting. Suffice it to say that we are continuing our work in the strong belief that the precepts upon which the League was founded are the only hope for the world and must triumph in the end'*.

With the onset of war, in September 1939, it was with bitter-sweet emotions that the girls at Fairfield would return to their beautifully modernised school.

CHAPTER SEVEN

WARTIME EXPERIENCES
1939-1945

They started the War as school girls and ended it as women of wide experience.

Britain announced that it was at war with Germany on the 3rd of September 1939. The next five and a half years would bring sadness and tragedy to many people.

That September the School was fortunate in that the new building and re-decoration had just been completed. In many other places the impending War had prevented work continuing on new school buildings. Nearby, the work on a new senior school for Droylsden, whose foundations had just been laid, was abandoned.

When War was declared the school was still on holiday but it had to quickly resolve the question of the evacuation of some of the pupils. Just over a quarter of the girls lived in Manchester and they were given the opportunity to evacuate. The Head Mistress and some of the staff returned to the school at the end of August and made arrangements for thirty three girls to be evacuated and continue their education at the Warehousemen and Clerks' School in Cheadle Hulme alongside girls from Manchester High School.[1]

The School had no air raid shelters and was unable to open as scheduled on September 14th. Work for the girls to do at home was organised and after three weeks, half-time attendance was arranged and the school re-opened for full time attendance a fortnight before the end of the term. By that time, half of the air raid shelters had been completed.[2]

ESCAPE FROM GERMANY

One twelve year old pupil who joined the school in January 1940 had made a long and emotional journey to England, on her own, to escape death-threatening persecution by the Nazis.

Fanni Bogdanow arrived on the "Kindertransport". This was the name given to the rescue mission that took place during the nine months prior to the outbreak of the War. Britain took in nearly 10,000 Jewish children from Nazi Germany and the occupied territories of Austria, Czechoslovakia, and Poland and gave them a home. The decision to start this rescue mission was made by the British Government a few days after the 9th November 1938. This date will always be known as 'Kristallnacht' (the night of the broken glass) and is usually associated with the burning of synagogues and the breaking of Jewish shop windows throughout the whole of Germany. However, Fanni remembers that far more happened on that day. During that afternoon the Jewish men and boys in her home town of Affaltrach were taken to Dachau concentration camp. Her eighteen year old cousin who lived in another part of Germany was taken to Buchenwald where he died within a month.

That night when only women and children were at home, the Nazis with their pickaxes broke into all the Jewish homes. They hacked down the front door, they hacked out the windows and window frames and they hacked holes in the walls. Not a piece of furniture was left standing, not a cup nor saucer was left whole. The following day all Jewish children were, by decree, expelled from the German state schools. And, as all Jewish teachers had the previous day been taken to concentration camps, Jewish children were left without schooling. By a further decree the remaining Jewish people were segregated into 'Judenhausser' (Jew Houses'}. Towns and villages where no Jewish people were left had a sign at their entrance saying 'Judenfrei' ('free of Jews).[3]

When Fanni's mother heard about the British offer of help she immediately put Fanni's name down on the list because, although it meant that she would have to part with her only child, she knew that it would probably save her life. Fanni didn't manage to get a place on the Kindertransport until the 26th June 1939 but while she waited her mother encouraged her to learn as much English as she could. Meanwhile, Fanni's father had been temporarily released from Dachau at the beginning of February 1939 and this meant that both her mother and father were able to travel by train with Fanni for part of the journey.[4] The journey, from Affaltrach in south west Germany to the port of the Hook of Holland in the Netherlands, started in the afternoon of the 26th June and ended at ten o'clock in the evening of the following day. They first had to travel to Stuttgart and then north to Frankfurt where Fanni met up with about a hundred other children all going to England. It was in Frankfurt that she finally had to say goodbye to her father - her mother had had to leave the train earlier. The children boarded a ship at the Hook of Holland and sailed for Harwich, arriving at eight o'clock the next morning. From Harwich they went by train to London.[5]

An organisation had been set up to establish transport and foster homes for the children, although there were children who arrived in London without any pre-arranged foster families and they had to go to temporary accommodation at summer holiday camps until they were found homes. Fanni was one of the fortunate ones. She was met in London by a relative of a Mr and Mrs Clement who had offered their help.

Mr and Mrs Clement were a Quaker couple, with two young sons, who lived in Haughton Green, near Droylsden. They were teachers and welcomed Fanni and looked after her as one of their own. In the six months from July to January 1940 they tutored her so that she reached the required standard to enter Fairfield High School and Mrs Clement's brother paid her school fees. Mr and Mrs Clement went on to have two daughters and when one of the daughters was about seven, she told Fanni *"you are our sister"* and Fanni says that to this day she has remained their sister and is in regular contact with them.[6]

Fanni was exceptionally clever, coming top of Fairfield's School Certificate list in 1943.[7] However, she had to leave Fairfield at the age of sixteen to earn a living and first went to work in Stalybridge Public Library and then at a School in Glossop. She began studying in her spare time (getting up at five o'clock in the morning) and enrolled on an External London University course. However, a member of the Refugee Children's Movement in Manchester suggested that she should sit for the Scholarship

Entrance Examinations at Manchester University. She sat for the first of the examinations on V.E. (Victory in Europe) Day, May 8th 1945. She remembers a note which was put on all the desks; it read *"If peace breaks out, the examination will continue!"* After the examination, she went out on to Oxford Street, and celebrations were already taking place and people were cheering and waving flags.[8] Fanni passed the examination with flying colours and was awarded the Alice and Edith Hamer Entrance Scholarship, the William Hulme Bursary and the Ashburne Hall Scholarship. These awards meant that she would be able to support herself while she was studying at the University.[9]

For nearly six years after leaving Germany in June 1939, Fanni had no idea what had happened to her parents. After she had left on the Kindertransport, her parents had continued, like many other Jewish people, to try to get out of Germany before the outbreak of war in September 1939, but despite every effort they were unable to do so. Fanni, as a twelve year old girl, had tried to help them. Only a few days after she had arrived in England she had written to the Home Office and the American Embassy in an attempt to obtain visas for her parents to come to England or go to America. But, as she was to say years later, her childish efforts were in vain. It was not until August 1947 when she was nearly twenty that she was re-united with her parents.[10]

During those years her mother and father experienced great suffering at the hands of the Nazis. Her father was a prisoner in a concentration camp in Wulzburg near Weissenburg in Bavaria until April 1945. Although it was not a death camp with gas chambers he was frequently beaten and survived on a starvation diet. When the Allied troops were nearing the camp the guards decided to march the prisoners out of Wulzburg. They were all very weak and could hardly stand. Fanni's father could not withstand this forced march and was left lying for dead in a ditch. He was rescued by an American soldier who picked him up and took him to an American military hospital.

Her mother's experiences were even more traumatic. She had to undergo forced labour and at the end of September 1943 she was sent by the Gestapo to Bergen-Belsen concentration camp. Her experiences there were horrendous and she was to tell Fanni that when she arrived there she thought she would never get out alive. The worst thing was the constant anxiety as to when one's last day would come. Quite miraculously, Fanni's mother and a number of other women were moved out of Belzen and transported west into France to a camp at Vittel. She did not know how they were selected or why they were being moved. Her mother's life was saved by a group of British prisoners in the camp there. (They had been caught up in France after the country had fallen to the Germans). They knew that she had a daughter who had escaped to England and they managed somehow to hide and protect her from the German guards and save her from being transported. The camp at Vittel was liberated by the Allies on 23rd October 1944.[11]

When the War ended neither of Fanni's parents knew that the other had survived, nor where they were, but they both had Fanni's address and through her they found each other. It wasn't until 1947 that Fanni managed to obtain a visa and was able to travel to Germany to be reunited with them. By that time they were living in a displaced person's camp in Bavaria.

Fanni Bogdanow with her parents in 1947, in Germany.

Fanni studied French at the University. She has said that because of her and her parents' experiences anything connected with Germany is a complete anathema to her. After she graduated she taught for two years at Stretford High School and then spent a year in Paris as a French Government Scholar, a year at Westfield College in London as the holder of a Research Studentship and a year at Liverpool University as a Leverhulme Research Fellow. She then gained an M.A and then a Ph.D. degree from Manchester University. When she completed her Doctorate she became an Assistant Lecturer at Manchester University and then progressed from Lecturer, to Reader and then Professor. She retired in 1994 as an Emeritus Professor and has spent her time since then researching medieval French literature which is a continuation of her life's work. For both her Master's and Ph.D. degrees she carried out original research into ancient Mediaeval French texts about the Legend of King Arthur, Merlin and Lancelot and later she also researched mediaeval manuscripts regarding the quest for the Holy Grail.[12] Fanni has published many books and in 1997 she was awarded the Prix Excalibur which was presented to her in France in recognition of her distinguished record of published work.

Fanni's father never recovered sufficiently to make the journey to England and died in 1959 but her mother joined her a few years later and spent the rest of her life living with Fanni at her home in South Manchester. She told Fanni that her time in England was the happiest years of her life and the first time that she had felt free and without fear. She often went down to the University and sat in on Fanni's lectures and the students became very fond of Mrs Bogdanow and "adopted" her.[13]

Fanni told me that her days at Fairfield had been very happy ones and that the teachers and fellow pupils were all very kind to her. She was immensely grateful to Great Britain for giving her refuge, to Mr & Mrs Clement who treated her like a daughter, and to the Allied Forces who liberated her mother and father. Fanni was very much aware that 90 per cent of the Kindertransport children never saw their parents again. Fanni didn't marry and was able to devote her life to her research. She died in August 2013 aged 86.

Fanni Bogdanow photographed in
March 2009

When Fanni arrived at Fairfield in January 1940 the air-raid shelters were all in place and the staff and pupils settled down to a life which would be affected, over the next five years, by many shortages, difficulties and tragedies, all of which would be faced with determination and stoicism.

Because there was a danger of an air-raid at any time, the girls always had to carry their coats, Wellingtons, gas-masks and 'iron rations' with them. The iron rations consisted of foods such as biscuits, cheese and fruit. They were only to be eaten if the girls had to stay in the shelters on the hockey field for a considerable length of time, although some girls remember that they had to replenish theirs almost daily.[15]

EVACUEES

Many of the girls who were evacuated didn't travel far. Their destination was Cheadle Hulme, a few miles south of Manchester. Dorothy Parfitt née Kershaw with her cousin Edna Royle and two girls from Manchester High School were billeted in a house across the road from the Warehousemen and Clerks' College where they were to continue their education. The evacuees went in the mornings one week and afternoons the next. They were very impressed by the College's swimming pool which they were allowed to use once a week but they weren't as enthusiastic about the bathing arrangements at the house. Every Friday night they were told to have a bath, but they all had to use the same water. They decided on a very fair arrangement whereby they took turns in going first.

These two Fairfield girls soon became quite homesick and when they were at school in the mornings they would often decide to make the bus journey back home and spend the rest of the day there. Soon it seemed that they were spending as much time in the 'unsafe' area as in the 'bomb free' zone and a decision was made to return home when a stray German plane bombed the Cheadle Hulme Golf Course, which was very near to where they were living.[16]

SCHOOL LIFE DURING WARTIME

Fairfield girls must have spent a lot of their free time knitting for the troops. During 1940 they made about two hundred knitted garments - socks, mittens, scarves and sailor's Jerseys as well as many blankets made from six inch knitted squares. They had a letter of thanks from the Commanding Officer of the new recruits of the 2nd/9th Battalion of the Manchester Regiment who were billeted in Fairfield Avenue and who were very glad to have the books, playing cards and other games that the school had sent them.[17]

To have a group of young soldiers billeted in the Avenue must have been quite a novelty for Fairfield Girls. One of the school rules was that the girls were forbidden to communicate with males (man or boy) whilst wearing school uniform. The only time this rule was relaxed was when a girl had to take a message to Sergeant Askew, the school caretaker. She was allowed to speak to him but only if accompanied by another pupil. For their part, the young army recruits must have found it rather amusing to be billeted close to an all-girls school. When the girls left school in crocodile form (never more than two abreast) the soldiers would approach them with requests that they carry their rifles or kitbags. It's reported that the girls kept their eyes firmly fixed ahead and never exchanged a word with them.

The summer of 1940 was warm and sunny and the girls were allowed a few extended dinner-hours to practise for Sports Day. The girls did not have any special sports dress. They just took off their tunics and practised in knickers and blouses. It was no surprise, therefore, that the young soldiers used to lean from the windows of their billets and cheer the girls on. It was not long after that, that Miss Edwards decided that tunics were not to be removed on the games field.

One Fairfield girl remembers that it was on such an extended dinner-hour that she heard that France had fallen to the Germans. She was extremely anxious because her father was serving in the army in France and she didn't know what had happened to him. She remembers that during a French lesson that afternoon the girls stood to give a heart-felt rendering of the French National Anthem, "La Marseillaise".

Apart from not talking to males, there were quite a number of other rules that the girls were expected to obey. Eating sweets whilst wearing school uniform was forbidden and the girls were not allowed to remove their school berets when wearing school uniform outside the school grounds and gloves had to be worn. Only girls from the Upper Fourth (Year Nine) upwards, were allowed upstairs on the buses. Purses were kept in knicker-pockets fastened with a press-stud (if a girl forgot to put her purse in her coat pocket when she left school it could be extremely embarrassing when trying to furtively locate her bus money.). Long hair had to be tied back, plaited or cut short.[18]

Life at Fairfield during most of 1940 was mainly uneventful. At Speech Day that year, it was even suggested that the "Blackout" had helped to make the girls healthier (during darkness, no lighting in the streets was allowed and so curtains had to completely "black out" the lights). Attendance had been excellent and the girls had withstood an epidemic of influenza extremely well. The Head Mistress attributed this to the fact that "blackout" conditions had curtailed festivities at night and this meant that the girls had more sleep and consequently possessed greater reserves of power. [19]

For more than five and a half years the War affected all aspects of life. Even small children knew that 'there was a war on' and they became familiar with the phrase *'when the War is over'*. They knew that *'when the War was over'* they would be able to eat bananas for the first time, taste real fresh cream, enjoy more than the small allocated ration of sweets and chocolate and, more seriously, look forward to Daddy coming home and not hearing the air-raid sirens ever again. We have to remember, of course, that for many thousands of children, Daddy would not be coming home.

For many Fairfield girls, home life was probably stressful and for them the school must have provided an atmosphere of friendly stability.

News about the War was becoming extremely grave. France had fallen to the Germans and the British Expeditionary Force had to retreat to the coast at Dunkirk where their evacuation began on the 26th May. During the summer another battle took place - this time in the air. Germany attempted to destroy the Royal Air Force but didn't succeed and the valour of our brave airmen will always be remembered as the Battle of Britain.

WARTIME BOMBING

Hitler was unsuccessful in his attempt to defeat the R.A.F. and he therefore turned his attention to bombing our cities. Coventry city centre was practically obliterated and Plymouth was extensively damaged, and, of course, London was bombed time and time again. Many thousands of civilians were killed. From the end of July, Manchester and the surrounding areas were bombed frequently and although quite a number of people were killed, the main targets had been various important sites such as Royal Ordnance Factories and steel works. As yet, the city centre hadn't been seriously bombed, so it was rather ominous when that year's School Christmas Party was interrupted by an air raid and the girls had to go to the shelters. A few days later, on Sunday 22nd December 1940, came the start of the biggest air attack on Manchester. The sirens, warning of an attack, were heard at 6.35pm and the long continuous note of the 'all clear' did not come until 6.28am the next morning. The bombing continued the next day from 7pm until just after midnight on the morning of Christmas Eve. The bombing of Manchester during those two days just before Christmas would always be known as the 'Manchester Blitz'.

The bombing caused vast destruction. In the centre of Manchester many important buildings and offices were destroyed including hospitals and schools and, in Manchester and the surrounding areas, thirty thousand houses were damaged.

The Manchester Blitz
1940

The scene of devastation
in the city centre

The Free Trade Hall, home of the famous Halle Orchestra, was badly damaged. Fairfield girls had attended concerts there, conducted by the permanent Conductor Sir Malcolm Sargent. After the bombing, the Halle concerts took place on Sunday afternoons at the Odeon Cinema.

During the two nights of the Manchester Blitz, 654 people were killed and 719 seriously injured in the Manchester, Salford and Stretford districts. On the following Saturday, the Bishop of Manchester conducted the funeral service at a mass burial of air raid victims in Manchester's Southern Cemetery.

Because the bombing, during these two days, was so devastating it is often assumed that the Manchester area experienced very little bombing after these dates. This was not the case. A close scrutiny of the Manchester and District Air Raid Alerts Log for the years 1940 to 1945 show that there were air raids on the 27th and 31st of December and for the first five days of the New Year, followed by one of the heaviest raids on the 9th of January. Bombing continued throughout 1941 during which a total of 119 air raids were logged.

Droylsden was not seriously affected by the bombing. The worst damage was caused by bombs being dropped near Greenside Lane. Three or four houses were badly damaged and a fire was started. A number of people were injured but no one was killed. Later in the War flying bombs fell in Clayton, an unexploded bomb landed near Fairfield Wells and later exploded and a number of houses were damaged in Denton. However, the Manchester Blitz caused deep concern. The people, in Droylsden, could hear the hundreds of planes overhead and see the bright glow of the Manchester fires, which were visible for many miles. Droylsden sent rescue and demolition parties into Manchester and the Home Guard helped to patrol the Manchester streets for several nights.[20] One Droylsden boy remembers walking in the Manchester streets the day after the Blitz. When he looked across Piccadilly everything was flattened. It was unrecognisable, just the odd doorway standing and there was still fire and smoke. Everywhere he went he was crunching through broken glass.[21]

Areas nearer to the centre of Manchester, such as Miles Platting, Collyhurst, Openshaw and Gorton suffered far more than Droylsden. The bombing in these areas resulted in many deaths and serious injuries. Some Fairfield girls lived in these areas of Manchester but many had been evacuated out of the city at the start of the War.

Bomb damage in Collyhurst, Manchester, Christmas 1940.
Phyllis Kershaw's home was nearby

SECRET WAR WORK

One girl, who left Fairfield a year before the War started, lived in the Collyhurst area of the city and experienced the trauma of seeking safety in the local air-raid shelters, whilst the noise of the bombs dropping all around could be heard. One evening, while she and her mother were hurrying down the shelter steps, her mother slipped and fell all the way down. She was seriously injured and died shortly afterwards. Phyllis blamed herself for her mother's death because she had urged her to be quick and had hurried her up. It took many years for her to be reconciled to the fact that if anybody was to blame it was Hitler.[22]

Phyllis Kershaw née Hawkins was an only child of working-class parents. Phyllis was a tiny baby weighing only 4lb 4oz when she was born in 1921and without incubators or central heating she was not expected to survive . She had luck on her side, being born in the summer and having an intelligent mother who made a make-shift incubator for her. Today's midwives will blanche to read that her mother kept her warm by wrapping her in cotton wool that had been soaked in olive oil and placing her in front of the fire.

Her father had fought at Gallipoli and had been much influenced by his time in the Army and his association with the 'Officer Class'. He had resolved to better himself and eventually bought a retail shop in the Collyhurst area. He realised the importance of education and encouraged Phyllis in her studies. Phyllis left school at sixteen after passing the School Certificate. She had excelled in languages, especially German and was also quick at problem solving and crosswords.[23] At the time of the Blitz she was working as a Comptometer Operator in Manchester but the experience of her mother's death made her want to do more for the War effort.[24] At the same time, the Government was becoming aware of the need to mobilize the whole country and in March 1941 all women aged between nineteen and forty had to register at employment exchanges where they were directed to essential work. By December of that year women were conscripted for the first time into compulsory wartime service.

Phyllis didn't wait for conscription to be made compulsory, but volunteered for the ATS (The Auxiliary Territorial Service - the women's branch of the Army). During initial tests her intelligence was recognised and she was selected for further tests, which she passed, and was sent to the Isle of Man as part of a very select group of girls for a six week's special signals training course. After successfully completing her training, Phyllis joined a large number of other ATS women at a large house called Beaumanor Hall, near Loughborough in Leicestershire.[25]

Phyllis in her ATS uniform

Beaumanor Hall

After she arrived she had to sign the Official Secrets Act and she knew then that the work she would be doing would be secret as well as important. Beaumanor Hall was a secret listening station, known as "Outstation Y" – one of several throughout the British Isles. It was connected to Bletchley Park which was to become famous for its work during the War in breaking the Enigma Code used by the Germans. The encrypted German messages, transmitted in Morse code, had first to be intercepted by the wireless operators at Beaumanor Hall and Phyllis was one of the many wireless operators who worked in shifts twenty four hours a day. She would sit with headphones on and continually tune and re-tune her radio to intercept the

Morse code messages. After a time it was possible to recognise the style of the 'tapping' of certain German operators. The intercepting took place in specially disguised huts which were built in the grounds of Beaumanor Hall. The huts were spaced far enough apart to avoid collateral damage in a bombing raid. They were brick-built, with walls made to withstand blasts. One hut was designed to look like a cart shed, another two looked like cottages, a fourth looked like stables and a fifth was disguised as a glasshouse block and the last was designed to look like a cricket pavilion complete with a false clock tower. All the cables and aerial feeds were located in underground ducts. Each hut had a pneumatic tube which was connected to the 'cricket pavilion'. A cylinder, containing the hand-written messages which had been received, was sent down this tube. This tube system was also underground and out of sight. The intercepted messages were sent by motorbike every day to the famous Station X at Bletchley Park for decoding.

Although Phyllis was very proficient at German, she didn't, of course, know what was in the messages as they were all encrypted. It wasn't until near the very end of the war that she intercepted a German message which was not in code, saying that they (the Germans) had lost the war.

In many ways Phyllis enjoyed her time at Beaumanor Hall. She told her husband that although it was hard work it was the best job she ever had. The camaraderie was fantastic, the men were officers and gentlemen, the girls were all well-educated and they were in a stately home. Added to that they knew they were doing important, exciting and secret work. Because of the secret nature of the work, it wasn't until years later that they would know how successful and really important it was. The team at Bletchley Park were able to crack the Enigma Code and this helped the Government to learn more about Germany's strategic plans. This knowledge helped Britain to finally win the War. Winston Churchill described the interceptors and code breakers as "the geese that laid the golden egg and never cackled". Phyllis didn't tell anyone about her War work until decades later when it started to be reported in the press.

Although the War in Europe ended in May 1945, we were still at war with Japan, and Phyllis, because of her language skills, was being taught Japanese and being prepared to travel to India. However, the Japanese surrendered and she eventually made her way back home to Manchester where she worked on early computers.[26]

Phyllis married her husband Jack in 1951. He didn't have to keep his War experiences secret. He was part of the D-Day landings in Normandy and drove a munitions truck across Europe and took part in the liberation of the Bergen-Belsen concentration camp. Between them, they must have thought that they'd had enough experiences to last a lifetime. They went on to have four children - two boys and two girls and all gained places at grammar schools. Diane and Lillian went on to university and subsequently followed careers in law, librarianship and computing. Andrew and Neil followed professional careers in accountancy and engineering. Lillian and the daughter of Phyllis's son Neil were both educated at Fairfield – three generations of the same family have now gone through the school. Later in life Phyllis did voluntary work and also helped with an adult literacy scheme. Like many Fairfield girls Phyllis was able to encourage her children to appreciate the value of education. [27]

In February 2010 Phyllis was finally honoured for her contribution to the war effort. Phyllis, along with all the surviving veterans who served at Bletchley Park and its outstations, was awarded a commemorative medal and certificate in recognition of the vital role played by the Government Code and Cypher School during the war.

Diane, their younger daughter has said that although their father was the main bread-winner, their mother always taught her daughters that, as women, they could not only be equal to men, but they could be better. Diane said *"She was "women's lib" before it was fashionable. We're so proud of her".*[28]

Miss Edwards who had been the Head Mistress of the school since it was taken over by the Lancashire Education Authority in 1919, just after the end of the 1st World War, retired in July 1941. In the School Magazine of that year the pupils paid tribute to her understanding, thoughtfulness and fairness which inspired confidence in all who came under her care.

In her final Report to Speech Day in 1941 Miss Edwards reported that there were now 405 girls at the school. She went on to say that she frequently had news from Fairfield girls now living in many countries including New Zealand, Egypt and the United States which led her to believe that even a moderately small school like Fairfield could have a far reaching influence.[29]

Miss Edwards' place was taken by Miss G. L. Bradley who was an enthusiastic forty one year old who came to be known by many of the girls as 'a force to be reckoned with'. She was keen for the girls to remember the traditions of their old school and endeavoured to ensure that her girls lived up to their motto of "The Utmost for the Highest".

ESCAPE FROM SINGAPORE

By December 1941 the War had extended to the Far East. The Japanese had invaded China, the Dutch East Indies, Borneo, the Philippines, Korea, Thailand, and Malaya and on December 9th they had attacked the American Hawaiian base at Pearl harbour. One Fairfield girl, living in Malaya, was to have her life changed dramatically.

Christobel Taylor (née Hall) was one of the five Fairfield girls studying for the Higher School Certificate in 1921. She lived in the Fairfield Settlement Square and her father was the town's Municipal Engineer and Surveyor. She gained a B.Sc. degree and then went on to study medicine, graduating with a MBChB degree in 1930. Just after she graduated she married Dr. Benjamin Taylor, a Bolton man who was working for the Malay Medical Service and she went out to Malaya with her husband that same year.[30]

A happy day in April 1930 Dr. Christobel Hall marries Dr. Benjamin Taylor of the Malay Medical Service at St. Mary's Church, Droylsden

The following year Christobel gave birth to twin daughters, Jane and Margaret, and in 1934 a son, Richard, was born. This meant that Christobel's time was taken up in looking after her family and she didn't practise medicine during her time in Malaya.

In 1941 Malaya was a British Protectorate and Singapore was under direct British rule. Singapore is an island which is connected to the mainland of Malaya, across the Jahore Strait, by a causeway. It had, over the years, become one of the most important ports of South East Asia due to its strategic position, both commercial and military, at the junction of routes between the Pacific and the Indian Oceans.

In spite of contact with Christobel's grandchildren and her Australian friends, it has been difficult to establish a complete picture of her and her husband's experiences during the Japanese invasion of Singapore. Thankfully, well before the invasion their three children had been sent to boarding school in Perth, Australia, but her husband, Ben, had become very seriously ill with a muscle/bone disease.[31]

The first intimation of an imminent invasion of Malaya came on the 1st December when Volunteer Forces began to be mobilised. Gunfire and planes overhead were first heard on the 6th December and many people in the country began a frantic evacuation to Singapore where they thought they would be safe. Most people never imagined that Singapore would fall. Some families who arrived in Singapore during the second week of December were not evacuated by sea until the last week in January. During that time they had to endure many air-raids and heard the news of the bombing of Pearl Harbour on December 7th and also the sinking of the Royal Navy ships the 'Repulse' and the 'Prince of Wales' which had left Singapore only days before. By the end of January all British Empire forces had withdrawn onto Singapore Island and from then on it was heavily bombarded by the Japanese, who then landed on the north-west of the island on the 8th of February and six days later they were on the outskirts of Singapore city. Singapore surrendered on the 15th of February. One hundred thousand troops were taken prisoner and hundreds of European civilians were interned.

Many women and children were evacuated before the end of January and Christobel was amongst them and because her husband was so seriously ill, he was able to accompany her on a ship which eventually landed at Perth,

Australia.[32] Other women and children who weren't able to leave the island until later, didn't fare so well. On the 13th of February about one thousand women, children and troops were waiting to be taken off from a stretch of waterfront when one group of people received a direct hit from a bomb and a number of women and children were killed. Eventually two large ships started off with their passengers to a nearby Dutch island but while they were just off shore they were dive-bombed by the Japanese. One ship sank immediately but the other settled down slowly. The survivors tried to get ashore as best they could on rafts improvised from wreckage or by swimming but the Japanese plane came back with machine guns and killed or wounded many of those who were struggling in the water. Over 400 were killed out of the 1,000 women, children and soldiers who had embarked. The survivors spent four days on the islands before being rescued by small craft escaping from Singapore.[33]

Christobel and Ben had left Singapore just before these dreadful events and arrived safely in Perth. Australia. They had very few personal belongings and were taken in and befriended by the widowed grandmother of Ann Fisher. It is Ann who has very kindly given me details of Christobel's life in Australia.

Christobel and Ben were reunited with their children and Christobel began working as a GP as soon as she could. She was fortunately able to go to work in a practice where the doctor had gone to serve in the War. Her husband's health deteriorated - if he so much as lifted a kettle he was likely to break a bone - and he sadly died before the War ended. A long and lasting friendship began between Christobel's and Ann's families. Christobel and Ann's mother met for lunch every Wednesday until Christobel's death in 1995 at the age of ninety three. Christobel delivered Ann's three children and remained one of her dearest friends. Ann speaks of her as having been a wonderful woman who was always held in very high esteem as a mother, wife, friend and doctor.[34]

It would not have been easy for Christobel as a widow with three children but, as a qualified doctor, she would have had the security of a professional career and the interest and personal contacts that it brought. There was to be more sadness in Christobel's long life. Her son Richard died in a car accident whilst completing National Service when he was nineteen and her daughter

Jane died from a brain haemorrhage while visiting her sister Margaret in England when she was fifty two.[35]

Christobel continued practising as a GP until she was at least sixty five and I am told that she still retained that 'joie de vivre' that had seen her through many adversities. Although Christobel had suffered much sorrow, the overwhelming impression given to me by her friends, is of a woman who was joyful, kind and much loved, someone of whom Fairfield can be justly proud.

Christobel (on the left) during her happy retirement. She is pictured here with the daughter of the lady who befriended her and her family

WARTIME MILITARY SERVICE

As the War continued, more and more Old Girls joined the three Services - the ATS (the Auxiliary Territorial Service), the WAAF (Women's Auxiliary Air Force) and the WRNS (Women's Royal Naval Service). Others enlisted into the Women's Land Army and the school had at least one representative in the Women's Timber Corps (female lumberjacks) and the National Fire Service.

One girl, who was nursing in St Albans, wrote that she had assisted during recent work in plastic surgery. This new development was to be of great importance in helping people with first degree facial burns and other facial injuries.[36] Another nurse spoke of her experiences in helping two severely injured RAF pilots who had crashed landed on the moors and who had been lost for two days. One recovered after sixteen weeks having had his arms and legs broken in several places; the other officer died shortly after being admitted to hospital.[37]

Others had less harrowing experiences. A new recruit to the WRNS (they became known as Wrens) was drafted to a small coastal station, attached to a larger Naval base. They lived and worked in a private house surrounded by lovely gardens. There was always someone on duty, because they had to keep a twenty four hour watch, but in between times they were able to sunbathe, play tennis, go to concerts, dances, the cinema and go on shopping expeditions. So, although the work was hard and sometimes tedious and free-time was liable to be curtailed at any moment, it was interesting and the time passed quickly. She mentioned that the girls in her group had all left very different jobs to join the Wrens - they included a dancing teacher, a designer of women's clothes, a university student, a governess and an actress. Our Fairfield girl was promoted to Lieutenant and was sent overseas in 1944. She survived the war. Her letter was written in 1941 and she poignantly ended her letter with these words … *"Every day the end of the war draws nearer, and with it the fulfilment of many of our hopes. Each one of us has her own particular dream of life after the war, yet all will miss the comradeship and the excitement of life in the WRNS"*. She didn't realise that what she had just experienced was the end of the beginning, the beginning of the end was still four years away.[38]

During those four years news from many old girls serving in the forces reached the Old Girls Association. Some suffered the cold and wind of lonely Scottish outposts, including one girl stationed on a small island in the Inner Hebrides working as a Wireless Operator. In contrast, near the end of the War, a Lance Corporal in the Army Welfare Service was stationed in Naples and had a view of the Isle of Capri and Mount Vesuvius from her window. Another girl had glorious working quarters in Cornwall in the house which was used as "Manderley" in the film "Rebecca".[39]

Some girls came under enemy fire. One got in the way of a V1 bomb and had to recuperate in hospital for several months; another experienced machine-gunning and bombing in Dover and one girl was blitzed out of her billet by flying bombs - she was on duty elsewhere at the time. But at least one girl found time for romance and married her Commanding Officer.[40]

One Fairfield girl was working as a Surgeon in a local hospital when the War started. She became a Captain in the Royal Army Medical Corp. and was posted abroad.

Some girls became drivers. One drove staff cars and ambulances and another drove convoys on the eve of "D-day". Another girl became an Air Mechanic servicing Fleet Air Arm planes. A number of girls worked on secret intelligence work and could not discuss what they were doing.[41]

The War gave most of the girls experiences that they otherwise would not have had and which certainly helped to broaden their outlook.

SCHOOL LIFE

Compared with the trauma and hardship suffered by many people world-wide as the War continued, the inconveniences and shortages experienced by the school could be viewed as somewhat trivial. However they were representative of what most people in this country were enduring. School dinners became increasingly difficult as numbers increased and rations diminished. The form gardens were used for growing vegetables and supplied a school dinner for the pupils on several occasions.

There were difficulties in obtaining uniforms and permits were required for the replacement of kitchen crockery and tea-towels and linoleum had to be cut up as mats for the dinner tables as tablecloths were no longer obtainable. (These were the days before Formica-topped tables). Paper was scarce and once pages in an exercise book had been filled they had to be turned upside down and the spaces between the written lines filled in. Supplies of new school textbooks were increasingly delayed and rubber soled gym shoes seemed to have disappeared completely.[42]

There was a noticeable change in the announcements of marriages and births in the School Magazine. At least a third of the bridegrooms and the new fathers were serving in the armed forces. So, although most of the girls at the school were not too adversely affected by the War, many 'Old Girls' were experiencing very stressful times, some as members of the armed forces themselves and others as wives with the ever-present anxiety of a husband away at War and sometimes a baby to care for.[43]

In the summer of 1942 the Lancashire Agricultural War Committee appealed to schools in the county to help with the harvest. Thirty five girls and seven mistresses from Fairfield answered the call and found themselves under canvas for a fortnight in August helping to bring in the pea harvest at a farm near Ormskirk. Despite a typical English summer of sunshine and showers, all the girls managed to pick their full quota and keep Hartley's canning factory supplied. The following year the farmer invited them back to help again.[44] Although many Old Girls remember these Harvest Camps with nostalgia quite a few heaved a sigh of relief when it was over. Conditions were very primitive – they had to make their mattresses by filling sacks with straw and the latrines were dug-out trenches with planks across on which the girls could squat. The girls made sackcloth screens for the latrines and sackcloth walled cubicles as washing areas.[45]

It would seem that the experience of war had not had a detrimental effect on the girls' academic achievements. At the school speech day in 1944, Miss Bradley was able to report that six girls were going on to University. One of these girls was Hilda Ridyard who was the first Fairfield girl to gain a place at Cambridge. Girls who qualified for University during War Time were not called up to serve in the Forces or to do war work so Hilda was able to go up to Cambridge where she studied Natural Sciences and Psychology at Girton. After graduating Hilda began work as a psychologist in the Personnel Department at the Rowntree Company in York and then joined the Civil Service Commission in London. While in London she met up again with a fellow Cambridge student and they married and emigrated to Toronto, Canada in 1953. Hilda worked as a supervisor in an insurance company for about a year until their daughter and then a son were born. After that Hilda only worked occasionally, in what she describes as rather unimportant positions. She says that staying at home and looking after your family was what was expected of a woman in those days. She and her family settled in Calgary, Alberta, and she later devoted a lot of her time to the Girl Guide Movement becoming a Girl Guide leader and Trainer of adults and then a Commissioner at various levels up to Provincial.[46]

In the same Speech Day Report Miss Bradley stated that she was seriously concerned about the increasing number of parents wanting to be released from their agreement to keep their daughters at school until they were sixteen. It was not easy for some parents to keep their daughters at school beyond the statutory leaving age of fourteen. Many Scholarship girls were from poor homes and many of their fathers were serving in the forces. In these circumstances it was often necessary for daughters to leave school and to go to work, and in some cases the girls themselves wanted to be independent and to support themselves.

A LIFE IN TELEVISION

Joan Riley née Bond was one of those girls. She left Fairfield when she was fourteen in 1944. She was a clever Scholarship girl from a very poor home. She was the eldest of eight children - six boys and two girls - who, along with their parents lived in a small terraced house in Gorton. The house had no hot water, no bathroom and only an outside toilet. She had to share a bedroom and the few clothes she had were hung on nails behind the bedroom door. Peg rugs and old coats took the place of blankets.

Joan sat the Scholarship exam in 1941 and unbeknown to her, her father chose Fairfield High School if she passed because he remembered it as the Moravian School for Young Ladies and hoped it might turn tom-boy Joan into a young lady.

Because Joan came from a large family and her father had a poorly paid job, winning the Scholarship also entitled her to free uniform, books, meals and transport. Joan and her mother then had the rather intimidating experience of having to shop for Joan's school uniform in the exclusive Manchester shopping area of St Anne's Square. It was certainly different from shopping on the local market. They managed to overcome their fears and came away with four blouses, a gymslip, indoor and outdoor shoes, a science overall, a swim suit and a gym outfit. They had to choose between a raincoat and a blazer and decided that a raincoat would be more suitable. Up to this point Joan's clothes had consisted of cast-offs and jumble sale purchases, so she really felt she was living through a dream.

Joan did well at school. The house must have been noisy and lively and it would have been difficult for Joan to do her homework but she was placed in the form which studied German - just one class down from the top Latin form.

For many years Joan's mother had been forced to use the services of the local Pawnbroker. Very early on Monday mornings she would take various items of clothing which wouldn't be needed until the following Friday. In this way she just managed to make ends meet using the Pawnbroker money to supplement the meagre income she had. Unfortunately, one Monday morning she mistakenly took Joan's school blouses to the Pawnbrokers and Joan had to wear one of her brother's shirts. Fairfield blouses at that time had square necks and no collars so it was clearly noticeable that Joan was not wearing school uniform and this was considered a rather serious misdemeanour. She was severely reprimanded by Miss Bradley and had to wear her science overall until she was able to retrieve her blouses. Miss Bradley was not told the true circumstances but it seems that she was told about Joan's poor background and obtained a second-hand school blazer for her. Joan's school clothing vouchers hadn't included one for a blazer and she had always wanted one. She felt so smart when she wore it and loved the embroidered school badge on the pocket showing the Lamb and the Flag. She wore it for the rest of her schooldays even when it became really too small for her and a little bit frayed at the edges.

When Joan reached fourteen she decided that she wanted to leave school. She had come to the point where having no clothes except her school uniform was becoming extremely distressful. She had seen many of her neighbours' daughters starting work and she felt she really needed to go out to work and be independent. By this time the financial circumstances of the family had improved a little because her father had been conscripted into the Navy and her mother received an allowance from the Navy for each of the children. Her father tried to persuade her to stay on at school. He would have liked her to have become a teacher but her mother was happy to see her leave school and wanted her to become a machinist. Her father insisted that office work was more appropriate for a girl who had attended a High School and she had no problem in gaining work in a local office, where among other things, she learned to type. Sadly her father, who had a responsible position on board a minesweeper, was killed a few months later when a German submarine scored a direct hit on his ship.

For the next few years Joan worked in an engineering office where she met her husband who was a draughtsman. Joan left work when she was pregnant with their baby son who was born in 1953. For a number of years after their son was born Joan worked on a part-time basis. She shared child-minding responsibilities with a neighbour who also worked part-time and her mother-in-law looked after her son during the school holidays. Then in 1960 Joan applied for a job which enabled her to have a fascinating and interesting career for the next thirty years.

The job that Joan applied for was that of a part-time copytaker in the News Room at Granada Television in the centre of Manchester. It was Joan's job as a copy taker to type the news stories that were dictated over the phone by local freelance journalists working throughout the Granada region. This 'copy' was then passed to the News team.

Joan and another copytaker worked a shift system, one sometimes working in the afternoon and the other on the evening shift and vice versa. It was on the evening shift on the 22nd November 1963 that Joan was to experience at first hand the breaking news story of the assassination of the American President, John F. Kennedy. She was one of the first people in the country to hear the news. Over the years there have been many arguments amongst broadcasters who have claimed to have been the first with the news on that momentous occasion. However, many years later Joan's account of what happened was acknowledged by Denis Forman, the former Chairman and Managing Director of Granada as being the authentic version and in the Preface to his book *'Persona Granada'* he quoted the file note that Joan had written about the events in the News Room that evening. Joan has described to me what happened on that occasion.

Joan and Terry Dobson, the News Editor, were the only members of the team on duty that Friday evening. Granada had an agreement with the Press Association that they would contact the News Room on a direct line if a major story broke. At 6.35pm they 'phoned Terry Dobson to say that news was coming through from America that Kennedy had been shot. There was an authorised procedure that whenever the Newsroom was informed of a big story the informer was told that Granada would ring them back. This action was in case the call was a hoax. Five minutes before this, Granada's local programme, "*Scene at Six-Thirty*" had just started and Terry Dobson immediately phoned through to the Producer, Barrie Heads who was in the Director's box in the *Scene* studio to alert him of the situation. Terry, at the same time, was quickly phoning the Press Association back on the direct line and they confirmed that the news was true. The Press Association had heard the news from a shortwave radio broadcast from Dallas and Terry could clearly hear this continuing in the background as he spoke to the Press Association. Terry passed this information on to Barrie Heads. The television was on in the News Room and Joan watched as Barrie got through to Mike Scott, the Presenter of *Scene at Six Thirty,* on the studio phone and Mike Scott immediately announced the tragic news. The viewers of Granada's *Scene at Six Thirty* programme heard the news of Kennedy's death thirty minutes before it was broadcast to the rest of the nation.

Joan remembers that there was feverish activity throughout that evening. The death of Kennedy came as a complete surprise. He was a young man who in normal circumstances would have lived much longer. Because of this, 'obituary' material had not been collected as it would have been for a much older man. Nevertheless Granada, with only a small group of people, managed to put out a programme about J.F.K. at eleven o'clock that night . Granada at that time only broadcast Monday to Friday so not all the people involved with current affairs were available on that Friday night. Joan remembers a sense of great urgency - no sooner had one script been snapped out of her typewriter than another had to be started. The end result was a fitting tribute to Kennedy and each member of that night's team received a personal note of thanks from Denis Forman.

Joan stayed working in the News Room until 1969 when she decided to work full-time. She then worked for a short time in the promotions and presentation departments and then went into Granada's Press Office. She was eventually promoted to Picture Editor where she was responsible for all pictures issued to the press. This involved press promotions for many television stars and programmes. She would sometimes go out on location and particularly remembers going to the stately home of Castle Howard which was used as the location for "Brideshead Revisited" which starred Sir Lawrence Olivier and Jeremy Irons.

Joan Riley

Another interesting experience came when she was talking to a rather worried member of the Casting Office who had been told that the "Coronation Street" team were in urgent need of some new ideas. As Joan had been brought up in a very similar street to Coronation Street she mentioned that what she thought was missing was a really rough family. Soon after, Hilda Ogden and her husband made their first appearance. Joan sometimes wonders whether her comments had anything to do with it.

For a short time after she retired Joan set up a small public relations company with the purpose of organising public appearances for the Coronation Street stars. Her reminiscences of her meetings with stars and prominent members of Granada's staff during her years as Picture Editor could fill a book and Joan has actually done just that. She has recently written two separate volumes about her life which are available on Kindle – '*The Age of Innocence (Memoirs of Wartime England')* and *'Moving on - (to a photo finish)'*.

Joan is grateful for the education she received at Fairfield. She is sure that without it she would have gone to work in a factory or mill and her life would not have been so fulfilling. Some years ago she did continue her education and studied A Level English Literature at night school. She achieved an 'A' grade which shows that given different circumstances she would probably have gone on to university. But then, of course, she might not have had such an interesting career.

Joan has been able to encourage her son and her granddaughter. Her son studied at University and went on to have a rewarding career in the electronics industry. Her granddaughter gained a Master's degree and was then awarded a course of study in China. She is now a consultant with the De Lloittes organisation.

Joan has come a long way from that crowded home in Gorton and she acknowledges that the few years she spent at Fairfield provided the first stepping stones to help her on the way.[47]

THE BEGINNING OF THE END

By the beginning of 1945 the Allies were gaining ground. In January Auschwitz concentration camp was liberated and in February the Yalta Conference between the US, Britain and the USSR took place where plans were discussed for Europe after the War. In April, Hanover, Vienna, Cologne and Arnhem were captured and Bergen-Belsen concentration camp liberated. It had been a bloody six years – millions of people had been killed.

As we have seen, the lives of many Fairfield girls were affected by the War – whether by their experiences in the Forces or completely life changing circumstances, as in the case of Christobel Taylor and Fanni Bogdanow and some girls suffered the early death of a parent as both Joan Riley and Phyllis Kershaw had done. Many had started the War as little more than school girls but ended it as women of wide experience – experience which would prove to be important in the post-war years as women continued to battle for equality.

CHAPTER EIGHT

THE END OF WAR AND A NEW BEGINNING 1945-1960

"You sure don't look like a physicist"

By April 1945 Germany was on the point of surrender and Victory was in sight. A few weeks later, on May 8, Victory in Europe was declared (V.E. Day) and nearly six years of anguish and trauma came to an end. The people of Droylsden, like most people in the country, celebrated with bonfires and parties. It seemed that every street or small community had their own celebrations and people even pushed their pianos into the street to accompany the sing-alongs. Fairfield, along with all other schools had a two day holiday.

Words in popular songs at the time spoke about "when the lights come on again" and "we'll get lit up". One of the abiding memories of war time had been the complete darkness in the streets and city centres. For a young child at the end of the War it seemed like wonderland when Manchester city centre gradually became 'lit up' with brightly coloured shop signs and advertisements. One Fairfield girl remembering the blackout had fond memories of when she used to meet her future husband in Greenside Lane in the dark. He used to whistle the Noel Coward song "Some Day I'll Find You" so that she would know it was him at their appointed meeting place.

SOCIAL ATTITUDES AND FEMALE STEREOTYPING

After the War married women were expected to abandon their wartime occupations and return to being full-time housewives. However, because of their work experience during the War, the attitude to married women working had altered and because of the need for more women to work in the new engineering and electrical industries, the employment of married women became acceptable. However, they were not viewed as permanent employees, staying at one job for twenty or thirty years as most men were expected to do. It was thought that most women worked for 'extras' and were not the breadwinner in the family. In that sort of position they could not expect to be promoted or to have equal pay. As it was, only 22 per cent of married women were employed in 1951; although this compared with only 10 per cent before the War.[1]

One Fairfield girl whose experience illustrates this situation had left Fairfield in 1943 having gained the School Certificate. After further training and attendance at the Manchester Commercial College one day a week she was, by the time she was twenty six, assisting in the running of the office for a sewing cotton manufacturer. She then decided she wanted to have children and when she gave in her notice her employers decided to advertise for a man to fill the post. Her husband successfully applied for the position and shortly afterwards his salary was increased to 50 per cent more than what she had been paid. Her husband stayed at the company and eventually became their Company Secretary.

Once a woman had children she was expected to stop working and stay at home. The cost of housing was far less than it is now and so there was often little necessity for two salaries coming in to a household. Additionally, there were very few child-care facilities available.

When a girl decided on her future career, it was often with marriage and motherhood in mind. There were often subtle pressures from her family, her peers and society, which made her think that she should be married by the age of twenty three or four. If that was the case, then five or six years of further education until she was about twenty two seemed somewhat pointless to a working-class girl. She often thought it was better to work and have some financial independence before she 'settled down' and often working-class families couldn't afford to support their children through a further five years of education.

It was, therefore, mainly girls from middle-class families who went into the sixth form and then on to higher education. There was only a minority of determined working class girls who went on to professional careers and they would nearly always have had the full support of their parents.

The Guest of Honour at the School's Speech Day in April 1946 was John Coatman, the North Regional Director of the BBC. In his speech he pointed out that *"women of today have a wider scope than ever before for their powers"* and mentioned several important positions held by women, including that of maintenance engineer at the BBC. Nevertheless, he thought it necessary to use the opportunity to emphasise that *"a woman's most important career still lies in making a home, since the future of civilisation rests largely upon women's ability to maintain the ties of the family.*[2] No change there then! It seemed that most men were still not expected to help in the 'making of a home'; their contribution being purely a financial one.

For many years women had been up against male attempts to undermine their confidence. Sometimes their techniques were quite subtle, at other times they could be downright rude. A typical example of this attitude was the treatment experienced by the first woman to work in the House of Commons Library (not a Fairfield Girl). Roseanne O'Reilly's appointment caused a mild sensation. She was much amused after a few weeks when a member put his head around the door and then backed out in horror, exclaiming: "Good God, they're not putting a girl in here, are they?" Gradually her confidence grew – though nobody spoke to her for the first year.[3]

In 1948 Fairfield girls were given the chance to challenge this male self-confidence. A team of four Fairfield girls visited Broadcasting House, Manchester, to take part in a History Quiz for Children's Hour. They were against a team from Stand Grammar School for Boys. Fairfield won by 48 to 41. They were helped by their knowledge of the Industrial Revolution which they had recently been studying. The quiz master on introducing this subject said it was one which would suit the boys rather than the girls. Fairfield girls managed to dispose of that attempt at stereotyping rather quickly.[4]

SECONDARY EDUCATION FOR ALL

The new Education Act had come into force in 1945. For Fairfield this meant that, from the beginning of the school year in September, no school fees had to be paid and text books were free. Every child in the country was to have a secondary education in what was known as the Tripartite System. There were three kinds of secondary schools - Grammar Schools for those children whom it was thought would benefit from an academic education, technical schools for those of a more mechanical or practical bent and secondary modern schools replaced the senior school section of the elementary schools for the rest of the children. The school-leaving age for secondary modern children was raised from fourteen to fifteen. The selection process was by examination at eleven years old - hence the name 'eleven plus exam'. As a former high school or secondary school, Fairfield High School for Girls was automatically considered as a Grammar School and for the next thirty five years it would educate the top 20 to 25 per cent of the girls in its catchment area. The modernisation and extensions that the school had completed just before the War had commenced in 1939 would be put to good use.

The new building

The tennis courts

The new school drive

That September saw the first intake of "11plus" girls. It seemed fitting that after the experiences of War should come the exhilaration of a new beginning. These new girls were full of enthusiasm to work and to take advantage of their new opportunities and proud of their uniforms including their navy berets with a green and white hatband. Miss Bradley was keen to foster the link with the Moravian Church and personally gave out the metal badges for the berets showing the Lamb and the Flag, explaining its significance. The sixth form girls were also given a new confidence by having their own distinctive uniform of blue blouses with ties and navy skirts. This was a far more grown up style than the school gymslip and more fitting for girls who would be young women by the time they left the sixth form.

In June the following year (1946), the School celebrated its 150th anniversary with a service of thanksgiving at Manchester Cathedral addressed by the Bishop of Manchester. School days carried on as usual with forty-eight pupils gaining School Certificate but only three passing Higher School Certificate. However, in the following year thirteen girls had gained this Certificate.

The Head Mistress in her Speech Day Report in 1949 discussed the future careers which were now available to girls. She mentioned that there were many interesting openings for girls with Domestic Science training or with science or maths degrees, but there were few posts for arts graduates who did not wish to teach. This seemed to be somewhat lacking in inspiration. Arts graduates were presumably needed as solicitors, barristers, social workers, civil servants, journalists and local government and hospital administrators, to name but a few.

At the beginning of the school year in September 1949, there were 511 girls on the register and there were four school certificate forms for the first time. There were now fifty nine girls in the Sixth Form. All the pupils, apart from those in the sixth form, were girls who had been admitted to the school after passing the eleven plus exam.

The early 1950s saw a number of important changes in the life of the school. In 1951 the old School Certificate and Higher School Certificate were replaced by the GCE (General Certificate of Education) examination at Ordinary (O) Level and Advanced (A) Level. In September 1950 the school uniform was completely changed. The rather sombre black square-necked gymslips and square-necked white blouses were replaced with navy v-necked tunics and 'apple green' shirt blouses and blue, green and white striped ties for the first three forms. The lower and upper fifth forms (years 10 and 11) had navy skirts instead of tunics. The sixth form uniform of blue blouses, ties and navy skirts remained the same.

POST-WAR EUROPE

France

In 1947 one group of girls went on the school's first trip abroad since the War. The girls stayed in a French convent and they had to bathe in a tub with their heads through the lids so that they couldn't view their 'nether regions'![5]

They were shocked by many sights - the battered port of Le Havre, Rouen's ravaged cathedral and Caen, a town laid waste, which had suffered 15,000 casualties. They thought at first it was an adventure to explore the gun emplacements at Vierville, but then they heard that the Allies only landed there after four bloody combats and much loss of life. Writing in the School Magazine, one member of the group spoke about the old father of the hotelkeeper at Grandcamp being completely bedridden after his leg had been shattered in the Allied landings. His son made them tea and spoke affectionately of Winston Churchill and Field Marshal Montgomery. They bathed in the Mulberry Harbour at Arromanches, and had a picnic on the beach but couldn't forget the wrecked ships and, on what was once the promenade, the monument inscribed "*Arromanches-Les-Bains, Port Winston d'ou sont parties les troupes Alliées pour la liberation de la France.*[6]

There were also pleasant memories of the holiday. The girls were particularly impressed with the cake shops or "patisseries". They were well-stocked with delicious cakes (chocolate meringues, éclairs, macaroons, cherry tarts and many other delicacies.) No doubt they compared this with the situation back home where shortages and food-rationing still existed. Although France had been occupied by the Germans during the War, they had not been faced with the heavy cost of fighting a War. Another girl, described a visit to Paris. She was impressed by the wide tree-lined streets and the outdoor cafes with little tables shaded from the sun by big umbrellas. It was difficult to realise that only two years previously Paris had been occupied by the Germans. It did not, of course, suffer from bombing raids as London had done and the city had remained practically unscathed.

The Ruhr, Germany

A few years later a number of Fairfield girls made independent journeys to Germany and their observations of a country with whom we had been at war only a few years previously, make interesting reading. One girl stayed in the heart of the Ruhr Industrial district not far from Essen. She was very impressed with the German shops which were full of things we never saw in England. Unlike in England in the early 1950s, there was no rationing but the goods were very expensive, particularly food, so in actual fact for most people things were rationed.

She was very shocked when she saw the bomb damage – large areas in the centre of the town were still no more than piles of rubble and it seemed that little had been done to try to clear up the damage. However, she was told that the people were very pleased with the way they had built up so much of the town and this made her realise how extensive the damage must have been. There was a great shortage of accommodation and she did not meet one family who occupied a whole house. The people in the mining areas seemed to be better off than the people in the country districts, where most of the children had no shoes.[7]

The Rhineland, Germany

Another Fairfield girl visited the German Rhineland a few years later in 1954. Her impression was one of contrasts. She thought that in England the War had now become a point in history, a period of time from which to date events, but in Germany it was still a present significance. She visited Cologne which she thought was one of the most beautiful cities she had seen but it was also the most mutilated. Whole streets were still in ruins devastated by bombs and the damage done to buildings of historic or artistic interest was colossal. Many buildings were being re-built and modern buildings were springing up from the ruins but big houses on the outskirts of the town would still remain in their mutilated condition for many years.

She saw many foreign soldiers – Belgians in Cologne, Americans in Bonn, French in Koblenz. Half the country to the East had been lost to the Russians and friends and relatives living there had not been heard of since the end of the war. Near Cologne there was a small settlement for refugees from Eastern Germany.

On a brighter note, she found that most cars on the road were new ones. This was because at the beginning of the war all private cars were seized by the German army. If an old car drove by it was taken for granted by the

Germans that it was English. She noticed that the Germans ate better than we did. They had creamier butter, more meat and the richest cakes she had ever eaten. In the afternoon the people flocked to cafes and in the evenings they filled the restaurants. The shops, too, were full of goods of a quality equal to or better than ours and at a more reasonable price.[8]

England

England was also suffering from the after effects of war. In the same year that our Fairfield girl visited the Ruhr the Headmistress was speaking about the problems experienced by the school. The meat ration per pupil was tiny and they had fuel sometimes for only two more days. There had been electricity cuts in an overcrowded building and the cost of paper continued to rise, roller-towels were no longer available and they had hastened to order drawing pins and pen nibs before they too disappeared. (The mention of pen nibs is interesting. It wasn't until after the War that Biros or ball point pens came into use but they were not allowed in schools at first and their use in examinations was forbidden for many years.) It was February 1953 before sweets and chocolates were no longer rationed.

NATIONAL HEALTH SERVICE

Apart from the new free secondary education for all there were other life-changing developments introduced by the post-war government. Chief amongst these was the establishment of the National Health Service in 1948. There was also a school health service and every girl had a medical examination once or twice during her school career. The school dental clinic occupied one of the houses on Fairfield Avenue and there was a daily list of dental appointments. Miss Bradley was determined that all the girls should learn to keep their teeth in good order rather than pay a penny a week to insure for 'pot teeth' by the time they reached twenty! This situation was astonishing but true. Lena Slack who was at school in the late 1930s wrote about the School clinics where children could have their teeth extracted without payment. She mentioned that extraction was usually the rule, as very few teeth were considered worth filling and it was quite common for girls, perhaps for cosmetic reasons, to have all their teeth out, and have a full set of dentures, whilst still in their teens![9]

General practitioner

One girl who was at Fairfield during and after the War was to work all her life in the National Health Service. Dr Joan Wilkinson MBE is a wonderful example of how a person with determination and a clear idea of their ambitions, can succeed where others with less perseverance fail. Joan, on her own admission, was mediocre at school, to such an extent that Miss Bradley forecast that she would never achieve her chosen goal of medical school. According to information from a number of girls, Miss Bradley seemed to be determined that a great many Fairfield girls should become teachers and Joan was no exception. Joan has told me that, if it hadn't been for her mother's perseverance, the Headmistress may well have succeeded. Her mother's persistence was all the more remarkable because she was an ordinary working-class woman who probably had little knowledge of higher education. Joan was to prove Miss Bradley wrong. She went on to graduate in 1957 and was, during the course of her career, closely connected with two of the twentieth century's pioneering medical advances.[10]

In January 1958 Joan took up her first post at Manchester Royal Infirmary as house surgeon to Mr D Lloyd Griffiths and Mr John Charnley - Consultant Orthopaedic Surgeons. At the end of February that year Mr Charnley performed the first ever hip-joint operation. Joan was responsible for the patients on the ward and got a first-hand account of proceedings in the theatre later in the day. However, her personal memory of the day was seeing Mr Charnley on a stool shaping the prosthesis with a penknife, to match the x-ray of the patient's hip! She started her ward round at 8.30am and Mr Charnley went to the theatre to put the precious prosthesis into the sterilizer.

Joan continued her training at Oldham where her fourth 'house job' was that of house surgeon in obstetrics and gynaecology to Mr Patrick Steptoe at Boundary Park Hospital, Oldham. During her time there Mr Steptoe got his first laparoscope (a fibre-optic instrument for insertion through the abdominal wall to enable exploration or diagnosis). Because of the small number on the staff and her increasing experience Joan was party to some of Mr Steptoe's early experiments.

Joan then left Oldham to train as a general practitioner in Leeds and then returned to Oldham as a principal in general practice. Over the years Patrick Steptoe's work developed and he met and collaborated with Dr Robert Edwards and once or twice a year they would update the local G.P.s on their progress.

In 1974 the government re-organised the health service. Each district was to be managed by a team of six: three medics, a nurse, a finance officer and an administrator. Two of the medics were elected by their colleagues. Joan was elected by the general practitioners and Patrick Steptoe by the consultants. A consequence of the changes at that time meant that Patrick Steptoe and Robert Edwards were not allowed to use hospital facilities for their research work. However, a previous colleague had built, endowed and bequeathed a general practitioner hospital which all the doctors used. It had a small operating theatre, where before the NHS, general practitioners had performed appendectomies, tonsillectomies, and dental extractions etc. Joan was able to arrange for Steptoe and Edwards to use a few of the beds there for their patients and they were thus able to continue their research.

The work of Patrick Steptoe and Robert Edwards culminated in the birth of the world's first "test-tube baby". Joan was the third person after the family to be told of Louise's safe delivery and was proud to have taken part in supporting this ground-breaking medical development.[11]

Joan found that there was minimal sex discrimination at medical school, although there was one male consultant at Manchester Royal infirmary who ignored female students on teaching rounds. She did find, however, in the early days, that she was not expected to join male colleagues when they were invited to the Manchester Medical Society Dinners. However, when she became a G.P. she was eligible to join the Medical Society and she and a female consultant managed to put an end to 'all male' dinners. She became the fourth female President and only the second lady doctor to preside at her own dinner.[12]

When Joan described some of her experiences in a letter to the Old Girls Association she commented that most people are very ordinary and that included her, but that didn't mean that they couldn't be on the side-lines of some great achievements and she felt privileged in having been involved in some small way in at least two great medical advances.

LIFE AFTER SCHOOL

The Micro-biologist

In 1952 Mary Cooke (née Palmer), who was the daughter of parents from a working-class background who had both managed to obtain a good education, gained a place at the Royal Free Hospital School of Medicine, London. Mary was exceptional, not only going on to University, but also pursuing her career in medicine and micro-bacteriology with hardly a break even though she married and had a family.

She married a Barrister and she thinks the difficulties of combining two careers were as great or greater then, than they are now. She moved twice, as necessitated by the requirements of her husband's career, but she did have tremendous support from him and they were able to employ a full-time resident nanny when the children were small.

Mary went on to have a distinguished career. Among the posts she held were Senior Lecturer and Honorary Consultant in Bacteriology at St Bartholomew's Hospital - only the second woman consultant appointed to Bart's and the first woman with an academic appointment to become a consultant there. She became Professor of Clinical Microbiology at Leeds University and Head of the Department of Microbiology between 1976 and 1979 and in1982 she was appointed Director of the Division of Hospital Infection at the Central Public Health Laboratory. She became Deputy Director of the Public Health Laboratory Service in 1989; a post which she held until she retired in 1994. She has published many articles in professional journals and written several books in connection with clinical bacteriology. She has been a member of various Government working party committees and groups, including those on clostridium difficile infection and the control of infection in hospitals. She was awarded the OBE in 1995 and was made an Honorary Fellow of Queen Mary's College, University of London, in 2008.[13]

In 1979 Professor Cooke was the Guest at Speech Day. During her speech she gave some general advice to the girls and I quote *"The possibilities for you as a group are considerable....Your immediate aims should be to get yourselves as well qualified as you can, but after that I hope you will look carefully at your own attitude to the problems associated with having a family and a career and that you will* *not lumber yourselves with pre-conceived ideas about what you <u>ought</u> to do. By all means listen to the advice that is given to you, but then you must make up your own minds. The needs of individual women vary enormously and what is best for one woman and her family, may be quite unsuitable for another, and it is, in my view, important that you look at your own situation and make decisions based on that alone"*[14] Thirty years on that advice is probably even more important as so many women "try to do it all".

Mary was at Fairfield just as school fees were abolished and a school place was determined by the passing of the eleven plus exam. This meant that more children from poorer homes were able to gain a place and Mary has told me that it was a deeply moving experience to visit the very poor home of one of her closest friends. It was a terraced house with no bathroom or inside toilet and just one room downstairs. However, her friend was fortunate in that she had one important advantage. Her parents were very supportive and were willing to make many sacrifices in order for her to succeed. She was a very clever mathematician and went on to gain a university degree. Mary said that their friendship had made her more aware of the difficult lives that many people had and it was an enduring memory of her time at Fairfield.

Mary has told me that she feels very indebted to the school and thinks that the science teaching was of an unusually high standard, particularly for a girls' school.[15] It was led by the Head of Department, Miss Dorothy Evans, who was an excellent Chemistry teacher and who had been at the school since 1923. The percentage of girls choosing to study science subjects was unusually high for a girls' school. The 'A' Level results for 1953 showed that almost 50 per cent had passed in science or maths subjects.[16] This was certainly higher than the national average. Nationally, there seemed to be a bias against science and mathematics as an appropriate study for the sensitive minds of young ladies. In 1956 a Ministry of Education Bulletin recommended that less laboratory space should be made available for girls' schools than for boys' schools. In the early 1960s the Industrial Fund, which was set up to improve the facilities for science teaching in direct grant and public schools, disposed of £3 million to 210 schools. Of these, 187 were boys' schools, 5 were co-educational and 18 were girls' schools. Even by the early 1970s only about 20 per cent of girls compared with 50 per cent of boys specialised in science subjects at 'A' Level.

High Society

The Deputy Head Girl in1952-53 was Mollie Rothwell and she too specialised in science subjects. Mollie came from a middle-class family and her father was the Chairman of the Governors and a J.P. Mollie, her elder sister Marjorie and younger sister Elizabeth, all went on to University and were awarded Lancashire County and State University Scholarships.[17] Mollie gained a first class honours degree in Chemistry from University College London in 1956 and was awarded the "Catherine Maude Pearce" Scholarship and also a scholarship from the Department of Scientific and Industrial Research.[18] She also did two years research in Biological Chemistry at UCL.

Mollie Brudenell

In April 1957 Mollie married John Michael Brudenell, and a year later, Timothy, the first of their four sons was born. Michael was an obstetrician and in February 1960 he assisted Sir John Peel at the birth of the Queen's son, Prince Andrew. Because of this, Michael and Mollie were invited to the Prince's Christening. Mollie had given birth to their second son, Jeremy only six days previously but was still able to attend. She wrote a lovely, intimate account of the occasion for the Old Girls' News Letter. The Christening took place in the magnificent Music Room in Buckingham Palace. Mollie described the silver-gilt font beautifully decorated with tiny freesia, lily of the valley, narcissi and grape hyacinths. These flowers were later removed and made into small sprays for the ladies. The whole of the Royal family were there including the Queen's aunts, uncles and cousins. The Prince was baptised by the Archbishop of Canterbury and the guests then went into an adjoining room where a buffet tea and champagne were served. The young Prince Charles and Princess Anne cut the Christening cake and the Queen then mingled with her guests stopping to talk and to show them her lovely baby. Mollie talked to the Queen and Prince Phillip for a short while. Prince Phillip was amused by the fact that Mollie had been "released" from hospital for the afternoon.

Mollie ended her letter by saying it was an occasion which she would always remember and cherish.[19] She didn't realise then that this would not be the only time that she would meet the Royal Family. Many years later there would be another important and more personal occasion.

In December 1962 Mollie gave birth to a third son, Marcus and their fourth son, Edward was born in September 1967. In 1964 husband Michael was a consultant obstetrician and gynaecologist at King's College Hospital and he attended the Queen at the birth of Prince Edward.[20] As a result, Michael and Mollie also went to his Christening, this time at Windsor Castle.

By 1960, when they had two small sons, Mollie decided to do part-time "supply" teaching and she taught Chemistry, Physics and Maths at various schools, depending on where they were living. However, by 1967 when they had four sons and Michael's work schedule was very unpredictable, Mollie decided the need for her to be at home was very important. She has always felt that she was very lucky not to have been obliged to work and to be able to put her efforts into being a housewife and mother. However, she has, over the years, done a tremendous amount of voluntary work. For more than thirty years she was a member, of the Ladies' Committee of the Medical Research Trust at King's College Hospital (including ten years as Chairman) and for more than forty years she was on the Events Committee of 'Birthright' (later 'Well Being of Women'), the charity of which the late Diana, Princess of Wales, was Patron.[21]

Mollie Brudenell meets the Queen Mother

In 1984 she again met members of the Royal Family; this time at the wedding of their son, Jeremy, to Edwina Hicks, the daughter of David and Lady Pamela Hicks and the granddaughter of Earl Mountbatten and the god-daughter of the Queen. Guests at the wedding included the Queen, the Duke of Edinburgh, Princess Margaret, and the Duchess of Kent.[22] One of Edwina's bridesmaids was her sister, India Hicks. She was Prince Charles' god daughter and her sister's wedding probably seemed something of an anti-climax as three years previously, in 1981, India had been a bridesmaid at the Wedding of the Decade – that of Prince Charles and Lady Diana Spencer.

Mollie's life has been a happy and fulfilling one. Her family has grown and she and Michael now have nine grandchildren and six great grandchildren. She has experienced a life far removed from her days at Fairfield, but none of this would have come about if she had not been well educated. Her intelligence and her higher education gave her the confidence to feel at ease with those in the very highest echelons of society.

The Journalist

The Head Girl in 1954 was Adele Judith Vincent (née Bagnall) - known during her school days as Judith. Adele gained County Major and State University Scholarships to study English at St. Hugh's College, Oxford where she graduated with an M.A. degree in 1958.[23] She wasn't daunted by

Miss Bradley's earlier predictions that it would be difficult for Arts Graduates to find work other than teaching and pursued her chosen career as a journalist and by 1960 she was one of the team compiling the *"This Week"* pages in the *"Observer"* Sunday Newspaper. She was promoted to the Editorial Staff and had her first article published entitled "The House that Mac Built"[24].

Adele was definitely one of *"the girls who walked away"*. On her own admission, she had grown up thinking England was a rather boring country governed by old men (Harold MacMillan was Prime Minister). Years of living in what she described as a rather sooty impoverished Manchester area after the war contributed to this attitude, as did many holidays taken on the Continent which seemed far more exciting.[25] At the end of 1963 she decided to work her way around the world, starting with America. She obtained a post as a journalist on the New York Times where Cupid promptly intervened and put a stop to her wanderlust. She met and married Geoffrey Vincent who was a fellow journalist and fellow Briton working on the paper. He was a widower with two children (a girl of ten and a boy of six).[26] Soon after they married Geoffrey was appointed Editor of the Courier-Journal in Louisville, Kentucky and Judith joined him on the staff. Their daughter Mary Jane was born in April 1966.[27]

At the end of the 1970's they moved to Columbus, a small town in Indiana where Geoffrey joined the public relations department of the Cummins Engine Company - a major diesel engine manufacturer with world-wide operations, particularly in Britain. It was here that Adele embarked on a second career working for the Cummins Charitable Foundation. Her work involved assessing and evaluating the programmes funded by the trust. The work involved a lot of the same skills of investigating and analysing that she used as a journalist but it allowed her to be more involved in what she was reporting and she found it very satisfying. The Charity supported activities in many communities around the world and this gave Adele frequent opportunities for travel - the thing she had set out to do all those years ago when she had left England for America. She retired as the Trust's Executive Director in 1998. [28]

Their elder daughter married in 1984 and Adele wrote to the Old Girls describing the ceremony. Apparently it was like something out of a Hollywood film. It took place at the home of the bridegroom. The house was large and attractive, built in the old Southern Colonial style with a large white-pillared portico and sited on a bluff overlooking the Ohio River in Louisville, Kentucky. The ceremony took place in the large hall, with the bridal procession coming down the wide staircase and music coming from two grand pianos in an adjacent room.[29] The scene must have seemed a far cry from the Droylsden that Adele had known in the 1950s.

TRAGEDY

A school is a microcosm of the world at large. Some girls are very successful, some are lucky and some will meet with tragedy. Over the years there were girls who didn't reach their full potential and there were some who died prematurely either from illness or accident and there have been those who have experienced the severe ill health or early death of a beloved spouse, child or parent. Girls who wish to remain anonymous include one whose mother did not want her to continue her education and, from the age of fifteen, made her pay for all her clothes, equipment and entertainment on a budget of ten shillings a week (50p). She survived and went on to university. Another pupil was kept awake until at least 11pm, or woken up at that time, so that her mother would not be alone when her father came home drunk. For years she survived on this sleep routine. Later in life another girl who went to live abroad, suffered the trauma of her daughter being murdered by her husband.

Joy Cooper was Fairfield's Games Captain in 1951 and when, in June 1957, she married Roger Byrne the Captain of the Manchester United football team, there was great excitement amongst the local Manchester United fans. It was a warm sunny Saturday morning and crowds of teenagers wearing their team's scarves waited for hours to catch a glimpse of the happy couple. Ten policemen and a police woman were needed to control the crowds which gathered round the church entrance. When Joy and Roger left the church they walked under an archway of muddy football boots fastened with red and white ribbons which were tied to the end of canes.[30] Joy, who was a chartered physiotherapist at Salford Royal Infirmary, had met Roger when he started studying on a day-release physiotherapy course. It was his intention to enter the profession once his football career was over.

Their happiness was to be short-lived. On the 6th of February 1958 it seemed

Joy Cooper marries Manchester United Captain Roger Byrne

that the whole world grieved, when the plane carrying the Manchester United Football team crashed at Munich Airport, but for Joy it was an almost unbearable tragedy. Roger died in the crash along with six other members of the team – Duncan Edwards died fifteen days later. Only a few days after the disaster Joy discovered she was expecting a baby and it was this and the support she received from family, friends and Sir Matt Busby and the United Officials that helped to comfort and sustain her in the months ahead.

Life for single mothers in the 1950s and 60s wasn't easy and even famous football players earned nothing like they do today. Joy had to work fulltime as a physiotherapist to provide for her young son. She also had help from both sets of parents and the football club. Her son went on to have a career in sports management. Joy met her second husband when he was teaching at her son's school and they married in 1976.

ROLE MODELS

In the 1950s only about 4 or 5 per cent of the population went to University. If you were working-class and female the percentage was even less. One of the main drawbacks, in the fight for female equality, was the lack of role models both for working-class and middle-class girls. In the great majority of working-class families there were no female relatives and very few male relatives who had pursued a professional career. Even for middle-class girls, professional females were thin on the ground. It was still assumed by the vast majority that a woman's role would be that of wife and mother.

A Typical 1950s Girl

I was typical of many girls who were at the school in the 1950s. My background was working class and nobody from my family, except a male cousin, had had an education beyond elementary level. My parents who were born at the beginning of the twentieth century, left school at thirteen and fourteen. My mother was a clever girl who was allowed to leave school on the day she was thirteen because she passed what was known as the "Labour Exam". This meant that the school couldn't teach her anything more. There had been no suggestion of her being entered for a scholarship. She had to stop working once she married and had to settle down to a life of domesticity whether she liked it or not. In 1936 my parents left their rented terraced house in Ardwick and took the important step of buying a small semi-detached house on one of the many newly-built private estates which were being developed in Droylsden. Their particular road was built on the site of the old Alderdale Farm which is marked on the maps of 1819 and 1847 which are illustrated in Chapters One and Two. The house cost £350 and was bought with a twenty five year mortgage costing £2 a month (or about ten shillings or 50p a week) which compared favourably with the seven shillings and sixpence (37½p) which they paid for a week's rent on their Ardwick home. It was just about affordable - although the ten shillings a week represented only one seventh of my father's wage of three pounds ten shillings. It must have been a pleasurable experience to live in a house that had a bathroom and an inside toilet. (Their house in Ardwick had no bathroom and neither had the homes they had lived in before they were married. Both my parents went to the local Public Baths early on the morning of their wedding day).

Through my parents, I can reach back to the early years of the twentieth century. I remember a day shopping in Manchester with my mother when she suddenly turned and said *"Do you know what's different in these streets from when I was a girl?* I thought she was going to say motor traffic, but she said *"All the children are wearing shoes now. When I was young there were always some children wandering around barefoot"*.

We had very few books in the house – a book on cake-making issued by a well-known flour manufacturer and a few Mills and Boon library books. We did have newspapers – the *Daily Mirror* during the week and *The People* and *Sunday Express* on a Sunday. I only remember my father reading two books. One was *"What Katy Did at School" by Susan Coolidge* which he read to me, and the other was the serialisation in a Sunday newspaper of *"Forever Amber"*, a bestselling novel of lust and love at the court of King Charles II by Kathleen Winsor. You could say his reading was comprehensive as far as women were concerned!

Just after the war as a six or seven year old, I practiced my reading on the strip cartoons every morning in the Daily Mirror, especially the one about 'Jane', the rather risqué damsel who always seemed to be caught wearing just her underwear. Years later I had the amusing experience of attending a lecture on the teaching of reading. The lecturer was a very experienced teacher and emphasised the importance of gaining the pupils' interest. He illustrated this by describing his experience just after the war when he was given the task of teaching a young Guardsman to read. The Guardsman had been told that he would have to leave the Army if he didn't succeed. The lecturer devised work sheets and 'flash' cards based on the 'Jane' cartoons. He realised that the Guardsman's interest would be sustained by following such a young lady and her antics. The students attending the lecture thought it was hilarious but none more so than me. I sat there remembering how I'd practised my own reading on the same cartoon at exactly the same time.

I loved learning and was overjoyed when I passed the eleven-plus exam to go to Fairfield. I looked forward to studying all the new subjects which would have been denied me at the Secondary Modern school where such subjects as great literature, languages, algebra, geometry, chemistry and physics were rarely on the curriculum.

The lack of role models and my working class background certainly affected my decision not to carry on with my education. The idea that professional people like doctors, lawyers and officials were an elite group of people (to which I didn't belong) seemed to be ingrained into my psyche. For many years I thought that a person with the title of Doctor (medical or academic) was a superior being. It wasn't until years later when one of my daughters gained a PhD that I realised that that certainly wasn't the case! Although I had a successful school career and was in the top stream and loved learning, I was definitely influenced by society's view that marriage and children would be my future and that another five or six years of education was not really needed. Added to this was the fact that my parents were unlikely to have been able to support me financially.

So, after 'O' levels, I ventured out into the commercial world of Manchester. I learned touch-typing and shorthand and attended evening classes in secretarial practice at the Manchester Commercial College and in 1959 I went to work on the Northern News Programme at Granada Television. Commercial television was in its infancy - Granada had transmitted its first programme in May 1956. My official job description was that of News Editor's Secretary but the set up in the News Room at the time meant that it involved much more than that. The production of the News Programme, which covered the whole of Northern England, including Yorkshire at the beginning, was the responsibility of a very small team. There was a News Editor, Assistant News Editor, a Sub-Editor, two copytakers who came in the afternoon (they typed the news stories dictated over the phone by journalists who were usually reporters on local newspapers in the Granada area), and myself who did the work that a Production Assistant would normally do on a programme, including arranging interviews, filming and photographs, keeping the diary, dealing with correspondence, typing the script and last but not least making sure all the freelancers or stringers were paid. The Production Assistant assigned to the News Programme came in just before the start of the broadcast to 'time' the newcast.

Granada TV's News Room – 1959

The News Room of fifty years ago was a far cry from today's modern large television news room with its electronic news gathering and communication equipment. The typewriters were not even electric ones and copies of the script were made using carbon paper. When many copies of material were needed a 'Banda' or Gestetner duplicating machine was used; it was some time before a photocopying machine was introduced.

The News Room, itself, was not much bigger than an ordinary living room. In the middle of the room was a large table made up of four office desks put together. On three sides of the table sat the News Editor, Assistant News Editor, and Sub-Editor and I sat on the fourth side on the left of the News Editor. News stories were shot on film by freelance cameramen living in various parts of the Granada area. The film reel was usually sent by rail to

Manchester and then rushed by taxi to the studio where it was placed on a telecine machine and edited.

It was a wonderful and stimulating experience and I felt very much part of the team and worked with many people who in the future became, not only well-known, but in some cases quite legendary. I was involved with everything that went on during the day and was thrilled to be part of such a dynamic team during a time which was later to be described as Granada's 'Golden Age'. The journalists were young men in their mid to late twenties, (including the News Editor, David Plowright, who went on to become the Managing Director and Chairman of Granada) and, like myself, they had been grammar school pupils who had not gone on to university, so in many ways I felt very much an equal. However, there was always the underlying impression that the male members of Granada's staff were the ones who had the responsible and creative positions. There were few women who got beyond the position of Production Assistant or Researcher. When, in 1963 Granada introduced its Graduate Training Scheme, it was mainly young men who were recruited. I can only remember one girl in the group.

As expected, I married when I was twenty-three and after seven years of working at Granada I left to have our first daughter. I found it difficult at first to settle down to being a full-time wife and mother without the day to day stimulus of work in an exciting environment but the arrival over five years of a further two daughters saw me doing my best to create a happy family home. The ten years I spent at home with my children were very happy ones and I can sympathise with and understand the dilemma faced by many professional women today.

When our youngest daughter started school I needed more than the routine of housework and childcare and I decided to continue my education. Over the next five years I studied for A levels and a degree and then taught in inner city comprehensive schools. I left teaching after a number of years and ventured once again into the commercial world where, among other things, I did research for a bank and later worked as an insolvency administrator. Not graduating until I was forty two meant that whatever career I chose, I was on the first step of the ladder, alongside colleagues who were young enough to be my children and any manager was probably going to be my own age or even younger . It is not a situation that I would recommend and it is not conducive to developing one's self confidence. My experience did, however, help me to encourage my own daughters to get well-qualified as early as possible and not leave it until their forties like their mother.

If I had not gone to Fairfield my life would have taken a different course. Childhood friends who went to the local Secondary Modern were offered jobs such as machinists or shop workers and so more than likely my work experiences would not have been so rewarding and I would probably not have had the confidence to continue my education and, most importantly of all, I would not have been in a position to encourage my daughters in their education and their professional careers.

The Physicist

Averil was a girl who managed to resist the social pressures of the period and steadfastly worked towards a professional goal. Although both her parents had received only an elementary education, she did have one important advantage and that was a role model in the form of her brother who was eight years older than her. He was a scholarship boy, who was educated at Manchester Grammar School and from there he went on to Cambridge University and Averil's ambition was to do the same.[31]

Averil says that, while she was at Fairfield, she was very conscious of her working-class background and she was led to believe that going to Cambridge was probably an unassailable ambition. In 1950 during her first year at school she was incorrectly informed by a teacher that no Fairfield girl had ever been able to get into Cambridge. Averil worked very hard - her strongest encouragement coming from the knowledge that her brother had been successful and from the Head of the Maths Department, Miss Auty, who was a Cambridge mathematician and who was still in touch with Lady Jeffreys who had been her Director of Studies at Girton College, Cambridge. Averil says it is difficult to say what part Miss Auty's personal connection played in getting her and another Fairfield girl, two years earlier, into Girton. However, Miss Auty was the only teacher at Fairfield able to get a girl into Cambridge in the 1950s. In the year before Averil had taken the entrance exam, three very bright girls, studying various other subjects, had not been offered a place.

In 1958 Averil went up to Cambridge on a Lancashire county Scholarship which was generous enough to cover all her tuition fees and a modest sum to live on.[32]

She says that she came across a number of prejudices at Cambridge, but being a woman caused no problems. In fact it was a decided advantage in those days, because there were so few of them! (in 1962 there were 680 women to 7318 men). They lived in single sex colleges but attended lectures etc. with the men. They were a small minority in the town, but because they lived with other women they didn't feel like freaks.

Being a Northerner was her first problem. Her accent immediately branded her as working-class. There were girls from wealthy Northern families but they had been educated at private day or boarding schools and had acceptable accents. A few of the girls were from ordinary grammar schools but the vast majority were from schools belonging to the Girls Public Day School Trust, Direct Grant Schools or top boarding schools like Cheltenham Ladies' College. Averil found that not only did the Grammar School girls have a social handicap, but the other students were much better prepared academically. She discovered that most undergraduates reading mathematics and science had already covered much of the first year curriculum. Those students without that advantage had to work extremely hard just to keep their heads above water. The lecturers went at breakneck speed, assuming that it was a review.

Lack of money was another problem that Averil had to face. She says it would have made life easier to have been able to afford a decent bike, good clothes, all the required books etc. She spent much time fixing her ancient bicycle and laundering and mending her few clothes. Most of the friends she made came up to Cambridge with at least one evening gown but Averil had to wait until half way through her three years before she took the plunge and bought one. Formal dress was required for so many events and Averil considered it was money well spent. She says it would have been a pity to have missed the wonderful formal balls and other social occasions. In these circumstances, women had the advantage. All she had to do was buy a gown. The men not only had to own a dinner jacket, they had to pay for the ball tickets, dinners, theatre ticket etc. All the men she went out with were from public schools and had plenty of money. She says that most grammar school boys didn't even attempt to join in that sort of social life and there were so few women around that it wasn't unusual for men to opt out of the social scene altogether.

Looking back Averil says that Cambridge was an experience that she wouldn't have missed but she sometimes wonders what it would have been like to have gone to a different university where she wouldn't have felt out of her depth socially and to a certain extent academically. But on the positive side, she knows that a Cambridge honours degree opens doors all over the world.

Although Averil had worked hard to gain her degree and was now qualified to earn a good salary for life, she immediately after graduating got married. This was to a fellow Cambridge student and Averil states that they planned out their future together with mathematical precision and no small measure of sexism. It was decided that she would teach Physics for three years to support them while he studied for a PhD degree. Most of the research students were male, many of them supported by their wives who were either teachers or nurses. There was a joke amongst the wives that they were getting their PhT – 'Putting Husband Through'. Their thinking was that the man would need to be the breadwinner for most of their marriage so it made sense to invest in his qualifications. After three years, Averil's salary as a teacher was roughly the same as her husband would have earned in a British Research Laboratory. It was no surprise, therefore, that he applied for and obtained a position with the Radio Corporation of America and Averil was persuaded to leave her much loved friends and teaching job and emigrate to America in 1965.[33]

Her first job in America was as a research assistant in an aeronautics laboratory near Princeton. She was the first woman they had hired who was anything more than a secretary and she was definitely a puzzle to them. At that time, women were not admitted to Princeton University and, even worse, it was "simply not done" for girls to study maths and physics, unless they were freaks. Averil got used to men saying to her *"You sure don't look like a physicist!"* Shortly after she started work in the laboratory she discovered that a young man working in the same company at a much lower level was being paid the same salary. When Averil queried this it was pointed out that she was a woman and salary scales for women were much lower. As she was the first woman to be hired in a technical position by the company, it made very little sense, but it soon became apparent that the traditional jobs for women with degrees, like teaching and nursing, were notoriously badly paid.[34]

Averil gave up her job when her husband said he was ready to have children. They had a boy and a girl and Averil didn't go back to work until her daughter Susan was in full-time school. She decided to go back into teaching, instead of research, because she wanted to be at home when the children weren't in school. She enjoyed her teaching career and felt very much appreciated. Averil feels that teaching is a low-level profession in America and a moderately good teacher trained in England is regarded as a superstar there.[35]

Averil said that, in the 1950s and 1960s, American women simply couldn't expect to compete on a level playing field with men. Girls in High School very rarely studied more than the minimum requirements in mathematics, and almost never took physics. The professions were dominated by men who had graduated from the major universities, many of which didn't admit women. The women who bucked the system, were regarded as freaks – maybe because they down-played their femininity.

Some years later she met the man who was to become her second husband. He's an American engineer and one of the least judgmental people she knows, but he told her in all seriousness that women were either intelligent or attractive – not both! Averil's expression must have spoken volumes because he hurriedly added that she was the first exception to that rule that he had come across! Averil thinks that maybe it was the requirements put on American women in order to be considered attractive – such as body deforming undergarments, uncomfortable clothing, elaborately styled hair, and thick make up that resulted in this attitude. A girl who didn't make the effort wasn't playing the dating game. Averil says that when the women's liberation movement took hold in the US, one of the first things that women did was to refuse to wear bras – the burning of them became a symbol of defiance against the strictures of a society that discriminated against them. The male population was delighted by the move, so it backfired in no uncertain terms!

Even today, Averil feels that women still face some discrimination in the US. A male politician who is forceful is considered strong – a female with the same behaviour is strident! On the whole, however, she thinks they have come a long way. Women are accepted, in almost equal numbers, at the major universities and it is illegal to discriminate on the grounds of sex. Today, a company would not get away with paying a woman less than a man doing the same job. [36]

In correspondence during 2010 Averil mentioned a statement by Shirley Chisholme who is the first African-American woman to be elected to the American Congress. Ms Chisholme stated that being a woman had put many more obstacles in her way than being black. Averil said that this was a huge comment, because Shirley Chisholme had grown up during a time of terrible racial prejudice in America. Shortly after receiving Averil's email, I watched Baroness Shirley Williams, the British politician, on television speaking about the drawbacks between being a woman and being black. She mentioned that, during the American Presidential Election, the abuse levelled at Hilary Clinton in television promotions, (using words like 'bitch' etc.), was the equivalent of using the word 'nigger' against a black person – something which would not be tolerated now. This discrimination in America is illustrated by the fact that women were not admitted to the Augusta National golf club until 20 August 2012 – twenty-two years after it admitted its first black member. Until that date the Club had operated a 'men-only' rule. It has to be noted here that golf in the U.K. is still a male 'strong-hold'. Three out of nine golf clubs on the prestigious 'Open' roster do not have any female members.

The Scientist

One girl, in the year below Averil, had a role model who was able to give her much support. Maureen Beattie (née Bustard)'s mother had been a pupil at the main Manchester high school in the centre of the city. Her school experience was unusual in that her father (Maureen's grandfather) was completely against her receiving a high school education – he thought it was unnecessary for a girl – and her attendance at the school was kept a secret from him. Maureen's grandmother brought in washing and did other work to ensure that her daughter was able to continue her education. Maureen's grandfather was rarely at home, spending most of his time either at work or in the pub. He never discovered that his daughter had attended the high school.

Maureen went on to gain a science degree and is very grateful for the guidance she received from Miss Evans the head of the science department. Miss Evans always told her to be proud of her achievements and qualifications and perhaps, just as importantly, to be wary of giving out too much personal information during job interviews. Miss Evans was very much aware of the sexual discrimination which was prevalent at the time, especially in the science industry. When Maureen went for a particular job interview she was the only woman out of twelve candidates. She took off her engagement ring before the interview and when she was asked whether she was planning to get married sometime in the future she asked the interviewer whether he had asked the other candidates the same question. She told him she expected to be judged solely on her qualifications and ability. She got the job. Her interviewer said later that he was impressed not only by her qualifications but also by her confidence and strength of character.[37]

The Government Minister

Another Fairfield girl who was at school in the mid- fifties became very much involved in work connected with the female struggle for equality. In 1990 Christine Bullen née Gallagher was appointed as Deputy Minister in the British Columbia Ministry of Advanced Education in Canada. Her particular department was set in place to advance the status of women educationally, socially, politically and financially. The work involved developing programs to support women and administer government grants to immigrant groups, native development programs and leaders seeking to advance women in science and technology. Her role involved much travel throughout the province and across Canada to meet women's groups and to represent the government at federal/provincial meetings, a great deal of public speaking to private and public-sector audiences and supporting the Minister in the legislature.

Christine came to this work after a very satisfying career in the UK and Canada as a teacher and guidance counsellor and school principal.. She was in the sixth form at Fairfield and went on to teacher training college. Although she appreciated the high standard of literacy and organisational skills she acquired at Fairfield along with a sense of duty and responsibility, she found the school very rigid and felt somewhat intimidated. She was once told that she would "never amount to anything" which was something she never forgot and which didn't enhance her self-confidence. This was an appalling thing to say and it would seem that it was the misguided opinion of just one insensitive and thoughtless teacher.

Her working class parents made great sacrifices to keep her and her two siblings at school until they were eighteen but it was not suggested that she should apply to university and Christine felt that this was something only middle class girls were more often encouraged to do. This is an attitude that quite a number of girls have said they experienced and it seems to reflect the general view of society in the 1950s that the majority of girls were expected to devote their lives to being housewives and mothers. She says that it wasn't until she went to live in Canada that she was able to fulfil her academic potential. She studied for a M.Sc. in Educational Psychology and then went on to gain her Ph.D. It was during her studies for her dissertation on "Women in Management" that she was recruited to join the Ministry.

Christine says that at the time there were comparatively few women in leadership positions but the government tried to set an example within their own ranks. They made progress and saw the proportions rise gradually. However, Christine says they were constantly battling with the thorny question of employment equality and male managers who wanted to keep it a closed shop. Christine feels that, although some progress has been made, women will always be at a disadvantage because of their child-bearing and rearing activities and domestic duties which are rarely equally shared. Although, she has noticed that her own sons do a lot more housework and child minding than the previous generation did, so it's a start![38]

The case studies in this chapter show that for those girls who had received a grammar school or university education, more career opportunities were opening up and a pioneering few were even demonstrating that it was possible to combine marriage and family life with an interesting career. However, it was just the beginning. There were still deep-rooted prejudices against women striving for equality and a chance to lead more independent and satisfying lives – the struggle would continue.

CHAPTER NINE

THE STRUGGLE FOR EQUALITY CONTINUES 1960-1980

Women demand equal pay and opportunity

By 1960 the school had eight hundred pupils, eighty of whom were in the sixth form and new extensions had been built. The school now had six laboratories and two science preparation rooms and employed two full time laboratory assistants. There were now thirty-seven mistresses and, believe it or not, six masters.[1]

UNIVERSITY EDUCATION

The 1960s saw the rapid expansion of university education. From 1962 students were entitled to maintenance grants to study away from home and the 1963 Robbins Report (the report of the Committee on Higher Education) stated that there should be a university place for anyone who was qualified to fill it. New universities were created and all Colleges of Advanced Technology were given university status. During the 1950s there had been only about 90,000 students and by 1967 there were 197,000. University education was free and money could no longer buy a place at university. All universities were required to select their students on the grounds of intellectual ability which chiefly meant "A level" results and a national agency was set up to channel university admissions.

It was hoped that these developments would lessen the gap between the social classes. At the time of the Robbins Report children from professional or managerial families were about twenty times more likely to go to university than those from the working-class. The situation has improved over the years - by the twenty-first century the gap had diminished to about five to one.[2] The coming years would see a greater number of girls gaining university entrance. Fairfield, with its established reputation for a high standard of teaching and scholarship, was in an excellent position to take advantage of these new opportunities in education. The coming years would see a greater number of girls gaining university entrance.

A WOMAN'S ROLE

By 1960 it was generally acknowledged that women's intelligence was equal to that of men. Many girls had received a grammar school education and a third of graduates were now women. However, once they left university they found themselves in a man's world, where men were seen as the breadwinners and women were dependent wives. One woman graduate who had been awarded a distinction for her research at university, where there had been thirty six men tutors but no women, was taken aside and told not to apply for a job there, because 'ladies don't do very well here'.[3]

Many people still felt that a woman's destiny was to be confined to domesticity and women's magazines continued to help perpetuate the idea that a woman's aim was to be a perfect housewife. The *"Woman's Own"* magazine, in its advice column, aimed at reinforcing women in their role as wives and mothers, cheering them up and enabling them to carry on. Katharine Whitehorn who worked on the magazine has written that if a woman complained of, say, a wandering husband, the answer would not be *'Yes, he's a rat, try putting too much salt in his food and starch in his collars'*. *'No, it must, surely, be your fault: you haven't been loving enough, you haven't responded to his needs, you've been coming down to breakfast in your curlers!*[4] In 1961, the magazine even told its readers that women were *"born to love, born to be partners to the opposite sex"*. The single most important thing a girl could do was to *"fix her heart on one man and to love and care for him with all the bounteous unselfishness that love can inspire"*[5]

Signs of Progress

Considering this attitude towards women, it was not surprising that the sixties were to see the first growth of the women's liberation movement. Feminist writers like Betty Friedan were to influence women and make them more conscious of their inferior situation. In her book *"The Feminine Mystique",* published in 1963, she discussed "the problem that has no name" – the unhappiness and futility felt by many women, dissatisfied with being just housewives. She challenged the prejudices against working mothers and emphasised the problems of the stay-at-home bored housewife, with her labour-saving gadgets. She suggested that their isolated and house-work dominated lifestyles were driving many women to drink and tranquillisers. She advised her readers not to view housework as a career and not to try to find complete fulfilment through marriage and motherhood alone, but to find meaningful work which used their full mental capacity.

Nearer home Mary Stott, a journalist on the *Manchester Guardian,* did much to encourage women to consider wider more important issues, other than the mundane domestic ones.

Being able to control the size of her family was a crucial factor in a woman's struggle for equality and the introduction of the contraceptive pill in 1961was an important step. This enabled women to plan their families and eventually employers would begin to see them as permanent staff members. In 1967 the Medical Termination of Pregnancy Act legalised abortion, if two doctors certified that it was needed on medical or psychological grounds and in1967 the Family Planning Act enabled local authorities to provide advisory services on birth control. Reform of the law relating to divorce, was achieved in 1969; a divorce could now be obtained on the grounds that a marriage had completely broken down after a separation of two years, if the couple both wanted to part, or five years if only one partner sought divorce. In addition, the Matrimonial Property Act, of 1963, secured the wife an equal share in family assets.

FAIRFIELD GIRLS

Looking through Old Girls' News Letters of the 1960s, it seems that many

Fairfield girls were pursuing independent lives and they were definitely a group who "walked away". A great many went to work abroad and their destinations and posts were many and varied. Those who went abroad independently, and not as a wife accompanying her husband, included those who worked as teachers in South Africa, France, Bermuda, Germany, Paris, Paraguay, Sierra Leone, Nigeria, the Sudan, Austria, Spain, Australia, and Mexico, as British Embassy workers in Teheran (under the Shah), Somalia, Berlin, Budapest, the Congo and Kenya, as nurses in Nairobi and New York; as an eye specialist in America, as a psychiatric nurse in Switzerland, as International Voluntary Service workers in Swaziland and the Solomon Islands and as "Bluebell" Dancers at the Lido in Paris.[6]

More than twice as many girls went to live abroad because of their husband's work, although some of them were able to follow their chosen careers in their new location. Many girls also moved to other places in this country because of their husband's employment. It seemed that it was still a man's world. I couldn't find a single case where a man moved to a different area because of his wife's work. It would be more than twenty five years before I found a Fairfield girl whose husband was willing to do this.

The Religious Vocation

Although the school was no longer connected to the Moravian Church there were still a small number of girls who went abroad as church workers alongside their husbands. Two of the girls who went overseas experienced completely different countries - one lived in the frozen North in Labrador and the other lived almost in the tropics, in Jamaica.

Marjorie Grubb's life in Labrador was particularly difficult. As well as supporting her husband in his work, she had six children to care for. Their Moravian Mission station, at Nain, had a ship, with which they used to visit the cod fishermen in the summer. One year the ship was partially destroyed by fire and it took months to restore it back into service.

The winter of 1962 was particular hard. There were more storms than usual and snow up to the roof tops. The spring was cold with harbour ice not breaking up and it wasn't until the middle of June that the fishermen could get their boats out. Almost immediately the arctic drift ice came sweeping in and prevented any supply vessels from getting through. The store ran out of milk, butter, sugar, canned meat and vegetables and, as fresh meat had been scarce all year, it was fortunate that they were able to catch rock cod and trout. Even in August, the outlying islands were still jammed with ice, seriously hampering the fishing, on which the Inuit people depended for their livelihood. The main event of that year was the installation of a telephone system with the switchboard in the boarding school. Eventually, an extensive road-building programme was started and an airstrip was built. This meant that mail and supplies were able to reach them more regularly.[7]

In contrast, Olive Linyard and her husband Fred's first post in 1962 was in the Jamaican countryside over 2,000 feet above sea-level where the temperature was relatively cool. It was a rural area where most of the people lived without electricity, running water or any other convenience and where there was little employment except on the not very productive land.

The day started soon after six o'clock when water had to be pumped and hens fed. Olive did have some domestic help and was able to teach housecraft on two mornings a week at the secondary school in the local town. Even at 2,000 feet it was usually too hot to attempt much work in the afternoon and most activities took place in the morning and between 4 and 6.30 pm. Fred looked after four congregations and Olive helped with an organisation for girls and young women called the Upward and Onward Society, Life boys, a Women's Fellowship and all the Church events that came along. She also had her own three young children to care for.[8]

Another Fairfield girl who shared her husband's missionary work was Judith Vernon (née Phillips). They lived among the Indians in a remote part of Argentina. It was a week's rail journey from Buenos Aires and there was no hospital within a hundred miles.[9]

Myra Dickinson (née Allcock) followed in Marjorie Grubb's footsteps in Labrador. Her husband was the Moravian minister in charge of the Hopedale Mission and Myra worked as the Principal of the village school.[10]

There were also girls who, because of their religious convictions, went on their own to live and work abroad.

Christine McQueen trained as a teacher and went to work in an Austrian convent boarding school in 1971. She stayed in Austria gaining a Teacher's Diploma and a BA from an American College as an external student. She was then awarded a Diploma for Interpreters and Translators and then studied part time for a Master of Philosophy degree at Innsbruck University. During these studies she was a house-mother at a school for 'difficult' boys. For many years she had wanted to become a Nun and three days after her last examinations in 1985 she entered the seventh century Benedictine Abbey of Frauenworth, on the beautiful island of Fraueninsel, on Lake Chiemsee, in Bavaria, between Munich and Salzburg - very much *"Sound of Music"* territory. She is now Sister Scholastica.[11]

In 1987 she took her first vows but was still serving her novitiate. These vows bound her to the Abbey for the next three years, after which she had to make a final decision, as would the religious community. In the same year she appeared on our television screens in an interview with Russell Harty in his television series about his Grand Tour of Europe. Russell Harty wrote of his meeting with Sister Scholastica in his book *"Mr Harty's Grand Tour"*. It was a heart-warming chapter. They spoke of love and the difficulties of a single life and also her choice of the name 'Scholastica'. It means 'pupil' and she told Russell that school in Droylsden had always been a very great joy to her. She said she wasn't particularly bright, but when she started school on her fifth birthday it was like a present. School meant everything to her. She had had to do exams all her life so perhaps Scholastica was the most appropriate name for her.

She went on to tell Russell that when she had served her novitiate, the sisters would vote for her with black and white beans. They would pop the little beans into a box and her future, maybe the rest of her life, would rest upon a bean in a box - but she felt in her heart that it rested with God. Russell wrote that he came away wiser, and happier and honoured to have met Sister Scholastica.[12]

Sister Scholastica wrote to the Old Girls' Association on a number of occasions. One Christmas she spoke about Sisters from the Ukraine, who had come to the Abbey to receive training to live in a community again. They had survived many years in the underground Church in the Ukraine, living in tiny huts in ones and two and would soon be returning to their homeland.

The island looks like a winter wonderland in December and Sister Scholastica gave a lovely description of the Abbey on Christmas Eve. *"All four candles are burning on the Advent wreath and the tree is waiting to be decorated. This is a task for the special time on Christmas Eve afternoon, when the brooms, buckets and dusters are stacked away, and the house is still, in expectation of the longed-for Guest"* This quiet scene seems so far removed from the sometimes frantic commercially orientated Christmases we experience here.

Sister Scholastica took her final vows and has been a member of the community at the Abbey ever since. She became responsible for the Guest House which during the year has about nine hundred guests. Since the girls' convent boarding school closed, their building has been used as a venue for international seminars and conferences. Sister Scholastica is responsible for these conferences. It is a big undertaking. Several hundred conferences using three large halls take place every year and people come from all over the world and from many different spheres of life. It seems that her religion is not restrictive, but is all-encompassing. When I visited her in 2009 she gave me a photograph of herself taken with three of the conference delegates - they were a Jewish lady, a Palestinian and an Iraqi. One of her other concerns is the education of disabled and failing children; she hopes that eventually she might be able to open a school for them.[13]

I mentioned to Sister Scholastica that I found it strange that somebody so independently minded like herself should be a member of a Church in which women are not really considered as equals. She said that she and the other Benedictine nuns had complete autonomy in the running of the Order and she felt that there were no restrictions imposed on them by the Church.

Gwen Carlisle was another girl whose religious convictions led her to service abroad. Gwen entered Fairfield in 1966 and after training and working as a teacher for four years, went out to Asuncion, the capitol of Paraguay in South America. She went to teach at St Andrew's College, which was set up by English missionaries and is connected to the South American Missionary Society. Gwen has now been at the school for nearly thirty years and is now their Head Mistress.[14]

Athletic success

The 1960s was a time when one Fairfield girl became a world-beater in Athletics. Christine Perera became interested in hurdle events whilst she was still at school. She first won the Lancashire 80 metre hurdles championships in 1964 and the following year she became English Schools Champion and in 1966 she again won the title with a record win of 11.6 seconds. During 1967 she held the world 100 metre hurdles record of 13.7 seconds. She represented Great Britain abroad several times. She won a bronze medal for the 50 metres hurdles at the European Indoor Athletics Championships in Belgrade and in Rome took third place in the 100 metre event, against top international competition. At the European Games in Athens, she reached the final of the 100 metres where she was the youngest competitor. In 1970 she gained a Bronze medal in the 100 metres at the Commonwealth Games in Edinburgh.

Christine Perera

During this time she was achieving star status in the local newspapers under headings such as *"World-Beater Christine to run in Belgrade"*, *"Ace Hurdler Christine again in great form"* and *"Champion Chris out to beat the world"*. The local papers also reported that during 1970 she had the distinction of being the fastest-ever British woman hurdler, when she finished the 100 metre hurdles in 13.4 seconds in a European Cup event in East Berlin.[15]Her main aim was to compete in the Munich Olympics, in 1972, but she was troubled with a leg injury for a year, and returned to serious competition just too late to make the grade in the Olympic trials. [16]

Chairman of a city's magistrates

For many girls a rather lack-lustre performance at school can often be followed by great success in later life. Many successful entrepreneurs and famous entertainers find the academic life at school rather stifling and boring and rebel against authority. One sixties girl who has recounted some of her rather unorthodox school experiences, achieved important and responsible positions in later life. Sharman Birtles (née Newth) began by saying that she was never particularly academic at Fairfield - she was too busy being mischievous! She held the school record for being given three detentions in four minutes and her most abiding memory was the occasion when she accidentally put her foot through a wooden door panel, when friends tried, jokingly, to lock her out of school. In Jive Sessions in the school hall during wet lunch hours she was delighted to win the Twist competition on one occasion.[17]

After this rather giddy educational start, Sharman went on to more rewarding times. She had a successful career in banking, becoming the Regional Facilities Manager covering Manchester, Leeds, Liverpool and Birmingham for a major Bank and in 1981 she became a Justice of the Peace, being the youngest magistrate in the County at the time. [18] In 2009 she was elected as the Chairman of Manchester City magistrates. This is a tremendously responsible position. There are 420 magistrates and there are eighteen courts a day – Manchester is the busiest Magistrates' court in the country and deals with everything from minor traffic matters through to serious assaults and thefts. Two years ago Sharman was appointed as a Deputy Lieutenant of Greater Manchester. She told me that, currently, 61 per cent of the Deputy Lieutenants for Greater Manchester are male, and 39 per cent female. This, however, is a big improvement on the situation in the past. Of those Deputies who have retired (over 75s), 86 per cent were men and 14 per cent women.

Sharman says that at the start of her career at the bank there were only whispers of a movement called "women's lib" and "girl power" certainly hadn't been invented. It was still extremely difficult for women to be taken seriously, particularly in the world of commerce. When she first joined the bank, all female staff were expected to learn to type and were not encouraged to take banking exams, as it was expected that they would soon leave their jobs to get married and have babies. Sharman says that things have changed since that time, but women still have to push harder to be recognised in almost every field. Because of this, self-belief is so important. She told Fairfield girls at a recent prize-giving ceremony *"We girls must always think big and have high expectations of ourselves. To achieve this it is important to work hard and to take advantage of the education that you receive at Fairfield"*.[18]

The role of women was gradually changing and, in the sixties, the career choices for the girls who went on to higher education became quite wide-ranging. There was news of a girl becoming an analyst at a steel works; another qualified as a pathologist; one became a dentist and another gained entrance to the diplomatic branch of the Civil Service. One girl who was at Fairfield in the sixties was working for the British Consul in Iran in 1979 when the Shah was overthrown. She managed to escape from the country in an RAF Hercules troop-carrier, just hours before Khomeini arrived and the Shah fled the country. She later went on to work in China as an English teacher.

With many Fairfield girls beginning to lead very successful independent lives and following exciting careers, it is difficult to realise that it wasn't until the next decade that the Equal Pay Act and the Sex Discrimination Act were passed. It would appear that quite a number of Fairfield girls were already in the vanguard of the march towards equality.

THE SEVENTIES

In 1971, the school celebrated its 175th anniversary. There were gatherings and exhibitions at the school and a service in Manchester Cathedral. The school uniform was far removed from that worn at the beginning of the century. The girls all followed the fashion of the time and their mini-skirts could not have been any shorter!

175th Anniversary Service 1971 in Manchester Cathedral

Fairfield continued to grow. By 1970 there were 136 in the sixth form. That year twenty three went on to university or polytechnics and a gradually increasing number of girls were gaining places at Oxbridge.[19]

THE STRUGGLE FOR EQUALITY GOES ON

The seventies saw a far greater interest in the fight for female equality. The first women's liberation conference took place in 1970. They demanded, among other things, equal pay, equal education and opportunity, the provision of nurseries and free contraception. There were many marches and demonstrations and the formation of local women's groups and gradually over the decade women's opinions and expectations were changed and the superior position of men challenged.

In the 1950's women teachers, civil servants and local government officers had won equal pay but it wasn't until 1975 that the Equal Pay Act was passed which stipulated that equal pay for men and women doing the same job had to be in place, within five years. The Act was eventually passed and many companies who wanted to avoid widespread industrial unrest, accepted that phased pay increases was the better of two evils. However, in 1976 the women workers at the Trico-Folberth windscreen wiper factory at Brentford in Middlesex had to go on strike for twenty one weeks until the company agreed to their demand to be paid the same basic rate as the men.

The Sex Discrimination Act was passed in 1975. It covered employment, training, housing and the provision of goods and services and established the Equal Opportunities Commission to see that the new Act was observed. It meant that sex discrimination was banned in education, job recruitment and advertising and women were entitled to have their jobs kept open for them if they stopped working temporarily to have a baby. Because of the Act women became more aware of the discrimination they faced and on the many occasions when a woman questioned her situation and faced opposition, a threat to contact the Equal Opportunities Commission, often had the desired effect.

One of the many groups campaigning for equal opportunities was "Women in Media". At the BBC only three women, out of a total of forty-seven, had been sent on production training schemes and very few women were on senior management courses.[20] I personally remember studying a book on media careers in the early 1970s. The writer pointed out that newsreaders and presenters and reporters on serious programmes had to be male. He could not envisage a time when a woman would have the authority and seriousness to be given such a job! Angela Rippon was the first female presenter of the nine o'clock news when she was appointed in 1975.

The 1975 Act was also supposed to make it easier for women to make financial transactions, such as obtaining a mortgage, or buying goods on Hire Purchase etc. but it was still extremely difficult for a woman to obtain credit or a mortgage without a male guarantor. I remember the formalities of obtaining a joint mortgage with my husband in the early seventies. Our solicitor informed me that I would need to attend his office so that he could explain the intricacies of the documentation to me. It was assumed that my husband did not need this help. I attended under duress saying "one moronic female attending for instruction". The solicitor was very embarrassed and apologetic.

Dame Jenni Murray, the Presenter of Woman's Hour, remembers the humiliation and a certain rage when, applying for benefits, she was told *"You can't have benefits because you are married and you have a husband and he's legally bound to keep you"*. She also recalls trying to get a mortgage after her divorce. *"You go along, you've got a job, you've saved up the deposit and they say no, no, no, we can't give you a mortgage unless you have a signature from your husband or father"*.

She threatened legal action under the Sex Discrimination Act and got her mortgage.[21]

Katherine Whitehorn in her autobiography *"Selective Memory"* criticised the banks. She once left a bank because, when she was trying to cash a cheque made out to her from a man, they asked her what it was for.[22] Even in the late eighties, when payments were made following the demutualisation of some Building Societies, these payments would go to the first-named person of a joint account which was generally the man . Katharine Whitehorn commented that" *considering women have to do most of the day-to-day juggling with money in most households, it's puzzling how this idea of their fluffiness with money persists.*"[23]

Katherine described an incident in the seventies which illustrates the male patronising attitude towards women. She recounted how government minister, Geoffrey Johnson-Smith, who was then in charge of co-ordinating government information, went to a meeting in Brussels with Barbara Hoskins, who was then his Parliamentary Private Secretary – that is to say, she was the one who actually had the briefing on everything he was going to negotiate. But she was expected to leave a high-level dinner with the ambassadors' wives, which she did, but she then returned. This outraged the diplomats but Geoffrey said she must stay. [24]

The 1975 Employment Protection Act made it illegal to force women to leave work once they became pregnant. The Act also gave women the right to six weeks' paid maternity leave and unpaid leave of up to twenty nine weeks.

Women were gradually realising that they could have a life outside the home. The size of families was now smaller and the use of modern labour saving devices meant that the time a woman was needed in the home was only a small part of her total life. If she was to have a rewarding and satisfying life, she would need interests and work outside the home. The more educated and qualified she was, the better position she would be in to follow her chosen career.

A few years later, the former Principal of St Hilda's College Oxford was the guest speaker at Speech Day. She compared a woman's life in the present day with that at the beginning of the century. She said that back then, women were fully occupied in maintaining their households, bearing and raising children and looking after invalids. Changes in the birth-rate, technology and public health had released women from the need to be fully occupied in the home and allowed them to use their energies in other fields. She told the girls *"you will have to be ready to turn your hand to anything that comes up. You have the vigour to produce a family of a dozen children - if you do not find an outlet for that vitality you will be a nuisance to your husbands and your families".*[25] Although it was certainly an interesting and somewhat novel comment to make I think I must question its validity. Many women in the past were drained of their vitality by the time they had given birth to twelve children and unless you were wealthy much child bearing often meant that women were either old or dead by the time they were forty.

SUCCESSFUL CAREERS

However, there were many Fairfield pupils who were able to illustrate their ability *"to find an outlet for their vitality"*.

Engineering
One girl who gained a PhD in Metallurgy worked for five years as a Project Engineer for British Nuclear Fuels and then took a postgraduate diploma in Micro-electronics. For the next eight years she worked as a software engineer/software account manager consultant until 1993. After having a young daughter, she lectured in Science and Technology at Cambridge University. [26]

Microbiology
Another Fairfield girl, having obtained a PhD degree in microbiology, worked on the breakdown of cellulose by enzymes, in the search for a new energy source. She then went to Sydney, Australia, to carry out research into the adhesion of bacteria to oral surfaces and to look into a heart condition known as infective endocarditis, which is caused by bacteria found in the mouth.[27]

Medicine
Fairfield girls continued to work abroad, often in remote and very poor parts of the world. Elizabeth Tutton, who was in the 6th Form in 1974, elected to

work at a Mission Hospital in Northern India, as part of her clinical education as a fourth year student at the Manchester Medical School. The hospital was in a very poor area and its 120 beds had to provide medical and surgical services in all fields, especially in eye diseases and leprosy. The patients came into hospital in a much more hazardous condition than they would in Britain and there were the additional problems of malnutrition and poor hygiene.

There were little rooms where the patients' relatives cooked food for themselves and the patients. There were two British consultants and twenty nurses. Compared to English hospitals, conditions were primitive and the beds were usually augmented by patients sleeping on the verandas along with dogs, goats and chickens. As well as her work in the hospital, Elizabeth went out into the village to give vaccinations and inoculations, and assisted at the weekly antenatal clinic.[28]

Elizabeth returned to England to complete her medical degree and started her training as a G.P. in 1980. She also married that year and in 1982 had a baby. She had to take some maternity leave and when she went back to work she became something of a pioneer, by taking her baby with her into hospital and breastfeeding. Elizabeth has successfully combined her work as a G.P. with that of caring for her family.[29]

Children's writer

Jill Marshall, who is now a successful children's author, started at Fairfield in 1976 and become the first Head Girl after the school became comprehensive in 1980. She had an outstanding school career although she does recall that she found the all-girls atmosphere at the school rather stifling and was happy to go on to a local sixth form college. She did, however, have a happy time at the school – the teachers were exceptional and she made many friends. There was a high expectation of learning and gaining good qualifications which set a standard for later life. She has told me that she is constantly looking for the same level of education for her daughter and failing to find it. She is still in contact with the friends she met at Fairfield and she commented that they are all solid, sensible, high-achieving women!

Jill went on to graduate from Cambridge University. Both her parents left school when they were fifteen; her father was first a joiner and then an industrial model maker. Jill was the first person in her family to go to university. After graduating with a Master's degree she had a successful career in the field of Human Resources, combining her work with bringing up her daughter as a single parent. She feels that being female did not affect her career and she was never overlooked for a position, although she suggests that this may have been because the field of Human Resources is particularly female-oriented.

It's embarrassing to report that Jill's first experience of sexism occurred at the school Speech Day when she was Head Girl. It was the practice then to ask the father of the Head Girl to say a few words. Her father was working away but they didn't ask her mother to take his place but asked her uncle instead. Her mother never said anything but Jill knows that she was highly offended.

Jill is now living with her daughter in New Zealand and she started writing about nine years ago. One of her most successful series is her Jane Blonde books (modelled on James Bond.) and her seventh book in the series, *"Spylets Are Forever"*, is to a very great extent set in a school hall. Jill tells me that this is based on Fairfield's school hall with the view from the stage that she became very familiar with over her five years at Fairfield. (She was very involved in the school drama productions). Her books have been translated into several languages and she has sold over half a million books.

Although Jill did not experience any sexism in her career in Human Resources, she says that publishing is a whole different matter. She has been told that her 'boy' books don't sell well because she is seen simply as a girls' writer and her publishers would definitely like to keep her in that mode. Overall, she has found that her gender hasn't been an obstacle in her progress, but she did say that she had found, from time to time (including at Cambridge), that her working-class, northern upbringing had thrown a few spanners in the works.

Jill put her writing and publishing knowledge to good use after the devastating earthquake in Christchurch, New Zealand in February 2011. She joined forces with another author to publish a children's book to help raise funds for the city in its struggle to recover from the disaster. This book went on sale on March 22nd, just one month after the disaster. This was a tremendous achievement as it usually takes a year or more to get to the publication stage. News from Jill at the end of May 2011 was that the book was selling very well. It had gone straight in at number 4 in the New Zealand Children's Best Selling List and profits were being sent to the Red Cross.[30]

Educationalists

Jill went to Cambridge with Judith Fenn, another Fairfield girl whose parents, like Jill's, were working class. Her father, who left school at fourteen, was wounded in the Second World War and worked in the wine and catering industry; her mother was a nursery nurse until she married. Like Jill, Judith was the first person in her immediate family to go to university. She says that her parents were very supportive and wanted her to go to university, although she thinks that the idea of Oxbridge never crossed their minds. Judith's mother died when she was fifteen and the support and inspiration she received at Fairfield and later at Hyde Sixth Form College, was greatly instrumental in helping her to achieve so much.

Judith says that, like Jill, she has never felt discriminated against because of her gender. She attributed this to the fact that both she and Jill were pretty straight talking, confident individuals. Judith found that being working class at Cambridge was hard at first and during her time there she did tend to gravitate towards other working class people who became and remain very good friends. She also felt that middle class, or privately educated people, seemed to have an in-built sense of confidence. However, since that time, because of her professional life, she has not been as aware of her background and the life she leads now is middle-class.

After graduating, Judith trained as a teacher and spent a number of years in the independent sector, becoming deputy head at The Godolphin & Latymer School. She now works for the Independent Schools Council where she oversees newly qualified teachers. She also liaises with Government Departments on teaching issues and is now working on the Government's review of teaching standards as the independent sector's representative on the review panel.

Judith says that she owes a great deal to the staff and ethos of Fairfield. She learned good academic habits, self-discipline and social skills and remains incredibly grateful for her education there.[31]

Rhiannon Wilkinson (née Fell) is another Fairfield girl whose career has been in education, She graduated from Oxford with an MA degree in

Modern History and completed her Post-Graduate Certificate of Education (PGCE) at Bath. She then taught for a time in state schools, before moving to Hong Kong, where she was Head of History and Head of the sixth form at the Sha Tin ESF (English Schools Foundation) school in Hong Kong, for six years. Rhiannon also spent four years as Deputy Principal at Jerudong International School in Brunei.

Rhiannon is married to Donald Wilkinson who is also a head teacher. When her children were young she returned to Manchester and completed an M.Ed in Educational Leadership and Management at Manchester University. Rhiannon then went on to teach at the public co-ed boarding school of Haileybury where she was Director of Studies (the first female in its 200 year history to hold the post) and then Deputy Head responsible for the girls in the school. She left Haileybury in 2009 to become Head and Chief Executive of the Harrogate Ladies College group of schools.

According to her personal assistant at the school, Rhiannon always spoke, both in public and private, about how wonderful Fairfield was and what an inspirational Headmistress she had in Miss Gleaves when she was there. I was also told that Mrs Rhiannon Wilkinson has (and I quote) *"brought life, leadership, excitement and vision to the College"*[32] Fairfield can surely ask no more from its former pupils! The latest news of Rhiannon is that she will be taking up the Headship of Wycombe Abbey School in September 2013.

Fairfield girls continued to travel and live abroad because of their husbands' careers but there were many girls who were following their own careers in many different fields, some of which until recently had been male dominated. Degrees were taken in a wide variety of subjects including Materials Science and Technology, Town & Country Planning, Computer Studies, Biochemistry, Metallurgy, Food Science, Engineering Science, Geology, Electronic Engineering, Nuclear Engineering and Geology and Oceanography.

As in the fifties and sixties many Fairfield girls were choosing to study science subjects and a high proportion of Fairfield girls were pursuing scientific and mathematics careers. One Fairfield girl writing a number of years later said that one of the joys of studying at Fairfield was having female role models who were definitely not 'odd' despite being scientists or mathematicians. Being in an all girls' school also helped because there was no stereotyping. The Fairfield girl studying Materials Technology at Sheffield University reported that her first year course was comprised of seventy five students of whom only six were girls. She also said *"in this man's world in which I am competing some still have the idea that "a women's place is in the home", but on the whole I am accepted quite readily".*[33]

In 1975 Miss Gleave, who had been the Head Mistress since Miss Bradley retired in 1960, moved to another school. She had been an enthusiastic and encouraging Head Mistress and during her time the girls had achieved increasing academic success. Her place was taken by Mrs Tracey who was to support the school during its transition to a comprehensive school in 1980, and a period of increasing unemployment and economic recession.

THE END OF THE DECADE

For Fairfield, like many places, 1979 was a particularly difficult year. In January there were numerous strikes and the one involving petrol and oil meant that oil was not available for the oil-heated section of the building and a rota system of attendance was put in place.(the fifth forms were not affected). On January 22 the school was closed due to industrial action of NUPE workers. In May, members of the National Union of Teachers started operating sanctions in connection with national discussions on pay awards and an additional welfare assistant was brought in at lunch times to cover for the withdrawal of teachers.

At the beginning of November notices about the introduction of Comprehensive education in Tameside from September 1980 were posted.

However, after a year of distraction and disruption, came the good news at the end of December that six girls had been awarded places at Oxford or Cambridge.[34]

At the end of the decade Margaret Thatcher became Britain's first woman Prime Minister. Whatever one thinks about her politics, her position as head of the Government must have challenged many male assumptions about a woman's place in the world and for many women she was an example of what could be possible.

CHAPTER TEN

EQUALITY AT LAST?
1980-2013

"Bringing home the bacon and having to cook it as well"

Kate Kerrigan

COMPREHENSIVE EDUCATION

In September 1980 the school experienced one of the biggest and most important changes in its long history. The comprehensive system of education had gradually been introduced nationally since the second half of the 1960s but the Tameside Local Authority had held out as long as possible. However, by 1980 the decision was taken to introduce Comprehensive education in all Tameside's secondary schools.

It had taken four years to reach this decision and during that time various provisional plans had been made regarding staffing and the curriculum. After the local elections in 1976 a decision was made to review the situation. There had been much publicity and many discussions - Thames Television transmitted a programme entitled "Education in Tameside" some of which was filmed at Fairfield - and then, even after the Secretary of State for Education announced his intention of seeking a high court action to compel the Education Authority to implement the Comprehensive System, the decision was made in 1976 to retain the selective system. However, by November 1979 the final decision to go Comprehensive was made and during June 1980 Fairfield's staff had to apply for the posts in the new system. At the end of the month Local Authority Officers came into school to appoint staff for the beginning of the new school year in September.[1]

For Fairfield, one of the most significant changes was the loss of its sixth form. The Upper Sixth stayed to complete their course but the Lower Sixth went on to the newly organised sixth form colleges in Ashton and Hyde. The change, from a school which had mainly concentrated on academic subjects to one that would also cover a less rigorous curriculum, was a gradual one. It would take five years before the school was completely comprehensive but the school's aim was to maintain its high academic standards as well as providing a sound education for the less academic pupil.

"All Girls" School

Fairfield was to remain an all-girls school. Angela Holdsworth, the producer of the television programme *Out of the Dolls House,* in her book of the same name, commented that girls in a co-educational school often achieved less than those in a girls only school. It was thought that there were a number of reasons for this, including the girls' conditioning and girls 'shamming it' because they thought boys would not like them if they appeared brainy .[2] An analysis at a Girls' Grammar school, which became a co-educational comprehensive school in the late 1970s, found that maths and physics were unpopular with girls who were convinced they were bad at them. The girls were not very ambitious. They recognised the need to work, but only to supplement the family income or support their children, if ever the need arose.[3]

ECONOMIC RECESSION

As the 1980s progressed, the economic and unemployment situation worsened. The country lost between 15 and 20 per cent of its manufacturing base and unemployment increased from 1.4 million at the end of 1979 to over three million by the end of 1982. The government's answer to this was to introduce a series of benefit cuts which caused much anxiety. Girls at Fairfield would not have been immune from these experiences and worries. The school is situated in the poorer east side of Manchester and the girls would be aware of the problems of unemployment and poverty facing many families. The Headmistress, in her Reports to Speech Day during the 1980s, frequently commented on the problems of unemployment. In 1982 she mentioned the world recession and that the unemployment situation was particularly bad in Tameside, where local employers were making cutbacks in recruitment and where unemployment was above the national average. A distressing number of the unemployed were school-leavers. Fairfield had faired reasonably well - of 145 leavers, 120 continued in further education and the others were in employment or on Youth Opportunity schemes. She stressed the importance of the educational qualifications needed for the new technologies which were being developed.[4]

The general use of computers, in the work place, was still in its infancy, but by 1984 the school was using computers within the normal teaching programme and "computer studies" were added to the curriculum.[5] The Headmistress commented that in future no girl would leave school without some appreciation of the effect the computer was destined to play in her life.[6]

Those who were employed probably enjoyed an improved lifestyle. New labour-saving devices were becoming available along with other commodities. Refrigerators, washing machines and freezers were becoming part of expected household equipment and the more affluent homes owned video recorders, microwaves and dishwashers.

FEMALE EQUALITY

By the age of eleven, girls were generally ahead of boys. In 1985 they outshone boys in 'O' level grades, but did fractionally less well at 'A' level. Although they made up 42 per cent of undergraduates and 37 per cent of postgraduates, only 15 per cent of lecturers and a mere 3 per cent of professors were women. Even in those professions where women were joining in numbers equal to men, few aspired to the top jobs.[7] (I should point out here that according to figures issued by the Higher Education Statistics Agency in 2012, 20 per cent of professors are now women and women now make up nearly 45 per cent of the academic workforce. So things are gradually improving).

Social customs also influenced girls' choices. Such things, as nursery stories, advertisements, stereotyping in school reading books and everyday language, were thought to be unhelpful and these gradually began to change.[8]

There were few women working in business managerial roles. Even by 1988, women held only 15 per cent of management or management-related positions. This was only 5 per cent more than in the 1970s and the increase was mainly in junior management in retail, hotels, catering and local government. By the end of the decade women made up only 6 per cent of directors and 10 per cent of senior managers in Britain.

Although, by the end of the decade, more women were entering the professions - the number of women becoming chartered accountants, bankers and solicitors had increased - it was still unusual for a woman to reach the top. Also, many women left the professions because of their family commitments.[9]

By the late 1980s two thirds of married women had jobs. Their main reasons for working were money and companionship, rather than ambition or personal satisfaction. However it was increasingly recognised that a second income was often necessary to pay the mortgage or weekly shopping bills.[10]

Many women with professional jobs did not want to abandon a promising career, when they had children, but they then faced the dilemma of childcare. Those working in the civil service were fortunate in that they were eventually able to work part-time. Angela Holdsworth wrote that this enabled high ranking female civil servants to make their way up the career ladder although at a rather slower pace than those who worked full-time.[11]

Although by the end of the 1980s women were making inroads into the male world of politics, banking, the police, industry and commerce they were still held mainly responsible for the well-being of the family. One in eight families were looked after by women alone (compared with one in two hundred by men alone). Childcare costs prevented many women from continuing with their careers and many women couldn't work because they had to look after elderly relatives. It is not surprising, therefore, that there were so few women in 'top jobs'. Even with the example of a woman Prime Minister, only 6 per cent of MPs were women. [12]

Barbara Castle, the Labour MP and former Cabinet Minister who introduced the Equal Pay Act, commented on women's social and economic progress in an article in *The Guardian* in October 1984. She felt that in some ways the situation for women was going backwards and the cuts introduced by the government ruthlessly reduced the services that liberated women from some of their traditional domestic servitudes - home helps for the elderly, day centres, nursery schools, NHS community hospitals, help for the mentally handicapped, had all been severely cut. She felt that a few women, with a lot of luck, had managed to achieve what they wanted to, but women were still undervalued and underused.[13]

The school continued to have excellent results in the 'O' Level examinations. In 1985 when the school was fully comprehensive, the results were better than in the years when it was composed solely of grammar school girls.

The school continued to grow. By 1983 there were 830 girls. However an inspection of the laboratories found that they were in a general state of disrepair and antiquity. Some aspects required urgent attention and the Education Service Committee recommended that £57,000 be spent on improvements. These improvements were implemented by mid-September 1984 and Fairfield was able to boast of six up-to-date and well equipped laboratories.[14]

GIRLS' CAREERS

The choice of degree subjects in 1982 still remained eclectic and among the twenty two known degrees awarded to Fairfield girls were ones in Computation, Archaeology with Latin, Materials Science and Technology, Applied Social Studies, Social Services, Accountancy, Law, Botany and Zoology. A year later Pharmacy, Food Science, Psychology, Applied Maths and Computing Science, Biochemistry and Economic Social Studies were added to the list.[15]

Fairfield girls continued to demonstrate their capabilities and many began to branch out into the male dominated workplace. One girl began studying "Meat Management", at Salford College of Technology, with the aim of becoming a meat inspector. Another past pupil, having graduated in Materials Science and Technology, gained a Ph.D. at the Royal School of Mines at Imperial College, London and then went on to work for the Ministry of Defence in London. [16]

Oil trader

Amanda Goodwin left Fairfield in 1981 when she gained a scholarship to continue her studies in the sixth form at Manchester High School for Girls. It was there that, for the first time, she met girls who had a far more privileged background than herself and she described this as "quite an eye-opener". Many of the girls lived in the Cheshire stockbroker belt and were given new cars on their seventeenth birthdays and their parents read the Financial Times and discussed stocks and shares at breakfast time. Neither of her parents, or any of her relatives, had gone on to higher education but her mother, who had also been a pupil at Fairfield, was adamant that she should go to university so that she could have a professional career and live independently, if she wished. Amanda went on to gain a Ph.D. in bio-inorganic Chemistry from Manchester University in 1989 and worked as a Research Scientist for ICI Fibres in Cleveland. After a number of years she accepted an internal transfer to Conoco Ltd, the oil and gas company and worked in their supply and trading department. This was a complete change of direction in her career, taking it into the financial world instead of the purely scientific one.

Amanda has stayed at Conoco which is now Conoco Phillips (UK) Ltd. It is part of an international company which is the third largest integrated energy company in the US and the fifth largest refiner in the world. Amanda has made great progress in her career and has worked in a number of very responsible positions. In 1995 she became the first female Oil Trader for Conoco in the UK and then went on to become their Regulatory Affairs Manager. This position involved lobbying the Department of Trade and Industry, M.P.s, the House of Lords and the European Commission in connection with legislation impacting on the oil and gas industry, such as the Competition Act and the Utilities Act. Between 2001 and 2005 she worked as a Commercial Negotiator, negotiating agreements for new UK off-shore developments. She then gained experience in other departments including work as a Joint Venture Manager and in July 2011 she was appointed as a Senior Commercial Negotiator developing new European business ventures working from their London Office. She is now the Director of Commercial Development in the Europe Commercial section of the company.

She met with considerable male opposition when she was working in a mainly male environment as an oil trader. Amanda says that she was the first woman in the company in the UK to be a trader, and the men hated it. She was excluded from conversations, excluded from social events, and deliberately given misinformation. When she did go out with the traders, they would make sure they went to places such as lap dancing clubs to try and get rid of her. She says she saw many sights she would rather not have done, all because she didn't want to let them win. She found the most annoying thing was the groping hands around the office. The only other woman was the admin assistant/secretary who used to sit on the men's laps and give them a kiss and a cuddle, which was not Amanda's sort of thing as she frequently had to tell the men. Eventually she took a career move out of trading and prided herself that she was there for three years – the next woman to become a trader left after only six months.

Amanda says that times have changed now and there are many women traders in the company. A number of years later, one trader who had been on the trading floor at the time Amanda was trading asked her why she hadn't complained about harassment. Amanda says that when she looks back now, she can see his point of view but at the time sheer determination kept her going and she would not have even considered a complaint that would have potentially damaged her career.

Not only has Amanda had a high powered career but she has married and is now the mother of two boys aged sixteen and eleven. She said this was only made possible by the steadfast support of her husband. He was an advertising executive but when they decided to start a family a decision was made that he would retrain as a teacher so that he would be available during school holidays . When their first son was born they employed a child minder when her husband, Michael, was teaching. When their second son was born the family moved to Aberdeen in connection with Amanda's work, and Michael gave up his teaching job and spent the first year purely looking after the children. He used to attend the mother and toddler events with all the mums. Amanda took six weeks' maternity leave, after their first child, and twelve weeks after their second. Now that she is working in London, Amanda goes down by train from their home in Cleveland on Monday mornings and travels back on Thursday evening. She works from home on Fridays and is able to pick up the children from school one day a week. Amanda says that she has kept in touch with the group of girls who were on her PhD course and although a number have married she is the only one with a family.[17] We will see later in this chapter that the experience of Amanda and her fellow PhD students is reflected in statistics published recently, as is the experience of Pauline Jones.

Corporate Lawyer

It wasn't just in the scientific field that Fairfield girls excelled and quite a number, like Pauline Jones, entered the legal profession. In 1986 she went to Nottingham University to study law and after a year at law school in Chester she went on to take a Master's degree at Leicester University. She worked as a corporate/ commercial lawyer for three years. Pauline enjoyed working on big corporate deals and the satisfaction of mergers and acquisitions. She felt, for her, it was more positive work than dealing with litigation. She herself didn't experience any discrimination because of her sex but some of her friends did – one made the big mistake of mentioning in an appraisal that she planned to start a family. She was also aware that senior women colleagues were definitely not offered Partnerships to the same extent as their male colleagues. She cannot recall any woman lawyer with a family working part time and it was unheard of, for a Partner.

Pauline then went to work 'in house' for Equifax, a US information services company, at their European head office in London for ten years. She enjoyed the business focus to her legal work and became their European Legal Director, responsible for their legal functions across their European operations and this work involved extensive travel around Europe. She also became a member of the European Management team, responsible for the strategic direction and management of the whole European business so her input and involvement was far more than providing legal expertise.

Pauline found working for an American company difficult in a number of ways. She commented that the Americans were not interested in understanding the different working culture in the UK compared to the US, and the very different culture again in their Spanish and Portuguese businesses. As a Director and a member of the senior management team, she would not have been able to work part-time if she had decided to start a family. Americans took far fewer holidays compared to the UK and Europe and believed that their employees should be contactable twenty four hours a day, seven days a week. They could never understand why most of their Spanish and Italian offices took the whole of August off.

Pauline says that her thirties were all about her career, enjoying the benefits of it and life in London, going to theatres, dining out, and weekends in Europe. She was able to travel extensively in South and Central America and South East Asia. She says that she does not regret any of it, but does think that she fell into the trap of focusing so much on her career in her thirties, that when she suddenly decided at thirty eight that she wanted something more, especially a family, she found she had left it rather late. Having been used to things going her way, she thought that having a family would be easy, and she is sure there are other professional women who are leaving it quite late and are just as blissfully unaware of the statistics, as she was.

Just over three years ago Pauline left Equifax to join her boyfriend (now her husband) in New Zealand. They live right by the sea and are only a ten-minute drive from the city of Wellington. Pauline says that it's a very different lifestyle from that in London. New Zealanders work very hard, but they are very good at leaving work on the dot of 5 pm and going to the beach, playing sport or going fishing. It is definitely more relaxed and Pauline thinks people are not as driven to work that bit harder and longer as they are in Northern Europe. Her husband says he does work harder than he did in England but the hours are shorter, plus there is a lot less commuting compared to London.

When I corresponded with her in 2011 she was not currently practising as a lawyer but was working as a volunteer with refugees accepted into New Zealand under the United Nations quota scheme. She took a deliberate decision not to find work as a lawyer in New Zealand as there was no point continuing in a high pressure job —- she could have stayed in London for that, and she wanted to take some time out so they could try to start a family.[18]

Police Inspector

Many Heads of Schools see it as their duty to give advice and to share their philosophies with their pupils at the annual speech day. Mrs Tracy and Mrs Fields, who was appointed in 1986, would be happy to know that the thoughts and ideas they shared with Fairfield girls were taken to heart and acted upon by many in their audience. One year it was stressed that ability alone was not sufficient - persistence and motivation was also needed. The girls were told to put maximum effort into all they undertook and, above all else, they should remember, they could never attain that for which they had not worked.[19]

Claire Galt, who was at school from 1985 to 1990, exemplifies such a Fairfield girl. Claire, for as long as she could remember, had wanted a police career but after gaining her 'A' levels she was still too young to enrol in the police. She had to wait until she was twenty one before she could apply but, after taking various tests, she became a police woman in 1996 aged twenty two.

Her two years on probation were served in Tameside, as part of their response team. She stayed at Tameside for another year and this was then followed by three and a half years with the Traffic Unit in Oldham. She was the only woman on this unit and whilst she was there she had the experience of helping to deal with the Oldham riots. These riots which took place in the summer of 2001 were the worst, racially motivated riots, in the UK for fifteen years. They were the outcome of a long period of inter- racial tensions and attacks between the local whites and the Asian and Muslim communities. Most violence occurred in the Glodwick area of the town. Five hundred youths were involved and one hundred riot officers were at the scene. The riots lasted over a period of three to four days. Petrol bombs, bricks and bottles were thrown against the riot police and several cars were set alight including an occupied police van. Thirty two police vehicles were damaged and twenty people injured, including fifteen police officers. There was extensive coverage by local, national and international newspapers and television. It was an experience that Claire would never forget.

The next year Claire successfully sat her Sergeant's examination and was promoted to Sergeant and transferred to Stockport in 2002. In 2003 Claire married Roger, who is also a police officer, and in the same year she sat the first part of the examinations for Inspector. The pass mark was 65 per cent and Claire scored 64.5 per cent and failed. This was something of a watershed moment at a time, now that she was thirty years old, when she needed to review her life and ambitions. Claire and Roger decided that they would like a child and two years later she was pregnant. Claire had not given up on her police career and she sat the first part of the Inspector exam again when she was eight and a half months pregnant. This time she passed and when her little boy was born she took four months maternity leave. She then applied for a position in the Performance and Statistics Unit which gave her more regular 7 am to 3 pm hours. Claire and her husband managed the care of their pre-school boy by being able to work on different shifts. They also had help from both sets of grandparents.

In 2007 Claire passed Part II of the Inspector exam and was promoted to Response Inspector at Tameside. From January 2009 she has been responsible for the Tameside West Neighbourhood (this covers Droylsden, Audenshaw and Denton). and heads a team of forty five people which include three Sergeants, twenty Constables, and sixteen Police Community Service Officers. As an Inspector she has many responsibilities. She has regular performance meetings with her team and is Chair of the Neighbourhood Action Team which is concerned with anti-social behaviour, the New Charter Housing Association, the Youth Service, Fire Service, Local Authority and the Probation Service. She has input into the action plans for offenders, which are compiled by the Probation Officers. Attendance at Football matches as part of the Police Support Unit of three sergeants and twenty one Police Constables is sometimes needed. On an average day she will receive about sixty emails.

On 18th September 2012 Claire experienced the most traumatic and painful event of her career. It was to shock and horrify the whole country. Pc Nicola Hughes and Pc Fiona Bone were shot dead by Dale Cregan from Droylsden outside a house on the Hattersley Estate in the Tameside South Neighbourhood. Dale Cregan had been on the run from the police since he had killed Mark Short inside the Cotton Tree Inn in Droylsden and had also murdered Mark's father David on the streets of nearby Clayton. Cregan had lured the two policewomen to the house and had used a gun and a grenade to kill them.

Many of Claire's team were involved in various aspects of the Cregan man- hunt and she and her staff were deeply affected by the shooting of their colleagues who were based at Hyde. Claire, along with most officers from Tameside attended the funerals of Fiona and Nicola and she said that it was just a very dark time from the day it happened until a long time afterwards.

Claire was involved in getting the Cotton Tree public house closed and in working to build up community confidence in Droylsden. Claire's colleague Steve Phillips completed a charity run in memory of the two policewomen in May 2013, running 230 miles over six days from Hyde to Bournemouth. Claire ran the first eighteen miles from Hyde to Macclesfield and her husband ran all the first day and the last day. They both felt they needed to do something positive.

Life, of course, has to move on. She leads a very busy life and acknowledges that juggling priorities is sometimes difficult. However, she tries to be very well organised both at work and with her domestic routines. On the home front many of the chores are shared with her husband. She is very active and often, as a way of relaxing after work, will go running for a mile or two. Claire says that she has always thrived on pressure. She loves her work and it is the career that she has always wanted to follow.

Claire says that she has not been the subject of any discrimination because she is a woman. She thinks that the ethos in the Police Force with regard to its attitude towards women, had changed before the late 1980's. She is judged on the quality of her work, not on her gender. [20]

At the end of the decade Fairfield had been a comprehensive school for nearly ten years. Many people in 1980 had been extremely apprehensive about its future and many had thought at the time that Fairfield would not be able to continue to provide the excellent standard of education which it had done in the past. Their worries were proved to be unfounded and its reputation remained intact. The difference now was that the excellent education it provided was available to many who previously would have been excluded.

THE 1990s

Fairfield started the 1990's by taking the dramatic step of appointing its first male Head Teacher. Mr Chris W. Penter was appointed Headmaster in February 1990 and he would be the instigator of the most important change in the running of the school since the move to comprehensive education in 1980.

Mr Penter fought hard for the school to be given Grant Maintained Status in 1993. This meant that the school would no longer be under the control of the Local Education Authority and would be funded directly by a grant from the government. Although the move did not provide large amounts of extra funding, it enabled the Governors to determine school related priorities and set in motion a development plan for the future. They were now able to go into the marketplace in search of value for money and this had proved of great benefit. Already improvements were evident in repair work completed around the school, more money spent on books and equipment and much improved financial management.[21] In 1993 the school achieved the best overall results in recent years and was placed in the Daily Mail table of the top 200 state schools.

In 1994 the Headmaster was able to report that during the year a new purpose-built technology block was due to be opened and that the Department of Education had agreed to fund the construction of six new classrooms to house the Geography and History Departments. He hoped that these would be ready for September 1996 and would be a fitting addition to the school during its bi-centenary year.[22]

BICENTENARY YEAR

1996 was an important year for the school. The school had been established in the last week of June 1796 and for two hundred years it had, without a break, educated girls from Droylsden and beyond. Fairfield is one of the oldest girls' schools in the country. There are a few girls' schools which are a little older but they are either private, co-educational, voluntary aided or partially selective. Research has found only one fully comprehensive girls' school which is older than Fairfield and this is the Sarah Bonnell School in London which was founded in 1777.

The bi-centenary celebrations began with a Service of Thanksgiving in Manchester Cathedral and continued in October with a visit by the Duchess of Gloucester.

The Duchess cut a ribbon to officially open the new six-classroom teaching block and visited the new technology building. The school also held an open-day celebration at the school when many former pupils from all over the country (and further afield) met and renewed old friendships. The Old Girls Association donated new Honours Boards which were placed in the newly refurbished School Hall.[23]

The elderly 'girls' gathering that weekend would have seen many changes during their lifetimes, none more so than in society's attitude towards women. The single girl was now seen as independent and successful. It was no longer seen as a failure if a girl didn't marry and if she did marry and have

The youngest girl in the school presents the Duchess with a bouquet whilst Deputy Head
Mrs Quinn looks on

children she could still pursue her career. Girls were more confident and
motivated at school and by the mid-1990s teachers were anxiously searching
for the causes of *boys'* not girls' under-achievement.[24]

THE CONTINUING STRUGGLE FOR EQUALITY

Women were continuing to make inroads into male dominated institutions.
In 1994 the first female priests were ordained by the Church of England and
after the 1997 General Election, 101 women Labour MPs entered Parliament.

However, although women had more freedom than ever before their
situation was often difficult and stressful. They often found that 'Having it
all' meant 'Doing it all' and from 1993 there was a steady increase in mental
disorders such as depression and panic attacks suffered by women. A NHS
study found that, between 1997 and 2000, these rose by 20 per cent, whereas
there was no increase at all among men.

An article in *The Guardian* in 1998 entitled "Get a life, girls" gave some useful advice. It suggested that *"the point of the whole sexual revolution was to give women fuller lives: it was not so they could grimly labour to earn only three quarters of what men did, then come home to nothing but housework and screaming children".* It went on to advise women that what they needed to have was some *"consuming passion"* that they would not allow anything to get in the way of, as men seemed to have, like watching sport or drinking with the boys. A woman would be more assertive if she had lots of things she liked to do. She would have a certain joie de vivre and would not be dependent on the approval of others."[25]

R.A.F. Squadron Leader

If one of your *'consuming passions'* was the work you did, then you were indeed fortunate. Squadron Leader, Karen Lofthouse (née McKnight) is one of these fortunate women and is definitely doing work which she is passionate about. Karen was Games Captain at the school in 1994 and her earnest wish was to join the Royal Air Force. In 1995 she was awarded one of sixty national RAF scholarships which enabled her to complete her 'A' Levels before going into the RAF. It also covered twenty hours of flying lessons, ten hours of which she flew solo. She successfully completed her Initial Officer Training course at RAF Cranwell and when she graduated as a Pilot Officer in May 1997 she was one of the youngest ever female officers.

Karen then went on to train as an Air Traffic Control Officer at the Central Air Traffic Control School at RAF Shawbury in Shropshire and worked in York and Lincoln and for a few months in the Falkland Islands. She received further training at the Air Traffic Control School in the use of area radar and was stationed at the main national Air Traffic Control Centre at Swanwick until May 2005. All high-level aircraft, all over the country, is under surveillance by the RAF. Their main role is the protection of UK air space and their knowledge is of the utmost importance on occasions such as the eruption of volcanic ash over Iceland in 2010. Karen then moved to RAF Leeming in Yorkshire where she controlled aircraft flying within north Yorkshire, up to sixty miles around Leeming.

In February 2005 Karen married Garyth, who was also an RAF Air Traffic Controller, until he retired in 2008. Their daughter Millicent was born in 2005 and their son Roman in 2007. They have been spared many childcare problems because soon after Roman was born they bought and shared a large house in York with Karen's mother and step-father who is retired

In 2009 Karen was deployed to Afghanistan for four months where she worked as the Deputy Senior Air Controller at Camp Bastion in Helmand Province. Before she went she was heavily involved in the pre-deployment training of her unit and during her time there she dealt with more than 12,000 aircraft movements a month. These involved the transport of troops and supplies, helicopter manoeuvres and medical emergencies. She told me that it wasn't generally known that Camp Bastion is the fifth busiest UK controlled airport.

She has a lot of energy and was still able to find time to raise more than £2000 for "Help for Heroes" by running a full marathon with the US Marine Corp in the searing 50 degree Afghan heat. She found it really difficult in the heat and the dust but was extremely happy to finish the 26.2 miles in four hours fourteen minutes. This Charity is very important to her. She said that the danger to the guys on the ground was really brought home to her when she saw an IED (improvised explosive device or roadside bomb) explosion from the Air Traffic Control Tower which sadly killed one of the U.K. troops. She hoped that the money she raised would go some way towards helping the injured and their families.

Karen arrived back from Afghanistan just before Christmas 2009. Her children had been well cared for but it took a little time for them to start relating to her again. Millicent was four and Roman was under three years old.

Karen left RAF Leeming in April 2011 to work as Deputy Senior Air Traffic Control Officer and Local Examining Officer at RAF Linton-on-Ouse - home to the No. 1 Flying Training Squadron.

In November 2011 she learned that she had been selected for promotion to the rank of Squadron Leader and she took up her post within the Flight Safety Division, at RAF High Wycombe, in February 2012. On 13th January 2013 Karen moved back to RAF Leeming to take up the position of Senior Air Traffic Control Officer, commanding a Squadron of thirty two people. This move meant that she could live back at home again and be with her family instead of only seeing them at the week-end. Karen told me that "living back at home and being a mum again is fab!" She is still keeping busy.

She has taken up triathlon and will be running in the York Marathon as well as ski racing for the RAF every January and February in the Inter Services against the Army and Navy.

When asked about the attitude to women within the RAF, Karen said she felt that it was sometimes difficult for a woman. They were seen as the weaker sex and had therefore to try harder and show that they had the strength and ability to lead their group. She said you have to be credible, you are very much part of a team and they look to you for leadership".[26]

Nuclear power engineer

Another Fairfield girl, who wanted to pursue a career in an area which was still thought of as being male dominated, is Rachael Harrison. Rachael left Fairfield in 1992 and graduated from Manchester Metropolitan University in 1998 with a B.Eng. Honours degree in Mechanical Engineering. Shortly after this she began working for British Energy at Heysham 2 nuclear power station. Rachael was the only female engineer and the first female graduate engineer that Heysham 2 had employed and she wrote to the Old Girls' Association saying that she hoped that her story would *"spur on current girls to keep pushing towards their chosen career - no matter how obscure"*. Rachael married in 2004 and in the same year became the Operating Experience Engineer where she was responsible for investigating events and reviewing investigation findings from around the world and ensuring that the knowledge gained was fed into processes at Heysham. In 2009 she became Head of the Technical Training Group which gives her the responsibility of managing the training of all Engineering Support Personnel at both Heysham Power Stations. [27]

Oil Company Engineer

Kelly Richardson who was at Fairfield from 1995 to 2000 is another pupil who has chosen a career in a male dominated profession. She studied for a BSc in Physics at Durham University and then gained an MSc from Heriot-Watt University in Petroleum Engineering. Since that time she has worked for BP as an Engineer in countries such as Norway, Canada, Angola and the UK. She works both onshore and offshore, working on rigs, boats and platforms and moved to Luanda, Angola in October 2012.

She has travelled extensively over the last few years and made many interesting visits which have included seeing gorillas in Rwanda, hiking up to the top of the Lost World Mountain of Roraima in Venezuela, driving around all of Alaska and visiting the beautiful city of Cape Town to celebrate New Year.

Kelly told me that the type of discrimination she has faced in the work place isn't the same as that experienced by women twenty years ago. However, she says that although she has never faced direct discrimination, there is constant pressure to act in a more masculine way and managers openly ask that certain traits, those which are seen as more feminine, are supressed. She told me that if she sometimes speaks passionately about something she is accused of being emotional. If in the course of her work she has to criticise somebody who has to report to her (especially if he is an older man) she is described as being hormonal or told that it's her time of the month – all of which distracts attention from a poor performance. She was once told in a performance review "you're good looking and you dress well. You'll get far" and that was a comment by someone who actually did respect her intelligence. She is asked when she will be taking time off work to have a baby and she is often mocked by older men with children for being "past her shelf life" as she is almost thirty without children. Kelly says that this is difficult to hear, especially as she knows that when the other female in her team had a baby she was then passed over for some of the more challenging work because she had a child. .

She feels that most women in her position face a dilemma with their life choices. When should they have children? They want a career and work hard early on in life, then soon they find themselves, at the age of thirty five, when having children is much more of a challenge. When do they choose to put their careers on hold to have the family they want and how do they balance the needs of both a career and a family when they are seen as both homemakers and bread winners? Kelly felt that men seem to have accepted women in the work place, but neither men nor women seem to want to acknowledge that there are essential differences between the sexes.[28]

Award winning charity fundraiser
Sarah Jones also started at Fairfield in 1995 and went on to study English at

Oxford in 2002. Like many other Fairfield girls who went to Oxbridge, her parents were not middle-class or university educated. At first she found it difficult to fit in but she persevered and after three years she could look back, not only at a wonderful experience that she would have hated to have missed but also on the many lifelong friendships she had made. Most of her group seemed to be very confident, privately educated, wealthy students – the sort of people she really hadn't met before. For their part, apparently, they had never met anybody quite like her. They were intrigued by her Northern accent and used to ask her to repeat various phrases! They said she reminded them of Julie Walters in 'Educating Rita' and Caroline Aherne the actress and creator of the 'The Royle Family' and "Mrs Merton". Her working class lifestyle was one that was completely unknown to them, although I suspect it didn't take them long to realise that Sarah was an intelligent and motivated young woman.

After graduating her life took a somewhat unorthodox course. She travelled in Brazil for a number of months before coming back to work in London for a short time. She then went to work as a volunteer in South Africa with Aids orphans and then in Cape Town as a volunteer, for a large charity, eventually being given free accommodation. Her experiences in South Africa were quite diverse. Her work with Aids orphans was in remote rural tribal villages and she was able to experience something of ordinary country life. Her life in Cape Town for the Amy Biehl Charity Foundation was entirely different. This charity organises cultural, educational and building programmes in the townships in an effort to reduce the levels of crime and HIV/AIDS and to give young people opportunities to live more healthy and creative lives. Sarah worked in the office of the Foundation in Cape Town. She said she lived and worked in a beautiful part of the town in a security-gated area housing many Europeans which didn't feel at all like the 'real' South Africa.

Sara worked for a year in South Africa and then came back to London to work and replenish her funds before she was off again, this time to Sierra Leone. Sierra Leone had suffered a devastating civil war for eleven years which had been resolved in 2000. It is, however, a very poor country and is ranked the eighth lowest country in the Human Poverty Index. Sara went out to Sierra Leone in October 2009 to work for the Welbodi Partnership as a fundraising co-ordinator. The Welbodi Partnership was established to support paediatricians in Sierra Leone. Child health statistics there are some of the worst in the world. One in four children die before they are five – mainly due to preventable and treatable diseases. The maternal death rate is one of the highest in the world. There is only one children's hospital in the country and only one qualified paediatrician in the country's public health service. The Welbodi Partnership has been working since 2007 with the Ministry of Health and Sanitation to help improve this Children's Hospital which is called the "Ola During Children's Hospital" and is located in Freetown, the country's capital. During her time there Sara raised £40,000 for the Charity and in so doing won the Vodaphone International Funding Competition.

When Sarah arrived at the hospital the country had no free national health service but on 27 April 2010 free health care for pregnant and lactating women and children under five was established. Sara was able to experience the excitement felt on that day and see the hundreds of young children who were brought to the hospital.

Sarah felt that living in Sierra Leone was a life-changing experience. Unlike her time in Cape Town she was living alongside the local people and could see at first-hand their problems and their poverty. On one particular day in the centre of the town Sarah watched a poor young girl of about nine who was trying to sell sachets of water. She was suddenly hit slightly by a vehicle which ran over and completely destroyed all her goods. The vehicle didn't stop and the young girl was left weeping in the road. She had been depending on the small amount of money she would have earned and now it had all vanished. Sarah felt she had to do something. Sarah says she will never forget the look of sheer joy, and relief on the girl's face when she handed her some money. Such instances as this certainly made her appreciate her home and family and the standard of living back in England and helped to put a lot of things into perspective.

Sarah came back to London to work four days a week, while studying part-time for a Masters' Degree in psychology. She graduated in July 2011 and worked as an Assistant Clinical Psychologist, at a school in Bournemouth for 16 to 19 year old boys who suffer from Asperger Syndrome. In July 2013 she returned to Manchester and is working for the N.H.S. as an Assistant

Clinical Psychologist with the Manchester Early Intervention Psychosis Team. She hopes that in the near future she will be accepted on a course to study for a Doctorate in Clinical Psychology – the career that she has been interested in ever since she was at Fairfield.[29]

Neuroscientist

Sarah's 'very best friend' at Fairfield and at Audenshaw Sixth Form College was Kelly Wild. Kelly went on to Lancaster University in 2002 to study Biological Sciences. While there, she suffered a terrible family bereavement but managed, although under tremendous stress, to achieve a good degree. Like Sarah, her career after university didn't follow a straight course. She had obtained a place on a PGCE (Post-Graduate Certificate in Education) course in Secondary School Science at Manchester University but because of her anxious last year at university she decided to take a year out from studying. She began work in the Clinical Radiology Department at the Manchester Medical School and the following summer she taught horse riding at a summer camp in upstate New York. She began her PGCE course on her return in September but was very unhappy on the course and realised that a teaching career was a wrong choice. She had thoroughly enjoyed working in an academic/medical setting in the Manchester University Medical School and had applied after she left for a PhD studentship although she had thought that she had very little chance of being successful. Much to her astonishment she was offered a fully funded three year studentship from the Medical Research Council to conduct Neuroscience research for her PhD.

Researching sensory motor integration in Autism gave Kelly the opportunity to present her work in places around the country including London, Birmingham, York and Cambridge. She also won a travel award to attend and present at the International Meeting for Autism Research in Philadelphia in 2010. She has also published a number of papers on her research in scientific journals. Kelly passed her PhD viva at the end of 2010 and was awarded a PhD in Neuroscience. She then took up a position with the NHS and is working as a Clinical Studies Officer for the Mental Health Research Network based at Manchester Royal Infirmary.

Kelly's story, like that of Sarah Jones', shows that even if things are not straightforward at the outset, perseverance in finding the right career path brings success in the end. Like Sarah, Kelly came from a working class background and could not have gained her PhD without full funding from the Medical Research Council. She had friends on the course who were on self-funded placements which cost up to £26,000 a year. She says that there was no way she would ever have been able to do that.

Like Sarah she was very much aware of her northern accent and sometimes felt like the comedy character at meetings. She also thought that sometimes she might not have been taken seriously. She realises that she was probably being over-sensitive and she has become less self-conscious as time goes by, but at the time it was a big issue for her.

In the team in which Kelly is working there are five females and only one male. She believes that the research world, especially in areas such as Biological Science and Medicine, is changing towards being female dominated. However, she says the vast majority of Principle Investigators and Consultants are still male, but these are of the older generation, and she thinks, in years to come, this will change.[30]

FAIRFIELD IN THE 21ST CENTURY

Fairfield's status as a Grant Maintained School was short-lived. With the change of government in 1997 came the news that Grant Maintained Schools were to be abolished with effect from the 1st April 1999 and Fairfield then become a Foundation School. The headmaster stated the Local Authority would once again exercise considerable control over the school, particularly in relation to both finance and admissions. He expected that the school's funds would be cut and said that some of the grants they were now receiving had already been reduced.[31]

School Performance
During the last ten years, Fairfield's academic achievements have been noteworthy and the results in the GCSE examinations for 2011 were outstanding. Fairfield was Tameside's top performing school with 99 per cent of the pupils gaining five or more A*- C passes and of these, 77 per cent achieved top grades in English and Maths; and the results for 2012 were even

better. The school was the best in Greater Manchester and the third best in the whole of the North West, when looking at "value added" scores. Mr John Hedley, who took over from Mr Chris Penter as head teacher in 2005, was notified early in 2012, by the Minister of State for Schools, that the 2011 results put Fairfield amongst the 100 top- performing schools, based on sustained improvement in each year from 2008 to 2011. Mr Hedley commented that the girls arrived with attainment levels equal to the national average and left with results way above. [32]

In April 2011 the school was offered the opportunity to convert to an Academy. Mr Hedley said that there would be no external noticeable change. The school would continue to be known as Fairfield High School and the word Academy would not appear in the school's name or stationery. The only difference would be that they would no longer be maintained by the Local Authority and the 12.5 per cent of the school's budget that had previously been retained by the Local Authority for administration would come directly to the school. This would allow the school more freedom to allocate funds to its own priorities and obtain best value for money.

This extra funding had enabled the school to employ a member of the 'Aim Higher' team. Mr Hedley explained that this organisation sought to raise the aspirations of young people. He pointed out that many Fairfield girls came from homes where the experience of higher education is less than half the national average. These girls didn't have a parent who would say "How about doing this or that". He felt that it was important that the school encouraged the girls to aim high and to realise that studying at Oxford or Cambridge or becoming an airline pilot was not an impossible dream. The 'Aim Higher' team member he recruited is supporting the school's careers advice and guidance service and establishing more solid links with the Universities.

It would seem that the school's outstanding results are partly due to the fact that Fairfield is an all-girls school. A report, published in March 2009 by the Good Schools Guide, followed 700,000 girls and found that those who sat GCSEs in single-sex state schools, all did better than could have been predicted by their scores at the end of primary school. By contrast 20 per cent of those who attended co-ed schools did worse than could have been expected from their school records at age of eleven. The publishers of the study said that they never expected to see such a difference.

There has been continued improvement in the school's technical equipment. By 2012 the school had eight hundred computers for the girls to use as well as others used by the staff and every girl was equipped with a computer memory stick that could hold, in text, the equivalent of the school library. There are also a number of classrooms which have 'idesks' – desks which convert to computers.

Sporting Achievements

It was not only in academic subjects that the girls excelled. In the sporting and athletic field they have had their successes. This was probably helped by the building of a large Sports Hall in the grounds in 2005. It is extremely well equipped and is used out of school hours by members of the local community. Fairfield girls have been successful in sailing, volley ball and the triathlon. Hannah Mitchell and her partner gained fourth place in the Youth World Sailing Championships in 2010[33]; Julia Whalley was a member of the England North Volley Ball team which won silver in the UK School Games in 2009 and she has played for the England Junior team[34] and Georgia Taylor Brown became the Triathlon European Junior Female Champion in 2012.

The sedate young ladies playing tennis in 1900 in their long dresses and straw hats would be amazed.

Olympic Torchbearer

Although no Fairfield girl gained a place on an Olympic GB Team, there was at least one girl who represented Fairfield in the 2012 Olympic festivities. Kelly Outhwaite, who was in her last year at school was chosen to run with the Olympic torch. She was chosen from a list of 12,000 and was nominated by her best friend who described Kelly's voluntary work with disabled children and the help that she gave to a couple who were deaf.[35]

FEMALE INEQUALITY

Reading the School Prospectus for 2005 it was interesting to note that it was still found necessary to stress that one of the aims of the school was to guide pupils to develop their potential, *unhindered by the possible limiting effects of sex stereotyping.*[36]

During the writing of this book it seemed that hardly a day went by without there being some aspect of female inequality being discussed in the media.

The Working Mother

In 2002 Allison Pearson brilliantly and amusingly examined the pressures of modern motherhood in her book "I Don't Know How She Does It". The fact that ten years later this book was made into a film would suggest that things have changed very little.

In 2007 the American, Leslie Bennetts published her book *"The Feminine Mistake"* in which she further developed the ideas which Betty Friedan had put forward in her 1960s book *"The Feminine Mystique"*. Leslie suggested that it was possible to combine work with bringing up a family and that having a challenging career, and earning money made women feel good about themselves. Leaving their jobs and becoming financially dependent on their husbands, led to unhappiness as well as insecurity, if their husband became unemployed or died.

By 2010 the number of 'stay at home' mothers was the lowest ever recorded. Of the seven million mothers in Britain, five million worked. It was found that money was the main reason for working but a survey by www.workingmums.co.uk, in the summer of 2010, found that this was not the only reason - enjoyment of their job, a boost to self-esteem, a need for adult company, a desire to get out of the house as well as wanting to do well in their careers were also cited. Most women, particularly once their children were in school found that having some kind of independent existence - financial, professional and emotional - outside the home was important.

In March 2010 a television programme was broadcast entitled "Women". It asked to what extent women were living the feminist dream. It found that, despite the fact that new figures in January 2010 had revealed that almost half of Britain's working women earned as much as their partner, and 20 per cent actually earned more than their husband or boyfriend, the majority of women were still picking up the bulk of the domestic burden. It seemed that because mothers enjoyed a longer leave period than fathers after a child was born, their traditional role as the main carer was reinforced. By the time a mother went back to work it was accepted as the norm that she would be responsible for the childcare and she then had to struggle with dual responsibilities. Although studies like the British Household Panel Survey, had suggested that younger men were doing more of the childcare, enthusiasm for their children wasn't matched by a love of washing or ironing! It seemed that, overall, the general feeling was that although quite a number of women were "having it all" they were also having to "do it all". As Kate Kerrigan amusingly expressed it in the Sunday Times, *"women were now bringing home the bacon and having to cook it as well."*[37]

Although 20 per cent of wives are now earning more than their husbands and more women now have higher education qualifications than men in every age group up to the age of forty-four, the challenge for society is what happens when these clever hard-working ambitious women have children. The present quite generous employment legislation (thirty nine weeks statutory maternity pay plus an extra thirteen weeks leave) seems to be becoming counter-productive. As early as 2008 some employers were beginning to look upon women of child-bearing age as a liability in the workplace. It is illegal to ask a woman what her intentions are - i.e. ask her whether or not she will be returning to work, if she is returning what hours she will be prepared to work and how she will balance work and child. Lord Alan Sugar pointed out that not being able to ask women whether they planned to have children, gave businesses an easy option *"Just don't employ them"*. An Equalities Review commissioned by the government found that more than 70 per cent of recruitment agencies had been asked by clients to avoid hiring pregnant women or those of childbearing age - which includes everyone from teenagers to women over forty.

The 2008 Equality and Human Rights Committee (EHRC) Report, found that women's progress in the workplace seemed to be falling away. In many professions the number of women holding top posts had decreased and women comprised only 10.5 per cent of chief executives of media companies in the FTSE 350.

Nicola Brewer, Chief Executive of the EHRC stated that Britain could not afford to go on marginalising or rejecting talented people who failed to fit into traditional work patterns. Women made up nearly three out of five recent first-degree graduates, yet in some workplaces discrimination still exists and they are still directed towards traditionally female occupations. The EHRC Report put much of the blame on our rigid, inflexible approach to work. Having children, outdated working practices, a long-hours culture and the absence of good-quality, affordable childcare, together with the expectation that women will look after the family and run the house, leads many women to decide the strain is too much. They take a less challenging role or leave employment altogether.

On 17 August 2011 the Equality and Human Rights Commission issued a new Report entitled "Sex and Power". It found that the results of the Report differed very little from those in the previous Report of 2008. EHRC Commissioner Kay Carberry was reported as saying that the gender balance at the top had not changed much in three years, despite there being more women graduating from university and occupying middle management roles. They had hoped to see an increase in the number of women in positions of power, however this wasn't happening.

Research carried out by the Institute of Fiscal Studies showed that in Denmark every woman is entitled to free childcare. The result is a happy workforce and a generation of fulfilled women. It is interesting to note that Helle Thorning-Schmidt became Denmark's first female Prime Minister in October 2011. She has two children aged eleven and fifteen.

Rosie Boycott in *The Guardian* commented that "*we might have won the battle for equal education, but that counts for little when that talent is squandered in later years. We tell girls to reach for the stars as they are growing up, only to tell them to reach for the door, the moment they reproduce.*[38]

In early August 2013 the law firm Slater and Gordon published new research into the experience of working mothers. Of the two thousand working mothers they interviewed, more than half considered that their employers' and colleagues' attitude towards them changed when they became pregnant and one in four believed they were subjected to discrimination either before or after the birth of their child. Nearly half felt that having children had halted their career progression, while a third described rising up the career ladder as a mum as 'impossible'. 42 per cent felt those younger and without children were prioritised in the workplace over themselves. One in four had even been made to feel they were no longer required in their current workplace and had had pressure put on them to leave their position or reduce their role. A representative of Slater and Gordon said that the Report showed that there were still negative perceptions of women with children and this kind of attitude was short-sighted and bad for business. She said it was in everyone's interest to ensure that working mothers were allowed to work to their full potential. .

Professional Women Remaining Childless

The problems that children bring may well be the reason why many women graduates are remaining childless. According to official statistics about one in five women in Britain is now childless and new research from America into women born between 1968 and 1989 suggests that the real number may be much higher. In the United States 42 per cent of educated professionals at the age of forty do not have children.

According to the author of the American study, Lauren Leader-Chivee, the trend is similar in the UK and many other countries around the world. 80 per cent of these women are married or in committed relationships and, while some of them have fertility problems, the majority of those without children have made a choice not to become mothers.

Portrayal of Women in the Media

The role of the Media, in depicting women as rather frivolous and not particularly serious, is a cause for concern. Kira Cochrane in *The Guardian* in November 2010 stressed that young women desperately need role models and what the media gives them are heiresses, sex objects, surgery addicts and emotional wrecks. She criticised the media for its portrayal of women as sex objects in turmoil, as wives and girlfriends and as appendages to powerful men as was seen in the general election campaign in 2010. While female MPs were almost invisible, the appearance of Sarah Brown and Samantha Cameron was reported in detail.

Kira Cochrane pointed out that as women have grown more socially powerful, it seems that the wider culture is pumping out images intended to put women back in their place. Cochrane went on to say that role models are more important to women than to men. In a male-dominated culture in which men make up 78 per cent of MPs and 95 per cent of FTSE 100 chief executives - men and boys, and specifically white, middle-class men and boys have an army of examples who show that success is possible.[39]

In August 2009 there was an interesting news story about Hilary Clinton,

US Secretary of State. She was asked at a Press Conference what her husband, Bill Clinton's, view was on a particular foreign policy issue. She replied that her husband wasn't the Secretary of State, she was. She went on to say *"You want me to tell you what my husband thinks? If you want my opinion, I will tell you my opinion. I am not going to be channelling my husband"* I noticed that when this news item was shown on Breakfast TV the male presenter suggested that perhaps she had got out of bed on the wrong side. Nobody made the suggestion that, if a male Secretary of State had been asked about his wife's views, the reply might have been even more robust!

FAIRFIELD GIRLS' QUESTIONAIRE

I wanted to find out what Fairfield girls of today thought about female equality and asked the Year Eleven girls in 2009 to complete a questionnaire. 133 girls completed this and their answers provide interesting reading.

Female equality

One of the questions asked "Do you think that the fact that you are female will restrict you in any way in the future?" Seventy six girls (57 per cent) answered "Not at all", fifty four (41per cent) said "A little" and only three (2 per cent) said "Very much so". The majority of the girls just ticked the boxes but some did give their reasons.

One girl who answered "Not at all" stated *"I will always achieve my goals to the best of my ability. The roles of men and women have changed a lot over the years but I will always fight for what I want"*. Another girl said *"If you want something you should work for it until you're satisfied, regardless of gender"*

The reasons given for "a little" were mostly centred on work. Most mentioned discrimination, stereotypes and prejudice in the work place. One pupil said *"because of stereotypes, I will possibly find it harder to get a more 'high flying' job than a man"*. There were also answers such as *"some men don't like women being higher up in business"* and *"some men think they are better than women and are sexist"*. The fact that men were paid more and still had different rights was mentioned. One girl thought that women were still looked down on but she added that maybe this would be different when she was older. Pregnancy was only briefly mentioned and childcare not at all. The majority of the girls were not yet sixteen so perhaps it's not surprising that the problems of motherhood had not occurred to them.   Two of the girls who thought that they would be very much restricted gave their reasons. One said *"women still aren't thought of as equal in the workplace so although we can get far I think there will be some prejudice"*. The other girl commented *"I feel that equality is still very distant between men and women and that there is still a huge lack of respect for women in society (in the work place and out of it)"*.

Careers

The questionnaire also asked the girls about the careers they were hoping to follow. Their answers showed their ambitions were wide-ranging. Teaching was the most popular career choice, followed by law, psychology and accountancy. Other choices included medicine, journalism, police, army, RAF, photography, social work, physiotherapy, veterinary work, floristry, biology, food science, politics, sport and plumbing.

Higher Education

The questionnaire found that, except for five pupils, all the girls were hoping to go to college. Of these five, one was going into the Army, two were taking up apprenticeships, one was hoping to work for the public services and one was going abroad. Forty eight girls specifically mentioned going on to university and a further nineteen gave career choices which would need a university degree but only "college" was mentioned. The number of girls hoping to go on to university has therefore increased tremendously over the last sixty years. In the 1950s there were rarely more than seven or eight girls each year who did so and by the 1980s the number was sometimes over twenty.

Leisure Activities

Girls were also asked about their leisure activities. Of the choices that were offered listening to music came top, closely followed by computers. Next in popularity were cinema and television. Reading and sport were the least popular. Of the activities specifically chosen by the girls, socialising or going out was the most popular, followed by shopping. Playing a musical instrument, art and dancing were chosen by a number of others. Organised activities such as guides, scouts or youth clubs were only chosen by a minority. There were a number of sporting pastimes which helped to balance the rather less-active choices. These included scuba diving, volleyball, Thai boxing and horse riding. It was interesting to note that there were no signs of crafts such as needlework, embroidery or dressmaking. The Fairfield girl of the nineteenth century, and even up to the mid twentieth century, would have been amazed.

Education

Fairfield's good reputation owes much to the excellence of its teaching staff and this did not go unnoticed by the pupils. They were asked "What are the best things about being educated at Fairfield". Over eighty pupils, - 60 per cent - stated that the teachers were the best thing and they thought it important enough to give their personal reasons and to mention individual teachers. They spoke about the teachers being inspiring, encouraging, and making lessons interesting. They were described as amazing, supportive, and enthusiastic as well as having well-disciplined lessons.

The next-highest group said that one of the best things about the school was the friendships that they had made. Some girls described the school as having a calm, disciplined and well-organised environment. Good examination results and the school's resources were thought to be important and quite a number thought that being in an all-girls' school was helpful - *"because it's all girls, you pay more attention and learn more"*.

Of course, you can never win them all. One girl said *"I don't like Fairfield"* and another girl, with a dry sense of humour, remarked that the best thing about Fairfield was that *"It's nearly over!"* I would suggest that 131 happy and contented girls out of 133 is something the school can be justly proud of.

It can also be proud of the number of Fairfield girls who have gone on to higher education, including Oxbridge, since the beginning of the new millennium. Among the degrees they chose to study have been such diverse subjects as cell biology and mediaeval women. However, it is too early to assess their careers, as even those pupils who started at Fairfield in the year 2000, would not gain their degrees until 2010 or 2011.

CONCLUSION

Our journey has taken us through more than two hundred years and women's lives during that time have changed enormously. Many women made tremendous sacrifices and worked in countless different ways to secure the freedom and independence that many of us have today. In writing this book I wanted to show how a group of really quite ordinary girls, who are representative of many others, have, through the years, contributed to this struggle for equality; a struggle that still has quite a long way to go.

There is a feeling that we are in a state of flux and much depends on what is happening at the "coalface" – the individual situations and relationships between the sexes. One of the biggest problems concerns baby and childcare but there does seem to be a very gradual realisation that the care of children has to be a joint effort and domestic chores need to be shared on a more equal basis. It has to be acknowledged that this is an immense radical change. Tolerance on both sides is needed if the children are not to suffer.

Shortly after I wrote this last paragraph Helen Fraser the Chief Executive of the "Girls' Day School Trust", which educates 20,000 girls in twenty six independent schools, spoke about this problem at their Annual Meeting.. She said that girls should think carefully and choose wisely when deciding on a partner. The man should be supportive and understand that it is important that a woman thrives and does well and he should see their working lives as a joint project.

On 10 July 2012, Frances O'Grady was elected as the first female General Secretary of the Trades Union Congress. Although this was welcome news, many women look forward to the day when such appointments are the norm and not particularly newsworthy. Only then will we know that women have finally achieved equality. In the meantime, it was one small step. Another small step was the announcement near the end of 2012 that female members of the Royal Family are to be given equality with men in the rules of succession to the throne.

I cannot finish this story without commenting on the present economic crisis that the country is going through and the very high cost of a university education. I hope with all my heart that it will not discourage present and future Fairfield girls and prevent them from reaching their true potential .

We have seen that earlier generations of Fairfield girls experienced not only two World Wars but also the dreadful recessions of the thirties and the eighties and I sincerely hope that the girls of today will have the same tenacity and capacity for hard work that enabled those past pupils to persevere and succeed.

I also hope that when they "walk away" on their last day at school they will echo the Fairfield girl of 1930 and *"press into the world ungrieving, knowing that they have gained all that school and work could win them"*. If they do, they are following in the footsteps of thousands of Fairfield girls who have gone before them and they will play their part in the on-going struggle for female equality.

SOURCE NOTES

CHAPTER ONE

1. Manchester Archives and Local Studies, Central Library, Manchester
2. Samuel Heywood, *Digest of the Law Respecting County Elections* (1790) p.158
3. Robert Speake & F.R. Witty, *A History of Droylsden*, (1953), p.49
4. John Higson, *Historical and Descriptive Notices of Droylsden, Past and Present (*1859) p.20
5. Ibid p.59
6. Ibid p.103
7. F. H. Mellowes, *A Short History of Fairfield Moravian Church*, (pub privately 1977, updated and reprinted 2007) p.9
8. Dr. John Aikin, *A Description of the Country from 30 to 40 miles round Manchester,* pub.1795
9. F. H. Mellowes, op.cit. p.14
10. John Higson, op. cit. p.58
11. F. H. Mellowes op. cit. p. 14 & 15
12. Ibid p. 38
13. Congregation Diary, Fairfield Moravian Church Archives.1793/1809, T/7/1527.
14. Fairfield Moravian Church Archives. Single Sisters' Diary T/8//4
15. James Muckle,*Bold Shall I Stand (Ockbrook since 1799),*(Ockbrook School), p. 18
16. Ibid
17. Joan D. Cooper, Article in the Fairfield School Magazine 1931
18. Mary Cathcart Borer, *"Willingly to School"* (Lutterworth Press, 1976). p.138
19. F.H.Mellowes, op. cit p.30
20. Ibid p.42

21. Ibid p.29
22. Information from John Beirne, present owner of Plantation Farm
23. John Smith Moffat, *The Lives of Robert and Mary Moffat* (Fisher Unwin 1885)
24.. Mary Smith's Journal,1819. L.M.S. Archives in School of Oriental and African Studies, University of London, Ref: CWM/LMS/Africa/Personal, Box 4, Robert Moffat papers.
25. John Smith Moffat, op.cit.
26. J.E. Hickey, *Dukinfield Past and Present* (Whittaker & Sons 1926) p.39-40
27. Mellowes, op.cit. p.29
28. Ibid p.61
29. Mary Tyrell, *"Memoirs"* Fairfield Moravian Church Archives, T/3/14
30. *Moravian Messenger Magazine* (September 1865) John Rylands Library, Manchester
31. Joan D Cooper, Article in the Fairfield School Magazine 1931.
32. Mildred Burlinson, Fairfield Remembered, 1992

CHAPTER TWO

1. Higson, op.cit. p.88
2. Ibid p.98
3. Ibid. p.101
4. Ibid p.23
5. Mellowes op. cit. p.50
6. Ibid p.66
7. Ibid p.61
8. Higson op cit. p. 164
9 Robert Speake & F. R. Witty, op.cit. p.137
10. Ibid. p.205
11. Higson op. cit. p.164
12. Ibid p. 21
13. John Higson, Op. Cit. p.56
14. James Bryce, *Studies in History & Jurisprudence* Volume II, (OUP, 1901) p.819

15. Colin Gibson, *Dissolving Wedlock* (Routledge 1993) p.51
16. Barbara Whitehead, *Charlotte Bront and her 'Dearest Nell'* (Smith Settle Ltd 1993)
17. Jenny Uglow, *Elizabeth Gaskell, A Habit of Stories* (Faber and Faber, 1993) p.77
18. Ibid p.61
19. Mellowes op.cit. p.69
20. Higson op.cit. p.107
21. Ibid p.138
22. Fairfield Moravian Church Archives T/31/2/23 & T/31/2/29
23. Ibid
24. Angela Holdsworth, *Out of the Dolls House, The Story of Women in the Twentieth Century* (BBC Books 1988) Reprinted by permission of the Random House Group Limited p.41
25. Dorothea Beale *"History of Cheltenham Ladies College 1853-1904.*
26. Emily Davies in Letters to a Newcastle paper.
27. *Moravian Messenger Magazine*, The John Rylands' Library, Manchester Volume I 1864
28. Ibid
29. Ibid Volume III 1866
30. Ibid Volume IV 1867
31. Harriet Ford, Letter in the Fairfield High School for Girls' Archive
32. *Moravian Messenger Magazine* op.cit. Volume XVI 1879
33. Mellowes op.cit. p.71
34. Ibid. p.78

CHAPTER THREE

1. Schools' Enquiry Commission1868 Volume IX Chapter 8, (Manchester Central Library)
2. Ibid
3. Ibid
4. James Muckle, *Bold Shall I Stand (Ockbrook since 1799),(* Ockbrook School, 2000)
5. Schools' Enquiry Commission, op. cit.

6. *Moravian Messenger Magazine* op. cit. Volume XV 1878

7. Mary Cathcart Borer, op. cit. p.271

8. *Moravian Messenger Magazine* op. cit. Volume XXI 1884

9. Ibid Volume II (new) 1892

10. Ibid. Volume XX 1883

11. Ibid.Volume II (new) 1892

12. Ibid. Volume IV (new) 1894

13. *Ashburne Hall, (Manchester University) Magazine* 1902

14. Dean John Burgeon, *To Educate Young Women,* (Oxford: Parker,1884) P.29

15. *Girls Own Newspaper* Sept. 1886 p. 770

16. Lucy Eagle – Letter in Fairfield High School's Magazine, 1946

17. Correspondence with Hugh Wilson, Rachel Wilson née Eagle's grandson

18. Head Mistress's Report to Speech Day 1925. Fairfield High School Archives

19. Prof. Edward Fiddes, Introductory Chapter, Tylecote ,*The Education of Women at Manchester University,* p. 10-13

20. Mabel Tylecote, *The Education of Women at Manchester University 1883-1933* (Manchester University Press 1941) p. 31

21 Ibid p.32

22. Miss E. Lang, Article in Owens College Jubilee Magazine 1901 quoted in Tylecote op. cit p.33

23. Owens College Magazine, October 1892 quoted in Tylecote op.cit. p.33

24. Miss E. Lang op. cit.

25. Miss Alice Crompton – correspondence June 1934 quoted in Tylecote op. cit. p.33

26 Dr.. Ward, *Manchester Guardian*, October 1899

27. Tylecote op. cit. p.34

28. Ibid. p.35

29. Ibid. p..51

30. Durham University Journal Vol XIII No.13 (1894)

31. Tylecote op. cit. p.38

32. Ibid p.44

33. Manchester High School for Girls' Archives
34. Rosalind Jones, Gwladys Powicke née Evans' granddaughter, correspondence with the author
35. Manchester High School for Girls' Archives
36. Tylecote, op.cit. p.114
37. Rosalind Jones op. cit. conversation with the author

CHAPTER FOUR

1. *Moravian Messenger Magazine,* Moravian Church Archives, London, Volume XVI   (1906)
2. Ibid, Volume XXI
3. Moravian School for Girls' Prospectus, Fairfield High School for Girls' Archives
4. School timetables in Fairfield High School for Girls' Archives
5. Fairfield Old Girls' Association News Letter 1969
6. Ibid 1986
7. Ibid 1970
8. Ibid 1969
9. Ibid 1993
10. Lucy Eagle, Letter in Fairfield High Schools' Magazine 1946
11. Mary Cathcart Borer op. cit. p.294
12. Head Mistress's Reports to Speech Day and *Moravian Messenger Magazine* op. cit. Moravian Church Archives, London
13. Vera Brittain, *Testament of Youth,* originally published by Victor Gollancz now an imprint of The Orion Publishing Group, London) p.33
14. Olive Schreiner, *Woman and Labour,* (T. Fisher Unwin, 1911)
15. Vera Brittain, Op. Cit. p. 73
16. Rosamund Essex. *Woman in a Man's World,* Sheldon Press, London 1977 P.5
17. Mildred Burlinson op. cit. p.8
18. Fairfield Old Girls Association's News Letter 1970
19. Head Mistress's Report to Speech Day, op. cit. 1916
20. Head Mistress's Report to Speech Day, op. cit. 1917

21. National Archives at Kew, Document WO399/4067

22. National Archives op. cit.

23. National Archives op. cit.

24. National Archives op. cit.

25. Lyn Macdonald, *The Roses of No Man's Land* (Penguin Books 1993) p.122

26. Ibid p.123

27. Ibid p.126

28. Speeke & Witty, op. cit. p.215

29. National Archives op. cit.

30. Ibid

31. Ibid

CHAPTER FIVE

1. Fairfield Old Girls' Association's News Letter 1969

2. Head Mistress's Reports to Speech Day op. cit. 1921 & 1928.

3. Conversation with Mrs. K Gordon-Ingram (Marguerite Johnstone's niece).

4. Fairfield Old Girls' Association News Letter 1969. School Archives

5. Ibid

6. Ibid 1970

7. Ibid 1969

8. Head Mistress's Report to Speech Day 1921. School Archives

9. Ibid

10. Fairfield Old Girls' Association's News Letter 1969

11. School Register for 1919-1921. School Archives

12. Fairfield High School for Girls' School magazine 1923 School Archives

13. Ibid 1922

14. School Magazine op. cit. 1924

15. Ibid 1928/1929

16. Fairfield Old Girls' Associations' News Letter 1992

17. Fairfield High School for Girls' School Magazine op. cit. 1925

18. Moravian School for Girls, Fairfield, Prospectus 1908, & FHS Prospectus 1920s School Archives

19. Head Mistress's Report to Speech Day op. cit. 1927
20. Ibid 1926
21. Head Mistress's Report to Speech Day op. cit. 1927
22. Ibid 1929
23. Ibid 1928
24. School Register op. cit.
25. Private family papers and correspondence from Simon Balfour-Browne, step-son of Frances Lotte Balfour-Browne née Stephens
26. Registers Volumes I and II, Fairfield High School Archives
27. Correspondence from Mr J Bates (Eva Bates née Dunks' son)
28. Headmistress's Report to Speech Day, op. cit. 1938
29. Ibid 1928
30. William Woodruff *The Road to Nab End* (first published under the title of Billy Boy by Ryburn Publishing Ltd 1993, Republished by Abacus 2002, Republished by Eland in 2011,Copyright © 2008 by Asperula, LLC reprinted by permission of Helga Woodruff). p.133
31. Betty Slater, *Droylsden and Audenshaw Voices*, compiled by Jill Cronin published by The History Press 2001 p.36

CHAPTER SIX

1. Fairfield Old Girls' Association's News Letter op. cit. 1996
2. Professor Sonia Jackson OBE, *3rd Joan Cooper Memorial Lecture.* 12 November 2008
3. Curtis Report (1946) Report of the Care of Children Committee, quoted by Professor Peter Wedge at the *Inaugural Joan Cooper Memorial Lecture,* 27 November 2003.
4. Professor Sonia Jackson OBE op. cit.
5. Professor Bob Holman, *Child Care Revisited*(The Institute of Childcare and Social Education -1948-1971. Quoted by Professor Sonia Jackson op. cit.
6. Dr. Denis Jones, correspondence with the author 15 May 2011
7. Sheila Rowbotham, *A Century of Women,* (Viking, (The Penguin Group) 1997), p.183.
8. Professor Sonia Jackson, op. cit.

9. Fairfield High School for Girls' School Magazine , School Archives, 1952

10. Professor Peter Wedge op. cit.

11. Ibid

12. Ibid

13. Fairfield Old Girls' Association's News Letter 1996

14. School Magazine, op. cit. 1932

15. School Registers op. cit. Volume II

16. Lena Slack, *Three Jumps to the Cupboard Door*,(Tameside Metropolitan Borough, (Volume 2 in the 'History in Your Own Words' Series)

17. School Magazine op. cit. 1950 (Old Girls' Section)

18. Lena Slack op. cit. p.5

19. School Magazine op. cit. 1934

20. Ibid, 1933

21. Ibid

22. Lena Slack, op. cit. p.44

23. School Magazine op. cit. 1932

24. Ibid, 1930

25. Ibid

26. Speake & Witty op. cit. p.257

27. Head Mistress's Report to Speech Day op. cit. 1938

28. School Magazine 1931

29. Ibid, 1937

30. Speake & Witty op. cit. p.257

CHAPTER SEVEN

1. Head Mistress's Report to Speech Day op. cit. 1940

2. Ibid

3. Author's correspondence with Professor Fanni Bogdanow 5 July 2008

4. Author's conversation with Professor Bogdanow 3 July 2008

5. School Magazine op. cit. 1940

6. Author's correspondence with Professor Bogdanow 5 July 2008

7. Head Mistress's Report to Speech Day op. cit. 1946

8. Author's conversation with Professor Bogdanow 2 November 2008

9. Author's correspondence with Professor Bogdanow 5 July 2008
10. Ibid
11. Ibid. 21 July 2008
12. Ibid. 5 July 2008
13. Author's conversation with Professor Bognanow 6 March 2009
14. Ibid 22 September 2010
15. Joyce Hallorth née (Keggen) & Brenda Firth née Cooke in Fairfield Old Girls' Association's News Letter 1993
16. Dorothy Parfitt née Kershaw in Fairfield Old Girls' Association's News Letter 1987
17. Head Mistress's Report to Speech Day 1940
18. Joyce Hallworth née (Keggen) & Brenda Firth née Cooke. op. cit.
19. Head Mistress's Report 1940
20. Speake & Witty op. cit. p.221
21. Fred Lord, *Audenshaw and Droylsden Voices* op.cit. p.99
22. Author's Conversation with Diane Demeger - Phyllis Kershaw's daughter
23. Ibid
24. Author's correspondence with Lillian Stevenson – Phyllis Kershaw's daughter
25. Diane Demeger, Press Release
26. Ibid
27. Author's conversation with Diane Demegar
28. *Tameside Advertiser* 18 February 2010 p.4
29. Head Mistress's Report to Speech Day 1941
30. School Magazine op. cit. 1930
31. Author's correspondence with Ann Fisher, Perth, Australia. 21 July 2008
32. Ibid 23 February 2009
33. *"Outpost"* (Nom de Plume), Singapore Nightmare, Pub John Crowther Ltd. c.1943
34. Ann Fisher op. cit. 19 October 2009
35. Ibid
36. School Magazine op. cit. 1941
37. Ibid 1943

38. Ibid 1931
39. Ibid 1945
40. Ibid 1944
41. Ibid 1945
42. Ibid 1943
43. School Magazine op. cit. 1942
44. Ibid 1943
45. Correspondence and conversation with Dr. Joan Wilkinson MBE
46. Correspondence and conversation with Hilda Lawson née Ridyard
47. Conversations and correspondence with Joan Riley over many years

CHAPTER EIGHT

1. Angela Holdsworth op.cit. p.77-78
2. School Magazine op. cit. 1946
3. *The Telegraph 'on-line' Obituary,* 25.February 2010
4. School Magazine, op. cit. 1948
5. Correspondence from Dr Joan Wilkinson MBE
6. School Magazine op. cit. 1947
7. Ibid 1951
8. Ibid 1954
9. Lena Slack op. cit. p. 21
10. Correspondence with Dr Joan Wilkinson MBE
11. Fairfield Old Girls' Association's News Letter 2010
12. Correspondence with Dr Joan Wilkinson MBE
13. Correspondence and conversations with Professor E. Mary Cooke OBE August 2009
14. Fairfield Old Girls' Association News Letter 1980
15. Professor Cooke's correspondence with the author 29 August 2009
16. Speech Day Programme, 12 July 1954
17. Ibid
18. Ibid, 29 October 1956
19. Fairfield Old Girls' Association's News Letter 1960
20. Ibid 1964

21. Mollie Brudenell's correspondence with the author 22 May 2011
22. Fairfield Old Girls' Association News Letter 1985
23. Speech Day Programme op. cit.
24. Fairfield Old Girls' Association News Letter 1963
25. Adele Vincent 's correspondence with the author 5 July 2009
26. Fairfield Old Girls' Association News Letter 1965
27. Ibid 1966
28. Ibid 2009
29. Ibid 1985
30. *Droylsden Reporter* June 20 1957 reprinted with permission from Tameside Reporter and Chronicle Newspapers
31. Averil Ipri's correspondence with the Author 29 June 2009
32. Ibid 30 May 2011
33. Ibid 1 June 2011
34. Ibid 18 June 2011
35. Ibid 31 May 2009
36. Ibid 18 June 2011
37. Conversations with Maureen Beattie née Bustard
38. Correspondence with Christine Bullen

CHAPTER NINE

1. Headmistress's Report to Speech Day op. cit. 1958
2. Robert Anderson, *BBC History Magazine,* June 2007 p.48-49
3. Angela Holdsworth op. cit. p. 195
4. Katherine Whitehorn, *Selective Memory* (Virago Press, an imprint of Little, Brown Book Group, 2007, p. 105
5. Dominic Sandbrook, *BBC History Magazine* March 2007 p.43
6. Fairfield Old Girls' Association's News Letters 1960s
7. Ibid 1963
8. Ibid 1962
9. Ibid 1962
10. Ibid 1967
11. Sister Scholistica's conversations with the author 9 September 2009
12. Russell Harty, *Mr Harty's Grand Tour*, pub Century Hutchinson

Ltd.1988 p.87-90 . Reprinted by permission of The Random House Group Limited

13. Sister Scholistica's conversations with the author op. cit.
14. Gwen Carlisle's correspondence with the author, June 2011
15. Trafford Athletic Club Archives
16. Fairfield Old Girls' Association's News Letter 1972
17. Ibid 1999
18. Sharman Birtles, correspondence with the author, September 2011
19. Head Mistress's Report to Speech Day op. cit. 1971
20. National Archives' File HO245/737 quoted in Mary Turner *The Woman's Century,* (The National Archives, 2003) p.144
21. Dame Jenni Murray interviewed by Aida Edemariam, in *The Guardian* 16 January 2010. (Guardian News & Media Ltd)
22. Katherine Whitehorn, op. cit. p.141
23. Ibid p.146
24. Ibid p. 191-192
25. Fairfield Old Girls' News Letter 1981
26. Ibid 1997
27. Ibid 1988 & 1989
28. Ibid 1979
29. Conversation with Elizabeth Tutton
30. Jill Marshall's correspondence with the author 1 February 2011
31. Judith Fenn's correspondence with the author 10 April 2011
32. Correspondence from Rhiannon Wilkinson and Harrogate Ladies College
33. Fairfield Old Girls' News Letter 1972
34. School Log Book

CHAPTER TEN

1. School Log Book
2. Angela Holdsworth, op. cit. p.57
3. Ibid p.59
4. Head Mistress's Report to Speech Day in F.O.G.A. News Letter 1982
5. School Log Book

6. Head Mistress's Report to Speech Day 1983
7. Angela Holdsworth, op. cit. p.57
8. Ibid p.58
9. Angela Holdsworth, op. cit. 84
10. Ibid p.84
11. Ibid p.84
12. Ibid p.202
13. Barbara Castle, article in *The Guardian* October 1984 quoted in *"Women of the Revolution"* pub. Guardian Books (Guardian News & Media Ltd)
14. School Log Book
15. Fairfield Old Girls' Associations' News Letter 1983
16. Fairfield Old Girls' Associations' News Letters
17. Conversations and correspondence with Amanda Goodwin July 2011 and July 2013
18. Pauline Jones' correspondence with the author
19. Fairfield Old Girls' Association's News Letter
20. Clare Galt's conversations and correspondence with the author June 2011
21. Fairfield Old Girls' Association's News Letter 1993
22. Ibid 1994
23. Ibid 1997
24. Sheila Rowbotham op. cit. p.561
25. Elizabeth Wurtzel, *The Guardian* 10 August 1998(Guardian News & Media Ltd)
26. Karen Lofthouse's correspondence and conversations with the author, September, October 2010, November 2011, August 2013
27. Rachael Harrison's correspondence with the author 26 April 2009
28. Kelly Richardson's correspondence with the author May 2013
29. Sarah Jones, correspondence and conversations with the author, March 2011
30. Kelly Wild correspondence with the author, June 2011
31. Fairfield Old Girls' Association's News Letter 1998
32. Head Teacher, Mr John Hedley, Fairfield Old Girls' Association's News Letter 2012

33. *Tameside Advertiser,* 8 July 2010

34. Ibid 13 May 2010

35. School's News Letter Spring 2012

36. School Prospectus 2005

37. K. Kerrigan, *The Sunday Times* 14 March 2010 (News International Syndication)

38. Rosie Boycott, *The Guardian*, 28 February 2008 (Guardian News & Media Ltd)

39. Kira Cochrane, *,The Guardian,* November 2010 (Guardian News & Media Ltd)

ACKNOWLEDGEMENTS

First and foremost I should like to thank all those Fairfield girls and their families who shared their stories with me. I hope that my narrative meets with their approval.

I was helped immensely by Fairfield Old Girls Association – without the information contained in the thousands of letters from Old Girls that they had safely kept over the last ninety five years there would have been no story.

I am grateful for the friendship and support given to me by Fairfield High School's Head Teacher, John Hedley and Deputy Head Teacher, Kathryn Quinn.

Thanks are also due to Claire Gillman of the Writers' Workshop for her expert editorial advice.

The support and expertise shown by the Matador publishing team was much appreciated.

The archivists Barbara Derbyshire at the Fairfield Moravian Church, Lorraine Parsons at the Moravian Church Archive in London, and Dr Christine Joy at Manchester High School for Girls gave generously of their time.

Lastly I should like to thank my husband and my daughters for their support and interest in my endeavour, and not least my husband for his computer expertise without which it's doubtful that the book would ever have been finished.

PICTURE ACKNOWLEDGEMENTS

Thanks are due to the following for permission to reproduce the illustrations listed below.

Sketch of Moravian Settlement, Fairfield	Moravian Church, Fairfield
Manchester University 1906	Manchester City Council
Photographs from the School Prospectus 1908 & 1925	Fairfield High School for Girls
Giant Stride	North London Collegiate School
Gwendoline Hughes' Record Card	National Archives'
Frances Lotte Balfour-Browne née Stevens	Simon Balfour-Browne
Eva Bates née Dunks & Headmistress's letter	Jim Bates
Professor Fanni Bogdanow & her parents	Professor Fanni Boganow
Wedding of Dr. Christobel Hall and Dr. Benjamin Taylor	Ashton Reporter now Tameside Reporter
Dr Christobel Taylor née Hall	Ann Fisher
Phyllis Kershaw née Hawkins	The Kershaw Family
Joan Riley née Bond	Joan Riley
Mollie Rothwell – Graduation Day	Mollie Rothwell
Wedding of Joy Cooper and Roger Byrne	Droylsden Reporter now Tameside Reporter
Sister Scholastica & guests	Sister Scholastica
Sharman Birtles née Newth	Sharman Birtles
Interior Fairfield High School's Sports Hall	Tameside Advertiser
Head Girl and Deputy Head Girl 2012	Tameside Advertiser
Police Inspector Claire Galt	Police Inspector Galt
Squadron Leader Karen Lofthouse (née McKnight)	Squadron Leader Lofthouse
Duchess of Gloucester at Fairfield	Fairfield High School
Sarah Jones & Ola During Hospital	Sarah Jones